W9-BXY-490

PERSONAL BENCHMARK

PERSONAL BENCHMARK

Integrating Behavioral Finance and Investment Management

Chuck Widger
Dr. Daniel Crosby

Cover design: Wiley

Copyright © 2014 by Chuck Widger and Dr. Daniel Crosby. All rights reserved.

Published by John Wiley & Sons, Inc., Hoboken, New Jersey.

Published simultaneously in Canada.

No part of this publication may be reproduced, stored in a retrieval system, or transmitted in any form or by any means, electronic, mechanical, photocopying, recording, scanning, or otherwise, except as permitted under Section 107 or 108 of the 1976 United States Copyright Act, without either the prior written permission of the Publisher, or authorization through payment of the appropriate per-copy fee to the Copyright Clearance Center, Inc., 222 Rosewood Drive, Danvers, MA 01923, (978) 750-8400, fax (978) 646-8600, or on the Web at www.copyright .com. Requests to the Publisher for permission should be addressed to the Permissions Department, John Wiley & Sons, Inc., 111 River Street, Hoboken, NJ 07030, (201) 748-6011, fax (201) 748-6008, or online at http://www.wiley.com/go/permissions.

Limit of Liability/Disclaimer of Warranty: While the publisher and author have used their best efforts in preparing this book, they make no representations or warranties with respect to the accuracy or completeness of the contents of this book and specifically disclaim any implied warranties of merchantability or fitness for a particular purpose. No warranty may be created or extended by sales representatives or written sales materials. The advice and strategies contained herein may not be suitable for your situation. You should consult with a professional where appropriate. Neither the publisher nor author shall be liable for any loss of profit or any other commercial damages, including but not limited to special, incidental, consequential, or other damages.

For general information on our other products and services or for technical support, please contact our Customer Care Department within the United States at (800) 762-2974, outside the United States at (317) 572-3993 or fax (317) 572-4002.

Wiley publishes in a variety of print and electronic formats and by print-on-demand. Some material included with standard print versions of this book may not be included in e-books or in print-on-demand. If this book refers to media such as a CD or DVD that is not included in the version you purchased, you may download this material at http://booksupport.wiley.com. For more information about Wiley products, visit www.wiley.com.

Library of Congress Cataloging-in-Publication Data:

Widger, Chuck.
    Personal benchmark: integrating behavioral finance and investment management/ Chuck Widger and Dr. Daniel Crosby.
        pages cm
    Includes bibliographical references and index.
        ISBN 978-1-118-96332-6 (hardcover); ISBN 978-1-118-96339-5 (ePDF); ISBN 978-1-118-96333-3 (ePub)
    1. Investment advisors. 2. Investment advisor-client relationships. 3. Finance–Psychological aspects. 4. Portfolio management–Psychological aspects. I. Crosby, Daniel, 1979- II. Title.
    HG4621.W46 2014
    332.601'9–dc23

                                                              2014020577

Printed in the United States of America

10 9 8 7 6 5 4 3 2 1

This book is dedicated to America's advisors.
Professionals who help investors achieve their goals.

Contents

Preface

The insight that inspired this book emerged in the spring of 2010 during an otherwise typical investment advisory discussion. My client, Rick, had investment needs. Like many investors, he wanted a conservative approach (low volatility) to managing his investments. Also like many investors, he simultaneously needed growth to increase his purchasing power. An inherent conflict. Thus, Rick called me to seek guidance on how to assemble a portfolio that would best meet his goals.

But Rick wasn't just any client. Rick was my longtime friend of more than 55 years. In the eighth grade, we played soccer together. In high school, we (along with our teammates) won the 1962 Pennsylvania State Championship. June 3, 1967, we entered Navy officer candidate school in Newport, Rhode Island together.

In 1970, I left active duty to join the finance industry. Rick went on to become a career Naval officer, rising to the rank of Captain in the Naval Supply Corp and earning a master's degree in computer science at the Navy's postgraduate school in Monterey, California along the way. He also prudently saved and invested his entire adult life.

Those of us who have the benefit of lifelong friendships know how special they are, especially at Rick's and my age. We shared a significant part of our youth together. Each of us was proud to serve our country. We each appreciate the career achievements of the other. And, importantly, we tease each other over minor missteps when we were young and a few misadventures we each have experienced as adults. There is an irreplaceable comfort in high quality, mutually respectful lifelong friendships.

Today, Rick and his lovely wife Dana have two children and three grandchildren. His personal goal is to provide for Dana on his death, and for his children and grandchildren on the death of the survivor.

Thus, when he turned to me in the spring of 2010 for investment advice, I was keenly aware of the discipline and sacrifice it took for him to assemble his portfolio. And I was intimately aware of the individuals who were trusting me for advice. So, as with any client, I took my advising role with Rick very seriously.

Rick knows from personal experience that markets are volatile. He also understands that at our age if he suffers a significant loss, he may not have time to recover. Thus, like many people, he prefers a conservative approach to managing his investments. Yet, his conservative bias is in conflict with another of his investment goals. Rick knows he must increase his purchasing power over time to maintain his standard of living. To increase purchasing power, investors must stay invested over reasonably long periods of time. Therein lies the rub: Rick is an action-oriented guy. Staying invested through good times and bad is at odds with his no-nonsense mentality of, "Don't just stand there, do some-thing!" when things get rough. When volatility strikes, he (like many others), wants to reduce his volatility and chances of loss, even if that means reducing the chances for growth. In short, Rick's conservative (low volatility) approach was stymying the growth component his portfolio needed.

As I thought about Rick's investment goals and risk tolerance, I intuitively saw that by establishing specific goals (low volatility, growth) for each purpose, I could confidently recommend a tested Brinker Capital investment strategy that I believed had a high probability of achieving each goal. I knew in periods of market volatility, I could point out the stability of the low volatility or safety allocation and note that, over time, the more volatile growth or accumulation allocation would compound and create more purchasing power. I now know what I had solved for Rick is the dilemma psychologists call "simultaneous risk preferences."

TABLE P.1		
Rick's Initial Portfolio Investment Strategy		
	Safety	**Accumulation**
August, 2010	Destinations Defensive (70%)	Destinations Moderate (30%)
Source: Brinker Capital, Inc. For illustrative purposes only.		

A Strategy

With this broad investment policy in mind, two different Brinker Capital investment strategies were selected initially to implement it. Each strategy is from Brinker Capital's mutual fund asset allocation program known as Destinations. Brinker Capital has eight different investment programs, with each based on the same multi-asset class investment philosophy that seeks to reduce volatility, while maintaining the opportunity for appreciation. Rick's initial portfolio investment strategy is pictured in Table P.1.

What I had intuitively done was use mental accounting, or buckets, to frame a portfolio investment strategy that both would create the investment experience Rick wanted and allow me to communicate with him in terms that he easily understands. Thanks to decades of research into human behavior we now know people naturally collect and simplify information through mental accounting. Framing information into discrete buckets allows for faster comprehension and more rapid decision making. This communication format creates an ongoing level of understanding that enables the management of normal biases through his investment life cycle.

Following implementation of this strategy for Rick's portfolio, in the second half of 2010, investors in equities achieved very attractive returns. Our Destinations Moderate model, as part of the Accumulation allocation, was up +16 percent during this period (as of December 31, 2010).

With ten months of experience, Rick became comfortable with the performance of his portfolio investment strategy. In the spring of 2011, I suggested to Rick that allocating 70 percent in Destinations Defensive

TABLE P.2		
Rick's New Portfolio Investment Strategy		
Safety	**Tactical**	**Accumulation**
May, 2011 Destinations Conservative (35%)	Crystal Strategy I (35%)	Destinations Moderate (30%)
Source: Brinker Capital, Inc. For illustrative purposes only.		

was much too conservative. He agreed. I then proposed, and he accepted, a change in his portfolio investment strategy.

We reallocated the 70 percent that was in Destinations Defensive: 35 percent to Destinations Conservative (a slightly less conservative strategy) and 35 percent to Crystal Strategy I Absolute Return, a global macro hedge strategy. His new reallocation is pictured in Table P.2.

By framing the portfolio investment strategy discussion and the performance discussion through the prism of mental accounts or buckets, Rick could easily see that:

- Using a Destinations Conservative strategy for his Safety bucket, a significant portion of his portfolio (35 percent) has the ability to remain stable during volatile periods. Knowing that his portfolio's safety is established, he can manage and put into perspective the pain of the more volatile accumulation strategy.

- Using Crystal Strategy I for his Tactical bucket, he has the potential to gain downside protection in volatile markets and the opportunity for appreciation in rising markets.

- Using Destinations Moderate for his Accumulation bucket, he has the potential to protect and grow purchasing power to sustain his standard of living in the future.

Once the first 24 months of the investment advisory relationship had passed, Rick understood how to view his portfolio through the prism of these three mental accounts. Our discussions on portfolio performance now takes place during periodic reviews and not during periods of volatility.

During the initial period of the investment advisory relationship with Rick, I had also begun to focus on the continued failure of the advice industry (investment managers, sponsors, broker–dealers and financial advisors) to apply the principles of behavioral finance in the investment advisory process. I soon realized that this was a key to more successful investing.

A Behavioral View of Finance

Through the efforts of noted scholars like Richard Thaler, Amos Tversky and Nobel Prize winner Daniel Kahneman, behavioral finance has established itself as a social science with a body of principles which are useful in predicting human behavior. During the last 20 years, many investment management firms have developed high quality presentations on behavioral finance. However, these firms neglected to develop investment offerings that integrate the principles of behavioral finance, even though individual investors continue to relate to their investment as human beings with behavioral biases, not just on the basis of return and risk (volatility).

For example, 30 years of data gathered by investment consulting firm Dalbar reveal that in periods of volatility, investors sell paper losses at bottoms and pile back in at market tops. This suggests that individual investors feel the pain of loss more than the pleasure of gain. As a result of this and numerous other behavioral tendencies or biases, actual investor performance materially underperformed commonly used indices for the 30-year period.

If, after the 2008–2009 Financial Crisis and Great Recession, former Federal Reserve Chairman Alan Greenspan (2014) can become "imbued with behavioral finance," why shouldn't the investment advice delivery system? If behavioral finance is good enough to be included in the macroeconomic models that guide macroeconomic policy, surely it is appropriate to include behavioral finance in the investment advice delivery system that guides the development of individual investment strategies.

In his book *The Map and the Territory: Risk, Human Nature, and the Future of Forecasting* (2013), Greenspan recounts his epiphany. In reflecting on the 2008–2009 period, he notes that most analysts and forecasters, both public and private, agreed with *The Economist's* view expressed in December, 2006 that "market capitalism, the engine that runs most of the world economy, seems to be doing its job well." He then asks and answers the question, "What went wrong?". According to Greenspan (2009), what went wrong is that economic forecasters like himself held too narrow a definition of animal spirits. Animal spirits, as defined by Keynes (2011), is the "spontaneous urge to action rather than inaction, not as the [rational] outcome of a weighted average of quantitative benefits multiplied by quantitative probabilities." On reflection, animal spirits should include behavior biases or propensities because there are systematic patterns to how people behave in periods of extreme economic stress. These patterns can be measured and included in economic models which are used to guide economic policy (Greenspan 2009).

In my view, if behavioral finance is good enough for Greenspan and the macroeconomic models that guide national policy (Greenspan, 2009), it's good enough for the investment advice delivery system used to guide the development of individual investment strategies.

It is a central thesis of this book that embedding behavioral finance principles into an investment management offering is needed to resolve the performance shortfall driven in significant part by individual investor behavior. When principles of investment management and behavioral finance are combined in an investment offering, the advice delivery system will materially improve the investor experience. In turn, investors may enjoy an appropriate mix of return and risk, and, most importantly, intentionally manage their behavior biases.

Clues about how to embed such principles can be found in Richard Thaler and Cass Sunstein's book *Nudge: Improving Decisions About Health, Wealth, and Happiness* (2009). In it, the authors note that people struggle to make decisions in the midst of complex or stressful situations. They persuasively argue that in such situations, people's decision making should be guided ("nudged"). They nudge using choice architectures, processes, or systems that take into consideration people's behavioral tendencies and that promote optimal (more helpful, less hurtful) choices. For example, they explained, nations with opt-*out* organ donor programs have more incidences of organ donation than nations with opt-*in* organ donor programs.

In the case of investment advisors, we are intimately aware that the number one source of stress is money (American Psychological Association 2012), and when this stress kicks in the quality of our thinking suffers. We forget the future, react ("Don't just stand there, do something!"), throw the plan out the window, and make what can be irrational comparisons to prior events. Having an investment advice delivery system that understands and anticipates these natural human reactions and tendencies is what investors need.

However, no delivery system has historically incorporated principles of behavioral finance or provided nudges and choice architectures that help investors voluntarily control their behavioral biases. Until now.

In later chapters, my co-author, Dr. Daniel Crosby, more deeply explains the concepts of behavioral finance that undergird Personal Benchmark, Brinker Capital's advisory model. Daniel has grouped 117 documented behavioral biases or tendencies exhibited by human beings into three categories of simple, safe, and sure.

In practice, we guide our clients to make allocations to safety, income, and tactical mental accounts. These allocations help clarify investors' personal goals, manage volatility, and harness the positive feelings linked to achieving personal goals. We still cannot predict short-term performance: No one knows what the market will do this month, or even this year. But over long periods of time, there is reasonable certainty that stocks will outperform bonds, and bonds will outperform cash.

The accumulation bucket in Rick's personal portfolio strategy recognizes this truth. By establishing a longer, appropriate time horizon for the performance of this mental account (bucket), Rick has a reasonable level of certainty, or surety, that he will grow the purchasing power he needs to sustain his and Dana's lifestyles. The accumulation bucket also brings even greater personal meaning because it provides the opportunity to provide for their children and grandchildren on the death of the survivor.

Thus, as Rick's story shows, our focus on presenting a limited number of mental accounts to design the broad investment policy simplifies clients' basic investment policy choices, presenting a choice architecture that frames information in a positive way, encourages action, and helps clients stick to a plan. In other words, our approach helps nudge our clients toward investing strategies that are appropriate for them.

Perhaps more importantly, this choice architecture helps investors connect their investment strategies to the production of the purchasing power they need to finance the life experiences, relationships, and charitable giving that make life meaningful, fulfilling, and purposeful.

By attaching purpose (the "Why?") to our investment strategies, we identify what matters to us personally. We establish our own "Why?," making it almost effortless to do the right thing in our investing and in our lives. This makes us more productive and our lives more meaningful.

Simon Sinek illustrated the power of "Why?" using the Apple company as an example in his 2009 TEDx talk. He explained Apple answered the three key questions ("Why?," "How?," and "What?") this way:

Why?   "In everything we do, we believe in challenging the status quo."
How?   "By making our products beautifully designed and user friendly."
What? "We just happen to make great computers."

At Brinker Capital, our "Why?" is challenging the status quo, our "How?" is by offering purpose-driven investing to help avoid the "behavior gap trap" known as the *Dalbar Effect*. Our "What?" is that we just happen to make great investment products. The latest of these is the Personal Benchmark solution, which provides a simplified approach to help investors cut through the relentless financial information that bombards us daily. It was this kind of simplified framework that made sense to Rick in 2010 and continues to make sense with countless other clients today.

Personal Benchmark: A Tool for Advisors

The principles of behavioral finance were embedded or integrated in the investment advisory process I offered Rick. Today, Brinker Capital's Personal Benchmark offers an elegant (simple, yet sophisticated) solution that is easily communicated by advisors and intuitively grasped by investors. Embedded within the tool is a formal integration of the principles of behavioral finance and investment management. The integration is an advance in the theory of investing because it increases the explanatory and predictive power of investing theory by including plausible psychological premises.

Of course, we believe investment advisors will continue to play a critical role in this enhancement to the advice delivery system. Through their relationship skills and professional expertise, advisors develop an understanding of the investor's personal goals and risk tolerance and can therefore guide the development of an investment strategy that will achieve the investor's personal goals. An investment offering that embeds the principles of behavioral finance empowers the advisor with important communication tools and discipline for managing behavioral biases. These tools are an important addition to the advisor's value proposition. By managing behavioral biases, advisors help investors avoid the "behavior gap trap" identified by Dalbar.

In numerous discussions with advisors, I have discovered that many advisors have clients with a mix of strategies, just like my friend Rick. Over the last six years, these advisors have put together investment portfolios that include individual strategies that separately provided safety, managed volatility and achieved growth or accumulation. Just as I intuitively set up individual strategies to satisfy the several separate purposes Rick had as an individual investor, many talented advisors, like Rob Burns, have done the same for their clients. Rob is a bright and service-oriented advisor from Exeter, New Hampshire. In discussions with Rob on his experience with Personal Benchmark, he noted he similarly had clients with whom he had developed portfolios with a "mishmash" of investment strategies. For Rob, Personal Benchmark is a solution that consolidates this "mishmash" into a single innovation providing both behavioral bias management tools and scalable practice management tools.

Glenn McKinney, a sophisticated advisor with offices in Tampa, Florida and San Diego, California echoes Rob's view. Glenn agrees that Personal Benchmark provides an easy-to-grasp, comprehensive solution that systematically incorporates several separate investment strategies, each with a different purpose. And, through the behavioral finance overlay, Personal Benchmark adds additional risk management alongside portfolio construction.

Personal Benchmark's bucket design combines several strategies into one individually managed unit. That single image paints a clear picture of each investor's life goal. All of the buckets are reported together 24/7 on Brinker Capital's website and on a quarterly basis through performance reports. The objective is to make information easy to use thereby making the advisor's practice more scalable. At heart we want the advisor and client to communicate comfortably using natural language and without tedious jargon.

Rob Burns indicates that when appropriate he will continue to guide existing clients to convert portfolios with a mix of strategies into the Personal Benchmark solution. He also notes that he will introduce prospects and new clients to this innovation. However, he notes that the media and the investment industry have conditioned (brain-washed?) much of the public to think about their investment portfolios in terms of performance against indices rather than performance that pursues and achieves personal objectives. Designing portfolios to beat indices is a significant cause of the behavior gap trap. Why? Because investors want the return but not the risk generated by the S&P 500 Index. When risk happens in bear markets like 2001–2002 and 2008–2009, investors bail and wait for the "all clear," piling in when markets recover prior peaks.

The tendency to measure personal performance against indices is a behavior bias. It is about keeping up with the Joneses. As Mary Mack, CEO of Wells Fargo Private Wealth Management, said at the Tiburon

Conference in April of 2014, "investment strategies are no longer about keeping up with the Joneses; they are about keeping up with the purposes (purchasing power goals) of the plan." Indices have a role in investor portfolio strategies; their role is not to set the purpose of or be the plan. Rather, the proper role of indices is to provide a grasp of the context within which the plan is operating (risk assets should be doing well, or non-risky assets are doing well) and to measure how well the individual managers are doing in performing their specific role in the investor's portfolio strategy.

As of this writing, more than 135 advisors have placed $152 million in Personal Benchmark. We expect the assets under management to reach $250 million by year-end 2014. Adoption by advisors and investors is taking place. *(Note: all forecasts are reasonably held at the time of this writing but are subject to change without notice by Brinker Capital, Inc.)*

Our goal in writing this book and in creating the Personal Benchmark solution is to change the investment advisory conversation and thereby help investors avoid the behavior gap trap. By embedding behavioral finance in an investment offering, which includes Brinker Capital's multi-asset class investment philosophy, we are confident we are adding a key element to the investment advisor's value proposition and at the same time leading the way to a better investment experience for investors.

Some Acknowledgments

It is said that "victory has one thousand fathers." This book and Personal Benchmark are the result of the insights and efforts of many, many people over the last three years. First, my co-author, Dr. Daniel Crosby, has provided an expertise in human behavior and behavioral finance that has been invaluable in writing this book and in designing the investment offering. To our joint efforts he has brought a sharp intelligence with an engaging clarity in his writing and presentations.

Many at Brinker Capital also made significant contributions to our project. Brinker Capital's Investment Group stepped up and contributed a coherent, well-written articulation of our firm's investment philosophy. Special thanks go to Amy Magnotta and Dan Williams from the firm's investment group. More than three years ago in a series of meetings, Amy first identified that what I was doing in my investment advisory discussions with Rick was using mental accounting. That was an a-ha! moment. The path to embedding behavioral finance in our investment management philosophy was opened up. Dan Williams did a first-class job in editing the chapter on Brinker Capital's investment philosophy. Bill Miller, Jeff Raupp, and Andy Rosenberger each made significant contributions to this chapter as well.

Ali McCarthy, Brinker Capital's National Marketing Director, has kept this project on track and has created excellent marketing materials that explain the concepts that are the foundation of Personal Benchmark. Avery Cook, Brinker Capital's Senior Product Strategist, did an excellent job in overseeing the technical design and manufacturing of Personal Benchmark.

Dr. Daniel Crosby and I extend sincere thanks to our editor, Karen Koepp, PhD. Karen is a superior writer who developed a firm grasp of the book's thesis and content. An especially important aspect of Karen's editorial efforts has been the effective blending of my and Daniel's different writing styles. When there are two authors, finding a single voice is a challenge. Karen has done a fine job in putting our voices in sync. She is a rare talent.

Critical to shaping the content of this book and the Personal Benchmark solution have been the insights, advice, and support of many advisors. It is simply not possible to develop a concept like Personal Benchmark without testing it with the advisors who will lead its adoption. So, a special thank you to Craig Beden, Darryl Bryant, Rob Burns, Michelle Curry, Roger David, Greg Davis, John DiCiaccio, Lance Drucker, Lee Gordon, Bob Fillmore, William Jones, Rollie Martin, Glenn McKinney, John Moore, Barbara Morse, Cathey Paine, David Poole, Rob Rinvelt, Bill Wallace and Dan Whittenburg. This book and the investment offering would not have been possible without your input.

References

American Psychological Association. *Stress in America: Our Health at Risk.* Washington: American Psychological Association, 2012. https://www.apa.org/news/press/releases/stress/2011/final-2011.pdf.

Greenspan, Alan. Strategas Research Partners Conference. Washington, D.C., March, 2014.

Greenspan, Alan. *The Map and the Territory: Risk, Human Nature, and the Future of Forecasting.* New York: Penguin, 2013.

Keynes, John M. *The General Theory of Employment, Interest, And Money.* CreateSpace Independent Publishing Platform, 2011.

Sinek, Simon. TEDx Talk, September, 2009. "How Great Leaders Inspire Action." http://blog.ted.com/2010/05/04/how_great_leader.

Thaler, Richard H., and Cass R. Sunstein. *Nudge: Improving Decisions About Health, Wealth, and Happiness.* New York: Penguin, 2009.

Introduction

Come this way, honored Odysseus, great glory of the Achaians, and stay your ship, so that you can listen here to our singing; for no one else has ever sailed past this place in his black ship until he has listened to the honey-sweet voice that issues from our lips; then goes on, well-pleased, knowing more than ever he did; for we know everything that the Argives and Trojans did and suffered in wide Troy through the gods' despite. Over all the generous earth we know everything that happens.

—The Sirens, Homer's Odyssey

Odysseus, Greek king of Ithaca, is best remembered for his arduous 10-year journey home after the Trojan War, as well as the Trojan Horse he used to gain surreptitious access to enemy fortifications. As the protagonist in Homer's epic poem "The Odyssey" and returning character in "The Iliad," Odysseus is painted as a fierce warrior whose strength was matched only by his cunning. And while Odysseus may be best remembered as a warrior, perhaps his most important action on his decade-long sojourn was an act of restraint rather than brute force.

In Greek legend, Sirens were dangerous creatures that enticed sailors to come close with their beauty and enchanting music, only to lead them to shipwreck along a craggy shore. In addition to their beauty, these femmes fatale were also thought to be wellsprings of knowledge that could be harnessed for personal gain, if not for the unfortunate footnote that hearing their words led to certain death. Odysseus and his men, aware that they would soon be sailing through the Strait of the Sirens, sought to capture this knowledge without succumbing to the Sirens' fatal wiles.

After consulting with Circes, Odysseus arrived at a solution; he would have his crew fill their ears with beeswax while he would have himself lashed to the mast of the ship. Thus, he would be provided access to the wisdom of the Sirens' song, but not be able to act in a way that would endanger his life. As expected, as Odysseus heard the song of the Sirens, he flailed and begged his men to be unfettered. But true to the original game plan, they ignored their leader's protestations until they were safely out of harm's way.

It is easy to paint ancient narratives like this as dusty and irrelevant to the hustle and bustle of modern life. However, Homer's story of Odysseus and the Sirens is remarkably telling when considering the Siren song of irrational behavior that shipwrecks so many investors. Like the epic hero, we are drawn to the promise of great returns and want to charge headlong into battle. Just as Odysseus was a man of strength and action, many investors have been successful based on lives of boldness and proactivity. But in Odysseus, we find an exemplar of the ways in which sometimes the most prudent action is restraint.

In *Personal Benchmark: Integrating Behavioral Finance and Investment Management*, we outline the ways in which a program of embedded behavioral finance, fueled by what matters most to you, can be your protection against the Siren song of irrational financial behavior. Along the way, you'll learn how to improve your investment experience, increase returns formerly sacrificed to misbehavior, and worry less about "The economy" as you become increasingly focused on "My economy." Welcome to a new way of investing, a new paradigm for conceptualizing wealth, and a system of turning emotion from your portfolio's worst enemy into its best friend!

This new way is coming none too soon, given that for the 30-year period ending December 31, 2013 the average investor underperformed the S&P 500 Index by −7.42 percent annually. This figure comes from the 2014 update of Dalbar's 30-year study, which reported the average stock market investor's annualized return for this period was +3.69 percent, compared to +11.11 percent for the S&P 500 Index.

Don Phillips, Managing Director of Morningstar and one of the investment industry's most respected voices, takes aim at this pathetic outcome and used the term *Dalbar Effect* to describe the tendency to make irrational investment decisions to the detriment of performance. Phillips noted at the Tiburon conference in New York City on April 8, 2014, "The *Dalbar Effect* happens even though many investors have advisors. The *Dalbar Effect*, therefore, is a collective report card for the advice industry." Phillips, recognizing an opportunity for advisors, demands, "We gotta manage the behavior gap."

This book introduces a breakthrough solution to manage the behavior gap. This innovation is Personal Benchmark, an investment solution that embeds the principles of behavioral finance in Brinker Capital's multi-asset class investment philosophy.

Initially introduced in May 2013, Personal Benchmark is attracting a diverse and expanding group of advisors as an elegant (simple to grasp, yet sophisticated) solution for advisors to use in designing and communicating investment strategies that both create purchasing power and manage the behavioral and investment conflicts that surface throughout the investment advisory process. Advisors are recognizing Personal Benchmark as a scalable investment solution that helps close the −7.42 percent shortfall in performance.

The behavioral gap is a stunningly stubborn problem. It continues even though the capital market and economic system intents that investors benefit from its incentives—incentives designed to animate a virtuous system that produces prosperity and a better standard of living for the people it serves. It persists despite a huge advice delivery system made up of financial services firms and individual advisors. The current system for the delivery of investment advice is premised on the belief that education and disclosure will lead to rational investor behavior and prudent decision-making.

That's all well and good; however, disclosure isn't working and education isn't taking place. Something more is needed. Thus, the current behavior gap persists, despite the tens of thousands of advisors, skilled experts, who are bringing remarkable professional and personal resources to the advisory relationship.

Given the 30-year behavior gap, the Dalbar study looks askance at the current system, recommending that a new system be developed for the delivery of investment advice. My recommendation is that the new system possess four elements:

1. It must identify the principles and best practices essential to successfully helping investors manage their behavioral biases.

2. It must be elegant, delivering advice in an intuitive, easy-to-use, yet sophisticated investment offering.

3. It must be adopted by talented, well-informed advisors, as these are the individuals who will raise investors' awareness and introduce them to the tools like Personal Benchmark that could protect them from normal behavioral biases and help them achieve their purchasing power goals.

4. It must offer a proven value proposition for advisors by supporting them in knowing their clients and constructing a portfolio that consists of asset allocation and investment strategy or manager selection, rebalancing and tax optimization (Envestnet, 2014).

What Dalbar fails to acknowledge is that these four elements are reflected in the principles of behavioral finance. Moreover, Personal Benchmark solution answers the call for change by incorporating these four elements in an innovative and elegant advice delivery system embedded in a multi-asset class investment theory. It has been designed for use by talented, well-informed advisors. This book explains the theory and principles underlying Personal Benchmark and offers a snapshot of how it works.

This is a book written for a wide range of advisors. Some advisors are wealth managers who offer a variety of services such as estate planning, employee benefits, retirement planning, and investment advisory. Others specialize in employee benefits or investment advisory. Throughout this book, the term *wealth advisor* is used to refer to an advisor who includes investment advisory services in his or her practice.

Part 1 examines why we need to look at investing differently. The need emerges from the idea that advisors tend to be optimists (Chapter 1), while investors tend to make financial decisions based on less than informed or rational bases (Chapter 2). Moreover, risk is seen as inherently personal, necessitating a shift in how risk is measured and managed (Chapter 3).

Part 2 provides an introduction to the Personal Benchmark solution, including an overview of Brinker Capital's multi-asset class investing philosophy (Chapter 4), using the concept of "buckets" to create a segmented approach to investing (Chapter 5), and outlining the practices for actively managing investment performance (Chapter 6).

Part 3 describes how a purpose-driven investment strategy can be executed. In this section, we begin with an overview of our goals-based approach to planning and monitoring the investment portfolio (Chapter 7) and provide encouragement and guidelines for pursuing your Personal Benchmark (Chapter 8). The remaining two chapters provide practical tools for the advisor to use, including an easy-to-use explanation of investing according to the Brinker Capital approach and Personal Benchmark (Chapter 9) as well as a practical illustration of the Personal Benchmark solution (Chapter 10).

This book closes with a conclusion that reviews what we have learned as well as an exhortation for advisors and investors alike.

References

Dalbar, Inc. *Quantitative Analysis of Investor Behavior*. Boston: Dalbar, 2014.
Envestnet Quantitative Research Group. "Capital Sigma Study." (May 2014). Chicago: Envestnet.

PART 1

Why Do We Need to Look at Investing Differently?

CHAPTER 1

Freedom in the Market and Advisor Responsibility

Chuck Widger

Between stimulus and response, there is a space. In that space is our power to choose our response. In our response lies our growth and our freedom.

—Viktor E. Frankl, *Man's Search for Meaning (1959)*

Within the securities market, investors have great freedom in that they are able to take risks through investments in exchange for the right to receive and keep interest, dividends, and appreciation. Yet, in the midst of this freedom, they experience various perils, such as volatility and subsequently, fear and anxiety. They may receive questionable advice. And ultimately, they often make costly and even devastating errors.

In the midst of the freedom of capital markets emerges responsibility. As advisors, we know our economic system is designed to create prosperity and that, properly guided, investors can successfully participate in its rewards. Thus, we have the responsibility to help investors engage with the world on the basis of clear, constructive thinking in search of positive outcomes. We have the responsibility of helping investors understand but not be overcome by emotional and behavioral pitfalls. In the words of Don Phillips, Managing Director of Morningstar, Inc., on April 8, 2014 at the Tiburon conference in New York City, "We gotta manage the behavior gap."

This chapter examines why and how we do that, as well as how we may have fallen short on this responsibility. First, we discuss the financial markets in terms of the freedoms and opportunities they offer and what these imply for investors and advisors. Next, we examine the problem and opportunity of investor behaviors. We then review what we have been doing for investors and what outcomes we have achieved. Next, we discuss what investors really want and need. Finally, we introduce Brinker Capital's Personal Benchmark solution as a means for helping us rise to the call of responsibility.

The Financial Markets

At some level of consciousness, all of us may comprehend that we live in a time of mass flourishing. These are the good times in human history. Today there are fewer wars, higher standards of living, better educational systems, and fewer people living in poverty than at any time in human history (Zakaria 2012). The good times are not an accident. They are the work product of the lessons of history and the evolved systems and cultural beliefs that support these systems. Compared to ages past, prosperity abounds, as does the opportunity to participate in it.

The central reason for the prosperity is a greater emphasis on human freedom. Human freedom, as defined by Professor Henry Louis "Skip" Gates Jr. (2014), Chair of African American Studies at Harvard University, is the ability to do as one pleases. The ability to do as one pleases requires economic freedom.

Economic freedom requires assets that generate the cash flow required to sustain each person's definition of wellbeing. For more than 200 years, the market economies of the West, Europe, and North America have been supported by democratic governments that protect individual human rights (including economic freedom) through the rule of law. These governments have been guided by cultural values that encourage and promote material wellbeing and applaud innovation and entrepreneurship. This virtuous system of governance, informed by cultural values supporting the spirit of individual exploration and innovation has spawned a standard of living unimaginable prior to the 19th century (Phelps 2013). Moreover, it is this market-based system that has brought hundreds of millions out of poverty into the middle class in Asia and Latin America over the last 30 years.

It is this system that inspired the people of Western Ukraine and spurred them in the natural human desire of all people for a better life. Secretary of State John Kerry, who flew to Ukraine's capital city of Kiev when Russia seized the Crimea in March 2014, shared the story of one man he met in Kiev. The man told Kerry he had been to Australia and had seen firsthand how others live a prosperous life and that he wanted to live as they do. Rather than having his wealth stolen by a corrupt government, he wanted the rule of law, markets, elections and the proper institutions of liberty. In short, he wanted freedom.

Central to providing the freedom and prosperity the man in Kiev witnessed are the financial markets. In America, we depend on the credibility of financial markets. The source of America's greatness is its capital markets. It's not debatable (Kauffman 2014).

The Purpose of the Securities Industry

The post-World War II American economy has been largely financed by providing individual and institutional investors with access, through capital markets, to the equity and fixed income returns generated by economic growth.

However, as the American economy continued its industrialization on a large scale into the 20th century, wealthy families could no longer provide enough capital to finance the remarkable American economic growth "machine." Investment was now needed by large numbers of smaller investors as individuals, through vehicles like pension plans, fueled continued economic expansion and increased standards of living for the American population.

Win Smith, in *Catching Lightning in a Bottle* (2013), his excellent written history of Merrill Lynch, explains, "By bringing Wall Street to Main Street and democratizing investing, Merrill Lynch helped countless middle-class individuals save and invest, and, in turn, helped thousands of companies, municipalities, and governments fund their growth." Merrill Lynch, along with other similar institutions, executed the financial intermediation process that helped the United States to grow into an economic powerhouse.

Creating wealth on a small and large scale is the purpose of the securities industry. The Securities Industry and Financial Markets Association (2013) explains that through the medium of capital markets, the purpose of the securities industry is to match the investment capital of private investors with the opportunities offered in a dynamic, free market economy, powered forward by entrepreneurial and innovative private enterprise (SIFMA 2013).

In turn, our capitalist, market-based economic system has produced significant economic growth and wealth for many millions of Americans who may not have otherwise participated. And economic growth means a higher standard of living and attractive returns on capital. Attractive returns on capital through interest, dividends, and capital appreciation are the incentives that a market system offers to investors to support entrepreneurs and innovators as well as existing enterprises. Attractive returns are intended.

Real Wins . . . and Losses

Over the last 30 years, both the economy as measured by real gross domestic product and the stock market as measured by the S&P 500 Index grew considerably. Real gross domestic product has grown from $6.99 trillion as of December 31, 1983 to $15.94 trillion as of December 31, 2013 (U.S. Bureau of Economic Analysis 2014). During that same period, the market capitalization of the S&P 500 Index grew from $1.22 trillion as of December 31, 1983 to $16.5 trillion as of December 31, 2013 (Haver Analytics 2014). Seen as a straight line these numbers are impressive.

However, the economy does not advance in a straight line. In fact, a free market economy is characterized by change and disruption. Today's goods and services become tomorrow's rubbish, as producers innovate, entrepreneurs introduce change, and consumer demand shifts. Capital markets also innovate and some investment innovations fail.

Government periodically get macroeconomic policy wrong. The result is swings, sometimes massive, in the value of securities. Volatility happens as disruption, discovery and change bring innovation and efficiency to the production of goods and services in a dynamic economy.

When economic growth lags or falls into recession as a result of capital market excesses or flawed governmental macroeconomic maneuvers, the imperative for a democratic government is to pursue policies that will produce economic growth, prosperity and a rising standard of living for its citizens. Moreover, in post–World War II America, with its rising tide of entitlement programs, the government must produce economic growth and tax revenues to finance its obligations. After economic downturns, when growth is restored, attractive capital market returns generally follow. The ebb and flow of economic growth and capital market performance act badly on the mind of investors. As mentioned earlier, over the 30-year period ending December 31, 2013, the S&P 500 Index performed at an annualized revenue of 11.11 percent, real gross domestic product has grown from $6.99 trillion to $15.94 trillion (U.S. Bureau of Economic Analysis 2014), and market capitalization of the S&P 500 Index grew from $1.22 trillion to $16.5 trillion (Haver Analytics 2014).

Disturbingly, investors did not keep pace. In fact, they lagged by a substantial margin. Despite the exciting story indicated by the amazing performance of the economy and stock market over the last 30 years the actual experience of many investors, individual and institutional, has been different, and often disappointing as participation in capital market returns has lagged. Why?

The Rot in Denmark

Anecdotally, all skilled advisors and investment managers know from personal experience that individual investors by and large are unwilling or unable to engage in the intentional study required to understand the often arcane language used in disclosure and inscrutable concepts that guide successful investing.

When this happens, inexperienced investors may rely on the media, friends, or the claims of investment firms touting investment funds with attractive recent returns and high ratings to make their investment decisions. Moreover, as discussed in greater detail later in this book, investors (okay, and advisors, too) unconsciously strive to keep things simple. In the pursuit of simple, we recall our most recent experiences, and tend to respond emotionally to those experiences and weigh short-term predictions heavier than long-term predictions.

The result? Often, investors end up with a mix of products that don't result in a cohesive strategy that achieves their personal goals and, in an even more brilliant move, they expertly act on emotion to sell low and buy high. Take the case of "George," a seasoned, 65-year-old lawyer client of ours. In March 2009, he proclaimed, "Move me out of stocks! I want bonds!" We don't want to be too hard on him: it is understandable that, given a $500,000 portfolio of which 60 percent ($300,000) is allocated to stocks, the anxiety of a 30 percent ($90,000) decline may be emotionally untenable. Many investors, like George, cried uncle: "I can't take it! Get me out!" And their advisors did.

This has been particularly true amid the increasingly risk-averse era of 2008–2009, as many investors fled the scene like a house afire, waiting for the all-clear signal to re-enter the market. They waited and they watched. They didn't miss a minute of watching for meaningful returns to happen for risky assets . . . and they watched all the way up to a 100 percent gain in the stock market from March, 2009 to April, 2013. The only problem is, they watched it happen for other investors.

As of January through May 2013, the S&P 500 Index was up more than 15 percent, apparently the signal investors were waiting to renew their interest in putting more money in stocks and other risky assets. George recently urged me, "Just talk to me about stocks. I don't want any more bonds." Accordingly, in June and July 2013, the Federal Reserve discussed "tapering" its bond purchases. Many bond investors, seeing the value of their bonds decline, have responded by selling their bonds. (I'm starting to see a pattern here . . .)

Selling low and buying high is one of the many pitfalls or behavior gap traps that investors fall into. The unfortunate consequence of the behavior gap trap is the serious misallocation of resources, leading to the failure to create the purchasing power needed to pay for our personal, financial, or lifestyle goals. The behavior gap is why the average investor meaningfully underperforms the average returns for asset classes over time. Yet, many can't resist the temptation of irrational behavior during nerve-racking volatility and irrational exuberance.

What we need to do as advisors is help investors close the behavior gap. In other words, help them actually do what we (and sometimes they) know they should do. We'll discuss that in detail later in this chapter (and throughout this book). First, let's take a look at what we've been doing and what we have to show for it.

What We've Been Up to as Advisors

Over the last 30 years, the interaction between academics and investment practitioners, as they have collectively and collaboratively assessed investors' capital market experiences, has produced a wealth of information. Experience is studied. Lessons are learned through inductive and deductive reasoning. Best practices are developed, and we as advisors rely on these tested principles and best practices to structure and execute financial plans and investment strategies that, in theory, helps our clients achieve their important personal goals.

Many of the current best practices have their roots in the 1970s. Two notable examples are asset allocation frameworks for portfolio investment strategies and fitting investment managers into style boxes and assigning the investment managers roles within the asset allocation. These two practices are at the heart of the principles and best practices used by institutional investors, consultants, and advisors. To individual investors, these are key tools used to manage risk or the volatility inherent in investing in capital markets while accessing return.

Another example is the efficient frontier concept, identified by Harry Markowitz in 1952. This concept teaches investment practitioners how to efficiently allocate portfolios into the different asset classes that make up an investment portfolio's strategy. David Swensen used this concept to pioneer the multi-asset class or endowment model at

Yale University in the 1980s. Simply said, returns are maximized and risk is minimized when using the efficient frontier concept. You are solving for the optimal combination of risk and return. (This is different than allocating capital to the most inefficiently priced asset classes.) However, the lessons of the 2008 financial crisis taught us that the optimal combination of risk and return must be augmented by factors such as liquidity needs and client objectives as well as opportunities created by market inefficiencies.

And so it is, through the application of tested principles and proven best practices, that talented, educated, and seasoned advisors experience meaningful success in serving their clients. This creates a positive feedback loop of helping clients achieve their personal goals, and advisors in turn develop a belief in their principles and practices they use, which rises to the level of professional conviction. John Moore, founder of wealth management firm John Moore and Associates of Albuquerque, New Mexico, explained, "Once you're in practice for a time, you experience delivering the positive outcomes clients seek. For me, as a practitioner, these positive outcomes are proof statements for the principles and best practices we follow as a firm. Successful outcomes are a positive feedback loop which reinforces advisors in the work we do for clients."

Successful advisors also become more persuasive over time because of their ever-growing grasp of market economies and the capital market system, which is integral to market economies. Imbued with understanding of the capital market system and how to benefit by participation in it, advisors become optimistic. They can serve investors at a high level.

I have observed over my 37-year career in working with advisors that the best advisors have pursued what I consider "the good life." The best take satisfaction in new insights, are thrilled by meeting challenges, take pride in making their own way as entrepreneurs, and find satisfaction in their personal and professional growth. They also recognize, in Moore's words, "it's a privilege to be allowed into a client's life. Once you've been let in, you apply tested principles and best practices to plan for and achieve client goals."

Despite our confidence and past successes as advisors, recent research suggests that the picture may not be as sunny as we think. The Center for Applied Research (2012); an independent organization funded by State Street Bank, conducted an extensive survey of 2,725 investors and gathered additional insights about what investors want from 403 investment providers and government officials. The researchers found that investors wanted something much different than the institutional mix of performance and services that have been developed over the last 30 years. They concluded that what investors want will determine the shape of the investment management industry in the coming years.

Providers of investment management performance and services as well as advisors to investors would do well to heed these insights. The researchers elaborated, "One thing is clear: When it comes to performance, one size does not fit all. The industry's value proposition must evolve to one that defines performance as personal. The current benchmark model does not speak to the needs of the investor. Relative performance-based peer groups or indices may serve the provider, but the investor's view of value is more complex and reflects their own personal blend of alpha seeking, Beta generation, downside protection, liability management and income management. In the future, the investor will be the benchmark."

We are not completely behind the eight ball, however. Over the last 15 years, investment advisory services have evolved to deliver these desired elements of perceived value. But, the actual products and services provided by investment advisors often fail to align with investor goals.

As a result of 30 years of professional guidance emphasizing index-oriented investing, many individual and institutional investors design and implement investment strategies which are not designed to achieve their goals. In most other commercial endeavors, investors are encouraged to believe they are unique and need personalized, customized products and services that treat them as the unique individuals they are. Like their burgers, they want to have their investments "their way." This brings us to an important frontier in serving our investors: Just what is it that investors want?

What Investors Really Want and Need

The current system for providing investment advice is premised on the belief that education and disclosure will lead to rational investor behavior and prudent decision-making. The *Dalbar Effect* proves the system hasn't worked. This suggests that what we are offering as advisors isn't what investors really want or need. In reflecting on our experiences as advisors and investors in the market, we've come up with what we believe are the key and often unspoken wants and needs of our investors.

Help Me Resolve My Conflicts

Investors bring conflicts to advisors for advisors to solve:

- Investors want safety and, on the other hand, growth.
- When markets are volatile, investors want advisors to do something to stabilize the swing in the value of their portfolios.
- Investors want an adequate pool of investment dollars in the future and, on the other hand, to enjoy consumption today.
- When the stock market is high, investors don't want bonds until the market corrects.
- Investors want equity-like returns without the volatility.
- Investors want to perform favorably against selected capital market indices while making steady increases in purchasing power.

These conflicting desires and the behaviors they inspire often lead to disappointing and even devastating results. It is our task as advisors to resolve these and many other conflicts that investors bring.

Help Me Achieve My Personal Goals

To encourage and create successful participation, advisors and investors should ask the question, what is it investors want? And in turn, develop the investment offerings that deliver what investors want. Unfortunately, this has not been a focus of the advice delivery system until recently.

One way to define "what investors want" is in terms of the personal financial goals they want to achieve. Goals may include:

- setting money aside for near-term spending or an emergency or rainy day fund.
- current income.
- some appreciation in investment value with reduced volatility.
- long-term growth to fund retirement.

Financial services industry leaders, such as the Money Management Institute (MMI), the $3.5 trillion industry association for sponsors (e.g. Morgan Stanley, Merrill Lynch, UBS, Edward D. Jones) and investment managers participating in the managed solutions industry (e.g., Lord Abbett, Nuveen, Lazard) have increasingly recognized that goals-based investing delivers a better investment experience for investors. For example, at the April 2014 (MMI) board meeting, members overwhelmingly approved the MMI's mission to embrace this approach as their primary focus in providing investment advice. At the April 8–9, 2014 Tiburon Conference in New York City, well-known industry leaders also emphatically embraced goals-based investing. Tiburon conference attendees are limited to C-Suite executives from prominent financial services firms. Chip Roame, Tiburon's CEO, emphasized, "We need to care about the fund owner doing well."

Mark Casady, CEO of LPL Financial, echoed Chip's message during his panel presentation at the conference when he said, "We should be about outcomes, not returns." On the same panel, Mary Mack, President of Wells Fargo Advisors, continued the argument for shifting from a relative return focus to outcomes. Mary identified raising risk consciousness as a significant opportunity for advisors. She noted, "It's no longer about keeping up with the Joneses. It's about keeping up with the plan." Present on another panel at the Tiburon conference was Don Phillips, Managing Director of Morningstar, Inc. Don amplified the emphasis on focusing on investor outcomes. "What matters is the investor experience. We as an industry will only thrive to the extent of good investor outcomes."

One way to define "what investors want" is in terms of the experience investors seek. This may include competitive returns, returns that are competitive with a capital market index, managed volatility, or return per unit of risk. This concept also can be understood in terms of what investors value, such as:

- returns: both alpha and beta.
- income management: the creation and management of income independent of earned income.
- managed volatility (too much is simply too much).
- transparency.
- objectivity.
- more predictable outcomes.
- communication.

Delivering an investment experience that contains the mix of these elements and which fits the investor's personal goals or desired outcomes is what advisors must do. Whatever the investors' personal goals and desired experience, these serve as the personal benchmark for the investing strategy advisors must develop and execute. Lee Gordon, CEO of Mesirow's Private Wealth Group and a 22-year veteran advisor, oversees $5 billion in assets and seeks to help investors finance the lifestyle they have worked hard to achieve. In Gordon's words, "To achieve your financial goals, you've got to get on and stay on the train, otherwise you'll never reach your destination."

Help Me Increase My Purchasing Power

Investors often talk about and think about comparing their investment strategy performance to capital market indices to assess their investment experience. The problem is, capital market return and risk is not relevant for achieving personal goals. Capital market indices measure speed, not the actual progress toward the goal. To determine progress toward goals, another metric is required: purchasing power. What gets measured gets done. Capital market indices have risk/return characteristics that tell investors of their rate of speed and the potholes (level of volatility) they may encounter, not their destinations.

The near-term tendency of focusing on capital market indices has been reinforced for more than 30 years as advisors adopted a common practice of guiding the development and measurement of investment strategies by these measures. A simple index might typically be a 60/40 blend of the S&P 500 Index and the Barclay's Aggregate Bond Index. The historical risk/return characteristics of these indices are well known, and, are typically seen as the best guide to the likely future investment experience. So, the theory goes, capital market index outcomes, or experience, will produce the desired return and acceptable risk for individual investors.

However, this theory simply hasn't played out in reality. Many investors do not want the risk experience or outcome that market indices at times provide. All too often the practice of using capital market indices to create investment strategies leads to a beat-the-index mentality. All investment advisors have had clients ask, "How am I doing in comparison to the S&P 500 Index? Did I beat it?" This leads to a discussion of relative return not absolute return. Relative return analysis is about comparing the client's investment return (and risk) to the S&P 500 Index's return for given periods. This is the wrong question and it leads to the *Dalbar Effect*.

David Poole, an advisor based out of Columbia, South Carolina, has built a very successful advisory practice through financial planning. In establishing client personal goals through the financial planning process, David emphasizes that the recommended investment strategies are designed to achieve purchasing power. Even though he emphasizes purchasing power, investor clients want to compare strategy perfor-mance to the S&P 500 Index rather than the purchasing power goals. David relates, "The consumer is so bombarded. It's in the water." He goes on to note, "Too much index comparison is a distraction from focusing on the goals developed in the financial plan."

The right questions investors should ask are: "Am I comfortable with the level of volatility in my portfolio and am I able to stick to my long-term plan?" Market indices can be used to provide context in various market environments, but the real performance comparison should be to the investor's long-term goals and objectives.

In short, articulated or not, the achievement of desired purchasing power is the investment experience most investors want. This makes purchasing power the objective and destination of a long-term investment strategy. Bill Wallace, a talented and successful advisor from Northern California, recently remarked that reasonably affluent and high net worth investors understand purchasing power. These investors say, "We like this world. What do we need to do to remain here? Give us strategies which will keep us here."

Help Me Weather Volatility

Potholes happen. Death and taxes do, too. But our focus here is potholes. And what happens when our investor's well-planned and well-implemented investment hits one?

Take the case of highly volatile markets like 2000–2002 and 2008–2009, when markets declined more than 40 percent. Investors developed a newfound intolerance for risk. They rushed to sell their risky assets (stocks) and moved into conservative assets (bonds). Whew, crisis averted. Or, was it?

The paradox is that the risky assets they dumped recovered because, in market-based economies, governments must pursue policies that promote economic growth. As we have witnessed in recent years, in order to remain in power, governments in democratic countries with market-based economies promote economic growth to sustain social benefits promised to their populations. To have sustainable economic growth, there must be investment, and in order to have investment there must be return on (and of) capital.

Capital market returns within recent years demonstrate these dynamics. Since March 2009, the Federal Reserve has pursued monetary policies designed to stimulate economic growth. Its two key monetary policies have been (a) a near-zero discount rate to stimulate lending by banks, and (b) the expansion of its balance sheet by buying U.S. Treasuries and mortgage-backed securities.

The large purchases of government securities have pushed down the yields on fixed-income securities to very low levels. Investors seeking income, or yield, are thus forced to buy or invest in riskier assets like high dividend paying stocks. The result is the value of riskier assets is "forced" up, while yields on less risky assets are "repressed." This monetary policy is called financial repression. It is a policy tool which monetary authorities, like the Federal Reserve, use when the ratio of the government's debt-to-GDP ratio is too high. Lower interest rates make it easier for the government to service its debt while increased prices for riskier assets encourage investment and consumption; increased investment and consumption are likely to produce, hopefully sustainable, economic growth.

So, although they were well-intentioned, the government's tactics didn't quite work out for those investors that fled from riskier stocks for safer havens. The result? Dramatic underperformance. From the equity market bottom in March 2009, the S&P 500 Index has returned an annualized 25.8 percent compared to a return of 4.9 percent for fixed income. Figure 1.1 reveals that for the 30-year period ending December 31, 2013, the average fixed income fund investor yielded a paltry 0.7 percent annualized return, in comparison to Barclays Capital Aggregate Bond Index (+7.67 percent) and the S&P 500 Index (+11.11 percent). This reveals a substantial performance gap between average individual investors and well-known asset classes.

This investor behavior during the 2008–2009 financial crisis is an example of why the *Dalbar Effect* exists.

The lesson from the last 12 or so years is that investors do not want high volatility. They did not enjoy nor do they want to repeat the bear market experiences of 2000–2002 and 2008–2009. These big potholes disrupted many plans for creating purchasing power, the desired destination.

Investment strategies guided by, or measured in comparison to capital market indices, delivered an investment experience like the

FIGURE 1.1

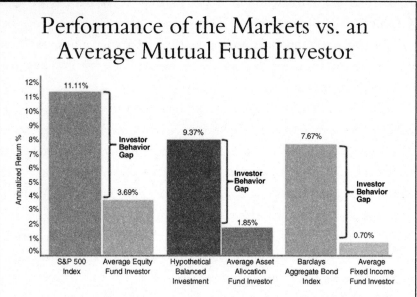

Performance of the Markets vs. an Average Mutual Fund Investor

Source: Quantitative Analysis of Investor Behavior (QAIB), 2014, Dalbar, Inc. www .dalbarinc.com. Data from January 1, 1984 to December 31, 2013. Average equity fund investor and average bond fund investor performance results are based on the DALBAR 2014 QAIB study. DALBAR is an independent, Boston-based financial research firm. Using monthly fund data supplied by the Investment Company Institute, QAIB calculates investor returns as the change in assets after excluding sales, redemptions and exchanges. This method of calculation captures realized and unrealized capital gains, dividends, interest, trading costs, sales charges, fees, expenses and any other costs. After calculating investor returns in dollar terms, two percentages are calculated for the period examined: Total investor return rate and annualized investor return rate. Total return rate is determined by calculating the investor return dollars as a percentage of the net of the sales, redemptions, and exchanges for the period. Hypothetical balanced investment based on the performance of an investment weighted 50% to the S&P 500 index and 50% to the Barclays Aggregate Bond Index and rebalanced monthly. Equity benchmark performance is represented by the Standard & Poor's 500 Composite Index, an unmanaged index of 500 common stocks generally considered representative of the U.S. stock market. Fixed income benchmark performance is represented by the Barclays Aggregate Bond Index, an unmanaged index of bonds generally considered representative of the bond market. Indexes do not take into account the fees and expenses associated with investing, and individuals cannot invest directly in any index. Performance of an index is not illustrative of any particular investment. Past performance is no guarantee of future results.

S&P 500 Index, which included declines of more than 40 percent in both of the aforementioned bear market periods. These declines meant that even if investors weathered the precipitous drops, they still required more time to accumulate or grow principal to create the needed purchasing power.

What this boils down to is that advisors must develop and oversee the execution of an investment strategy that anticipates the inevitable potholes and stays the course of efficiently compounding the investment portfolio to create purchasing power. This requires both the management of the investment portfolio and the management of investor behavior. Skilled, experienced advisors know that one of their most important responsibilities is to help investors avoid making emotional decisions when volatility is high or when markets are irrationally exuberant.

Now Explain It to Me Like I'm a Four-Year-Old

Listening to all of these requests, let's assume we helped our investors resolve their conflicts, work toward achieving their personal goals, increasing their purchasing power, and weathering volatility. One more vital request is left. In the words of Joe Miller, the attorney played by Denzel Washington in the 1993 movie, *Philadelphia,* when he wanted to thoroughly understand something, he (and our investors) say: "Now, explain it to me like I'm a four-year-old . . ." Or, for aficionados of crime dramas, our investors, like Paul Newman's character in the 1967 movie, *Cool Hand Luke* may quip, "What we got here is a failure to communicate."

In any case, the dilemma for many investors is that they do not receive the sophisticated investment advice they need in an easy-to-understand, intuitive format that helps them discipline their emotional biases. Many years ago, Rollie Martin, a talented advisor from Minnesota, offered his approach by explaining his value proposition to clients. Rollie impressed upon me that his goal is to help clients and prospects avoid three disastrous decisions over their investment lifetime, referring to the all-too-enticing urge to sell at the bottom of the three bear markets any given individual likely will experience in his or her lifetime.

These various concepts reflected in investors' wants and outlined in this section are reflected in Dalbar's (2014) four recommendations to advisors:

1. Reframe the advice discussion to properly set investor expectations. Reframing begins by emphasizing capital preservation through allocation to lower volatility investments, as safety is desired by all investors.

2. Reframe investing in comparison to investor goals rather than to average market returns. The Dalbar report explains, "Linking the investment to a personal desire keeps the attention focused on that desire and avoids the distraction of market volatility that leads to bad investment decisions." In short, a goal helps advisors and investors manage risk.

3. Monitor risk tolerance, understanding that investors' risk tolerance varies over time and is based on investors' purposes. In other words, an investor's portfolio likely will reflect a range of different risk tolerance levels, depending upon each group of resources allocated and its purposes.

4. Use probabilities rather than certainties when discussing risk and return outcomes. Possible outcomes for specific asset classes vary widely. Probabilities give investors a rational basis for making allocation decisions.

The challenge is to design an advice delivery system that incorporates the Dalbar recommendations while addressing investor wants, needs, and biases.

A New Investment Advice Delivery System

In order to satisfy a complex set of investor wants and needs, while remedying the shortfall known as the *Dalbar Effect*, a new investment advice delivery system needs to be created. Successful explanation and implementation of investment advice requires an investment advice delivery system that incorporates the Dalbar recommendations and includes a choice architecture that nudges investors in the direction of choices that control their behavioral biases.

A nudge is to push mildly in the ribs to alert, remind, or gently warn. A choice architecture is an organized approach for making decisions, an approach that focuses on the small details and points people in a particular direction that will have beneficial effects (Thaler and Sunstein, 2009 p. 4).

Thaler and Sunstein illustrate the choice architecture concept with a story about a school district dietician. The school district dietician and a friend with an expertise in statistics developed a theory about arranging the presentation of the food in school cafeterias to encourage students to make healthy food choices. The dietician, as a choice architect, realized that if she put the desserts first and the fries at eye level students would tend to pick the desserts and fries rather than vegetables, fruits, and other healthy choices. After experimenting with various arrangements in different schools, the dietician created a choice architecture, or arrangement of food choices, that improved student diets by 25 percent (Thaler and Sunstein, 2009 p. 1–3).

The use of choice architecture to create a positive influence on people's choices is characterized in *Nudge: Improving Decisions About Health, Wealth, and Happiness* as libertarian paternalism. It is libertarian in the sense, as Milton Friedman might have put it, that people are "free to choose." It is paternalistic in the sense that the choice architecture is designed to influence people to make choices that are likely to have a positive effect on their lives. Six principles should guide the design of an effective choice architecture. The six principles are:

1. Avoid inertia or status quo bias by establishing a default option that is generally perceived to produce positive effects, or by establishing a required choice.

2. Expect error at times and incorporate the opportunity for people to correct their decisions.

3. Provide feedback.

4. Map the consequences of people's choice in ways they understand.

5. Structure complex choices to affect outcomes.

6. Make incentives salient.

Thaler and Sunstein (2009, p. 74) recognize that constructing and managing portfolios is a complex task that average people do not face in the flow of everyday life. Moreover, most people lack the tools necessary to create the appropriate feedback as well as the capacity to translate investment concepts and tools into easily understood terms.

As a consequence, people make a lot of mistakes in constructing and managing portfolios. They can benefit from a helpful and forgiving investment choice architecture, which, for example, manages the tendencies to think short-term and not long-term and use inapplicable rules of thumb. A managed account can be a helpful solution (Thaler and Sunstein, 2009, p. 121–122).

Brinker Capital has built a solution that incorporates the Dalbar recommendations and includes a choice architecture that nudges people toward the successful management of their behavioral biases. This new solution is called Personal Benchmark. Following the Dalbar recommendations, it reframes investor expectations through an emphasis on allocations that manage volatility by focusing on investor goals, managing a range of risk preferences, and discussing the probabilities of different risk and return outcomes.

This new solution provides a choice architecture that avoids inertia, or status quo bias, by establishing a system for investors to easily understand and make required choices.

The complex choices to be made are structured to affect outcomes. The consequences of these choices are mapped or shown through intuitive graphics. The incentives for each alternative choice are salient. And, the choice architecture is flexible, creating the opportunity for correction through a feedback system.

This new solution, Personal Benchmark, creates a new advice delivery system. Let's take a look.

Brinker Capital and Personal Benchmark

Throughout Brinker Capital's 27-year history as a firm, it has been and will continue to be an innovator and entrepreneur. Founded as a platform to provide investors with access to high quality, top performing separate account investment managers, Brinker Capital has evolved to be one of the nation's finest independent investment management firms.

A History of Innovation

Its history is accentuated by innovations (see Figure 1.2) that improve the advisor and investor investment experience. Included among its innovations are being one of the first independent fee-based clearing arrangements (1989), one of the first multi-asset class mutual fund offerings (1995), a fully automated proposal system (among the first, in 1995), an automated monthly distribution system for retirement accounts (2005), and the award-winning Crystal Strategy I Absolute Return portfolio (2009).

FIGURE 1.2

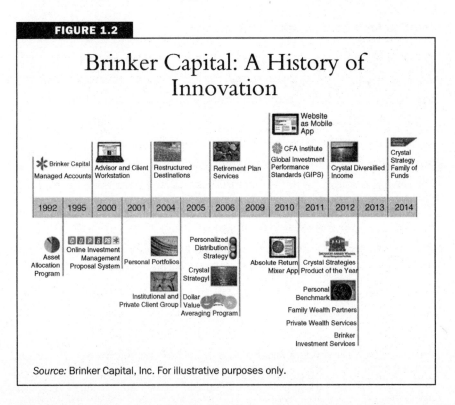

Brinker Capital: A History of Innovation

Source: Brinker Capital, Inc. For illustrative purposes only.

One of Brinker Capital's most recent innovations is the Personal Benchmark solution, which was introduced in 2013. Personal Benchmark has been designed and developed to help investors manage their emotional biases while achieving the attractive returns needed to finance the lifestyle they seek.

We believe this scalable solution is a multi-faceted tool that will enable advisors to efficiently sort through the conflicts and confusion investors bring to advisors in their search to find the appropriate strategy for achieving their personal financial goals.

The solution is founded upon Brinker Capital's theory of investing which is multi-asset class investing. It is made up of a body of principles that have been studied, tested, and formalized over a long period of time, some of which are rooted in hundred-year-old observations and insights. These core principles frame Brinker Capital's multi-asset class investment theory and include diversification, innovation, active management, and equity-like bias.

The Personal Benchmark Solution

Personal Benchmark is an elegant (simple to grasp yet sophisticated) solution for advisors to use in designing and communicating investment strategies both which create purchasing power and manage the investment and behavioral conflicts which surface while advising investors.

Our approach or solution focuses on the investor's purchasing power and risk management goals throughout the advisory process. The investor's purchasing power and risk management goals each guide the design and execution of the investor's investment strategy and make up of his or her Personal Benchmark.

The investment strategy design begins by framing the discussion with the investor with an easy to grasp model. Behavioral finance tells us people naturally account for mathematical or financial activity through mental accounting, or buckets. We naturally account for, or keep track of, our basic banking and investing tasks through a checking account, a savings account, and an investment account. If this is how we naturally account for numerical activity, then why not "mentally account" for or frame our investment strategy in a similarly, simple, easy to understand fashion?

Most investors will have four basic goals. Each of these goals can be "mentally accounted" for as separate accounts, or buckets, as defined:

- Safety: To preserve principal and reduce overall portfolio volatility.
- Income: To generate cash flow while limiting volatility.
- Tactical: To manage volatility and focus on opportunity for appreciation.
- Accumulation: Appreciation and acceptance of greater volatility for the purpose of increasing future purchasing power.

Obviously, each of these buckets meet a tangible investment goal such as income for spending and/or income for spending needs and less risk. Not as obvious, but just as important, each bucket also solves for intangible investor misbehaviors. In the next chapter we will introduce common investor mistakes/tendencies under three pillars described as Simple, Safe, and Sure. These pillars provide the motive or the answer to the question why four buckets make for the best investor experience.

Brinker Capital offers a range of portfolios and has determined with reasonable accuracy the risk/return characteristics of each strategy. This enables his or her Personal Benchmark to guide the selection of the strategy most fitting for the investor's goals, as indicated by the bucket allocations. Taken as a whole, the investment strategies for each bucket constitute the investor's portfolio strategy. Following implementation, the advisor reports to the investor on whether the strategy for each bucket is achieving the goal set for each bucket.

The Case of Jim and Jane Dodd

Let's look at a simple hypothetical example to illustrate how Brinker Capital's new solution and advice delivery system works. Assume an advisor's client is a couple, Jim and Jane Dodd. Jim and Jane are each age 50, both work, and each has maintained a personal savings program. Jim has $300,000 in a personal savings account and $100,000 in an IRA. Jane has $500,000 in a personal savings account and $100,000 in an IRA. Jim and Jane are still concerned about investing in capital markets because of the 2008–2009 Financial Crisis and the Great Recession. While they want their investment portfolio to grow, management of the portfolio's volatility is very important to them. Currently the couple is drawing about $20,000 each year for personal cash flow needs and wants to continue these distributions from the investment portfolio. Jim and Jane want to keep track of their investment portfolio on a combined basis at the household level.

This data provides the advisor with the essential information needed to create a portfolio investment strategy for Jim and Jane Dodd. The advisor can then turn to Brinker Capital's proprietary proposal system either with Jim and Jane present, or on his or her own, to develop the appropriate sophisticated multi-asset class investment strategy that is presented in an easy-to-communicate format of mental accounts or buckets.

Creating the Proposal

Figure 1.3 depicts the Brinker Capital proposal screen that the advisor uses to intuitively determine the appropriate asset allocation for Jim and Jane. In the center of the screen is a continuum slider bar labeled "More Conservative" on the left and "More Aggressive" on the right. By moving the slider along the continuum, the advisor visually identifies the mix of risk and reward they are most comfortable with. Part of the visual experience is that as the slider is moved along the continuum, the content of the cylinder at the lower right of the screen changes. If the slider is moved toward More Conservative, for example, the percentage of portfolio assets to the Income and Safety accounts, or buckets, will increase while the percentage allocated to the Accumulation and Tactical accounts will decrease.

Next, the advisor confirms the answers to the classic questions in a risk tolerance questionnaire presented by the system, clicks "Next," and is presented with the visual depiction of how Jim and Jane's assets are allocated on a combined basis or household level (see Figure 1.4). At the same time, the Brinker Capital systems and the custodian maintain separate registration of each of the specified accounts.

This screen also displays a description of the investment strategy selected for each of the four buckets. For example, the Accumulation bucket, which has $500,000 of allocated assets, is executed by a Brinker Capital investment strategy called "Destinations Moderate."

FIGURE 1.3

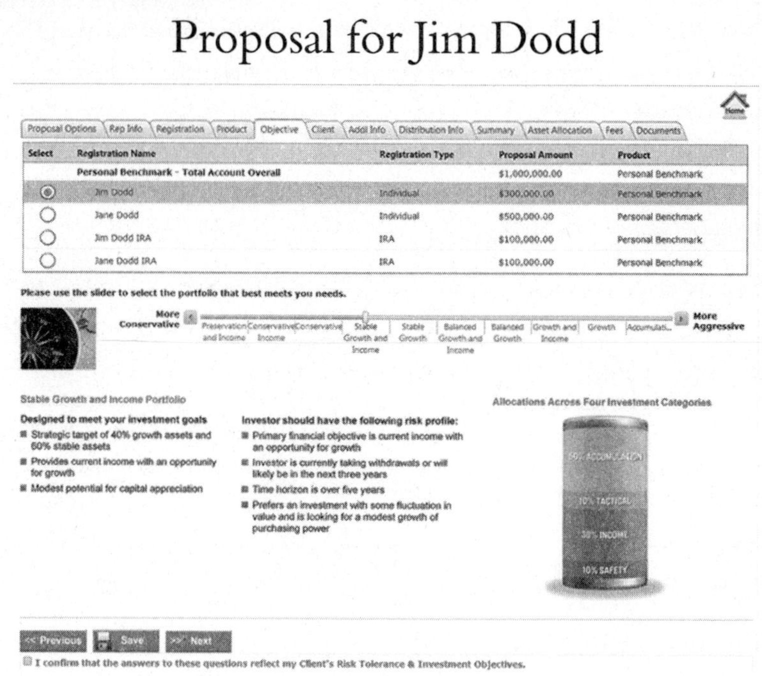

Proposal for Jim Dodd

Source: Brinker Capital, Inc. Hypothetical example for illustrative purposes only.

FIGURE 1.4

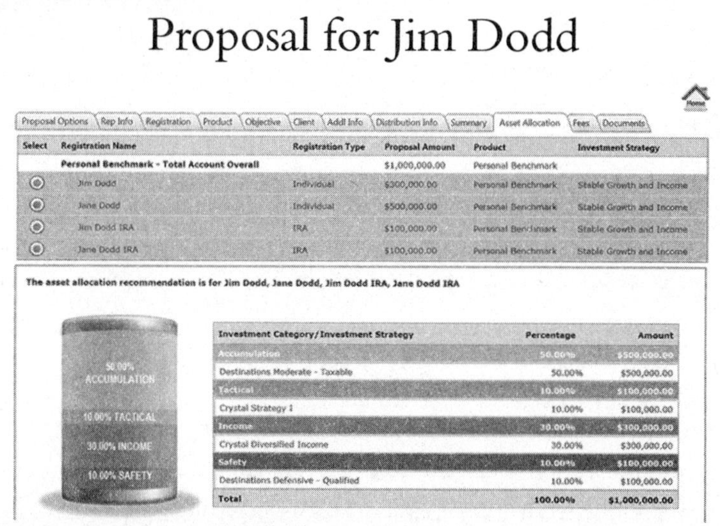

Proposal for Jim Dodd

Source: Brinker Capital, Inc. Hypothetical example for illustrative purposes only.

Destinations Moderate allocates up to 60 percent to equities (domestic U.S. and international). The balance of the strategy is allocated to the other four asset classes (fixed income, private equity, absolute return, and real assets). The purpose of the accumulation mandate for the bucket is to grow purchasing power by achieving annualized returns of CPI plus 4 percent over a 10-year period. To obtain current portfolio performance, contact your financial advisor or a member of the Brinker Capital Service Team.

We also see in Figure 1.4 that $100,000 has been allocated to the Tactical bucket. The strategy selected to implement the Tactical bucket is Brinker Capital's "Crystal Strategy I Absolute Return Portfolio."

Crystal Strategy I is a multi-asset class global macro strategy which hedges to reduce volatility. Its goal is to produce absolute return not relative return. Its purpose is to deliver returns which exceed CPI plus 2 percent over a three year period. To obtain current portfolio performance, contact your financial advisor or a member of the Brinker Capital Service Team.

The Income bucket is funded principally from the $300,000 allocation to this bucket. The strategy selected to execute the Income bucket is "Crystal Diversified Income."

Crystal Diversified Income is a multi-asset class strategy that uses hedges to reduce volatility. Its return goal is a yield of greater than CPI. To obtain current portfolio performance, contact your financial advisor or a member of the Brinker Capital Service Team.

Jim and Jane want muted volatility, provided by the 10 percent allocation to the Safety bucket. The strategy selected for this bucket is "Destinations Defensive."

Destinations Defensive is a multi-asset class strategy and its goal is to generate positive returns in each rolling 12-month period. To obtain current portfolio performance, contact your financial advisor or a member of the Brinker Capital Service Team.

The advisor proceeds through several more screens after what we see in Figure 1.4 in the Brinker Capital proposal system before clicking on the proposal Print button.

The individual investor proposal and the institutional investor invest-ment policy serve the same purpose or function. Each intermediates or connects the investors personal or institutional goals with the risk, return, and other statistical measures of the selected investment strategy. In other words, for the individual investor the proposal personalizes the mathe-matical expression of the level of risk and return created by the selected investment strategy. The Personal Benchmark proposal transforms the mathematical description of return and risk into a statement of the investor's goals by framing the description of investor goals as individual mental accounts or buckets. Through the proposal, the investor is focused on his or her goals and views the investment strategy as the means for achieving the several separate investor goals.

Presenting the Proposal

Just as the proposal system is intuitive and easy-to-use, so is the proposal itself. The proposal communicates Brinker Capital's investment philos-ophy, the combined recommended investment strategy for Jim and Jane, and the strategy's historical performance. The first page of the proposal presents Brinker Capital's multi-asset class investment philoso-phy in a clear, succinct fashion (see Figure 1.5).

The next page of the proposal displays the calendar showing annual performance of Brinker Capital's six asset classes, illustrating that a multi-asset class philosophy presents a broad opportunity set and various ways to win (see Figure 1.6).

Next, Jim and Jane's proposal presents the empirical proof statement for multi-asset class investing. Figure 1.7 shows that for the 42-year period ending December 2013, a multi-asset class investment strategy compounds more wealth or purchasing power than either the S&P 500 Index or a blended 60/40 index. The multi-asset class strategy outperforms because it com-pounds off higher lows. The top line represents the equally weighted six asset class index. The fact that it compounds off higher lows is clearly indicated within the circles, which are the 2000–2001 and 2008–2009 bear markets.

Up to this point, the proposal has included standard educational pieces that all investors receive. The remainder of the proposal presents

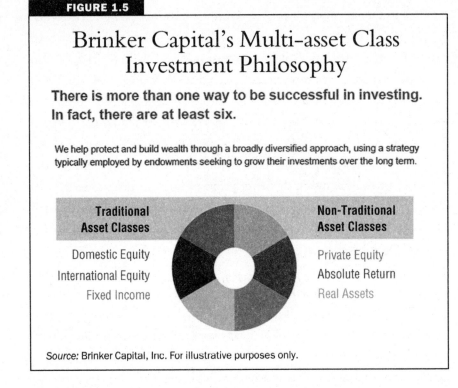

FIGURE 1.5

Brinker Capital's Multi-asset Class Investment Philosophy

There is more than one way to be successful in investing. In fact, there are at least six.

We help protect and build wealth through a broadly diversified approach, using a strategy typically employed by endowments seeking to grow their investments over the long term.

Traditional Asset Classes	Non-Traditional Asset Classes
Domestic Equity	Private Equity
International Equity	Absolute Return
Fixed Income	Real Assets

Source: Brinker Capital, Inc. For illustrative purposes only.

information customized for the investor, based upon the selected investment strategies.

Figure 1.8 presents a summary of the recommended combined investment strategy, including funds allocated, strategies chosen, and overall diversification.

Figure 1.9 communicates the strategy through the mental accounting framework of the four buckets. Just as humans account for their basic financial activities through their checking account, savings account, and investment account, Personal Benchmark establishes a mental accounting framework for communicating Jim and Jane's investment portfolio. This page also displays the overall investment objective, goals, and risk profile.

Of course, Jim and Jane want to know how the combined recommended investment strategy has performed in the past. Figure 1.10 depicts year-to-date, one-year, and three-year annualized performance, as well as the performance since the strategy was launched for them (upon

FIGURE 1.6

Annual Performance of Brinker Capital's Six Asset Classes

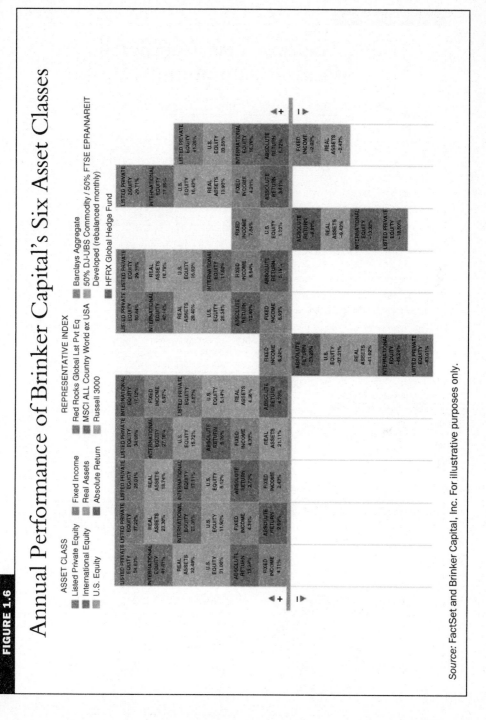

Source: FactSet and Brinker Capital, Inc. For illustrative purposes only.

FIGURE 1.7

Presentation That Additional Diversification Compounds Wealth

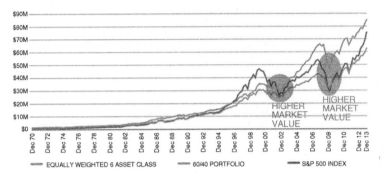

━━━ EQUALLY WEIGHTED 6 ASSET CLASS   ━━━ 60/40 PORTFOLIO   ━━━ S&P 500 INDEX

Source: Brinker Capital, Inc., Fact Set, Cambridge Associates, NCREIF. This Growth of $1M chart is for illustrative purposes only. No representation that the results represent performance of actual client accounts is intended. The chart is intended to demonstrate the impact on a traditional portfolio of diversification through the inclusion of additional asset classes over a long-term investment horizon. Data from January 1, 1971 through December 31, 2013.

FIGURE 1.8

Dodd's Combined Recommended Strategy

Detailed Investment Strategies

Account Registration	Brinker Program	Assets
Jim Dodd	Personal Benchmark - Crystal Diversified Income	$300,000
Jane Dodd	Personal Benchmark - Destinations Moderate - Taxable	$500,000
Jim Dodd IRA	Personal Benchmark - Crystal Strategy I	$100,000
Jane Dodd IRA	Personal Benchmark - Destinations Defensive - Qualified	$100,000
Total		$1,000,000

Overall Diversification

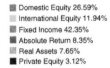

■ Domestic Equity 26.59%
□ International Equity 11.94%
■ Fixed Income 42.35%
■ Absolute Return 8.35%
▨ Real Assets 7.65%
■ Private Equity 3.12%

Source: Brinker Capital, Inc. Hypothetical example for illustrative purposes only.

FIGURE 1.9

Recommended Investment Strategy: Personal Benchmark

Portfolio Holdings

Investment Category/Strategy	Registration Name	Target Allocation	Target Allocation
Accumulation		**$500,000**	**50.00%**
Destinations Moderate - Taxable	Jane Dodd	$500,000	50.00%
Tactical		**$100,000**	**10.00%**
Crystal Strategy I	Jim Dodd IRA	$100,000	10.00%
Income		**$300,000**	**30.00%**
Crystal Diversifield Income	Jim Dodd	$300,000	30.00%
Safety		**$100,000**	**10.00%**
Destinations Defensive - Qualified	Jane Dodd IRA	$100,000	10.00%
TOTAL		**$1,000,000**	**100.00%**

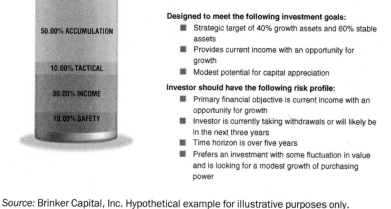

50.00% ACCUMULATION

10.00% TACTICAL

30.00% INCOME

10.00% SAFETY

Overall Investment Objective: Stable Growth and Income

Designed to meet the following investment goals:
■ Strategic target of 40% growth assets and 60% stable assets
■ Provides current income with an opportunity for growth
■ Modest potential for capital appreciation

Investor should have the following risk profile:
■ Primary financial objective is current income with an opportunity for growth
■ Investor is currently taking withdrawals or will likely be in the next three years
■ Time horizon is over five years
■ Prefers an investment with some fluctuation in value and is looking for a modest growth of purchasing power

Source: Brinker Capital, Inc. Hypothetical example for illustrative purposes only.

implementation). This figure also depicts the varying performance of the asset classes executed by the strategy. This quilt chart offers perspective on asset class performance trends as well as nearer-term variability in performance.

The proposal also illustrates the growth of a $100,000 investment of the previous five years, as illustrated in Figure 1.11.

Once the Dodds accept the recommended strategy, investment advisory agreements are executed and assets are transferred to an independent custodian. Brinker Capital then directs the investment of the Dodd's assets in accordance with their investment strategy.

FIGURE 1.10

Performance of Recommended Investment Strategy: Personal Benchmark

Performance Through 06/30/2014

Annualized	QTD	YTD	1 Year	3 Year	Since Inc. (1/1/2009)
Recommended Investment Strategy	2.59%	3.77%	11.62%	7.40%	9.93%
CPI	0.87%	1.32%	2.08%	1.85%	2.15%
Calendar Year	2013	2012	2011	2010	2009
Recommended Investment Strategy	11.06%	9.92%	1.49%	9.43%	19.66%
CPI	1.51%	1.76%	3.02%	1.42%	2.81%

Historical Table of Investment Returns

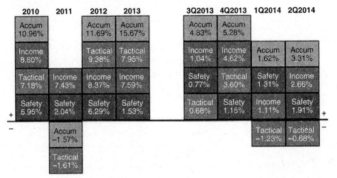

Source: Brinker Capital, Inc. Hypothetical example for illustrative purposes only. The performance information for the Personal Benchmark strategies presents back-tested performance of a hypothetical account invested with the specific investment strategies (or a proxy thereof) included in the Recommended Investment Strategy and not the historical performance of actual accounts invested in the Recommended Investment Strategy. Calculations assume annual rebalancing of the account to the target allocations in the Recommended Investment Strategy. No representation that any actual account has achieved such performance is intended. The performance information does not reflect the deduction of advisory fees payable to Brinker Capital or other expenses for services not covered by the advisory fee. These fees and expenses will reduce an investor's return.

Reporting Performance

Each quarter following implementation, Brinker Capital provides a performance report of the investment strategy and its progress in creating purchasing power.

FIGURE 1.11

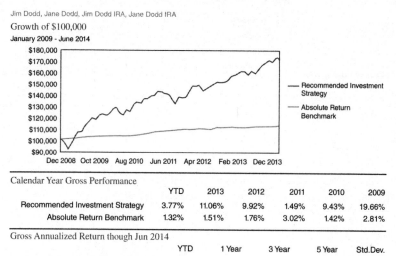

Historical Performance of Recommended Investment Strategy: Personal Benchmark

Jim Dodd, Jane Dodd, Jim Dodd IRA, Jane Dodd IRA

Growth of $100,000

January 2009 - June 2014

Legend:
— Recommended Investment Strategy
— Absolute Return Benchmark

Calendar Year Gross Performance

	YTD	2013	2012	2011	2010	2009
Recommended Investment Strategy	3.77%	11.06%	9.92%	1.49%	9.43%	19.66%
Absolute Return Benchmark	1.32%	1.51%	1.76%	3.02%	1.42%	2.81%

Gross Annualized Return though Jun 2014

	YTD	1 Year	3 Year	5 Year	Std.Dev.
Recommended Investment Strategy	3.77%	11.62%	7.40%	9.70%	7.00%
Absolute Return Benchmark	1.32%	2.08%	1.85%	2.05%	0.67%

Source: Brinker Capital, Inc. Hypothetical example for illustrative purposes only. The performance information for the Personal Benchmark strategies presents back-tested performance of a hypothetical account invested with the specific investment strategies (or a proxy thereof) included in the Recommended Investment Strategy and not the historical performance of actual accounts invested in the Recommended Investment Strategy. Calculations assume annual rebalancing of the account to the target allocations in the Recommended Investment Strategy. No representation that any actual account has achieved such performance is intended. The performance information does not reflect the deduction of advisory fees payable to Brinker Capital or other expenses for services not covered by the advisory fee. These fees and expenses will reduce an investor's return. The standard deviation shown is for the length of time displayed on the Growth of $100,000 Chart.

Figure 1.12, consistent with the proposal, presents the investment strategy in terms of its mental accounts in the upper-left portion of the figure. The lower-left portion identifies the strategies that execute each bucket, including amounts allocated in absolute, percentage, and target terms. The bottom-right portion reports performance for the bucket and

FIGURE 1.12

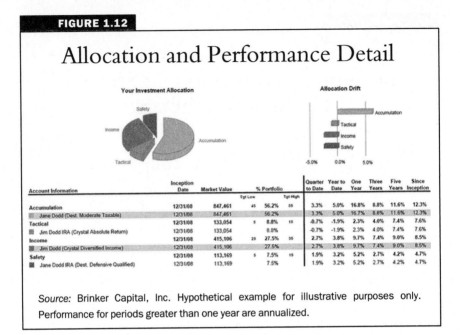

Allocation and Performance Detail

Source: Brinker Capital, Inc. Hypothetical example for illustrative purposes only. Performance for periods greater than one year are annualized.

each of its strategies. The upper-right portion of the screen shot depicts the direction of drift from the target for each bucket's value and identifies the need to reallocate among the buckets.

Figure 1.13 provides an additional tool for performance evaluation. Here, the advisor and the investor concentrate on performance of the mental accounts, or buckets, against their plan and within the context of the performance of the buckets in the current year's quarters and in three prior calendar years. The upper-left portion provides conclusions on achievement of CPI goals while the lower-left reports the year-to-date and since-inception return. The lower-right offers an area chart which pictures how each bucket is trending over time. Safety, for example, at the bottom is preserving capital as it is supposed to do while the accumulation account is growing ever larger, creating more purchasing power.

Figure 1.14 depicts the next performance report page, which graphically illustrates how each bucket has been performing in terms of its stated purpose. For example, the black line in the upper left portion shows the Safety bucket maintains value, while risky assets

FIGURE 1.13

Personal Benchmark Evaluation

Period Ending June 30, 2014

Performance Versus Plan

Accumulation ACCUMULATION
Goal: CPI + 4% over a 10 year period
YTD Return in the Accumulation pool exceeds the stated goal
Since Inception Return in the Accumulation pool exceeds the stated goal

Tactical TACTICAL
Goal: CPI + 2% over a 3 year period
YTD Return in the Tactical pool trails the stated goal
Since Inception Return in the Tactical pool exceeds the stated goal

Income INCOME
Goal: Yield greater than CPI
YTD Return in the Income pool exceeds the stated goal
Since Inception Return in the Income pool exceeds the stated goal

Safety SAFETY
Goal: Positive return for a 12 month period
YTD Return in the Safety pool exceeds the stated goal
Since Inception Return in the Safety pool exceeds the stated goal

	YTD	Inception
Overall	3.9%	10.1%
Accumulation	5.0%	12.3%
Tactical	-1.9%	7.6%
Income	3.8%	8.5%
Safety	3.2%	4.7%

*Returns prior to Inception Date are hypothetical and derived from the composite return of the underlying products listed on this page. Account returns are used from your inception date forward. Past performance is no guarantee of future results.

Historical Table of Investment Returns for Investment Pools*

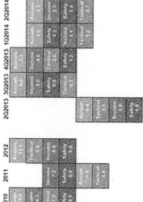

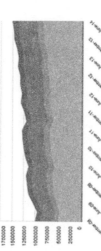

Historical Growth

Source: Brinker Capital, Inc. Hypothetical example for illustrative purposes only. *Returns prior to inception date are hypothetical and derived from the composite return of the underlying products listed in this chart. Account returns are used from the investors inception date forward. Past performance is no guarantee of future results.

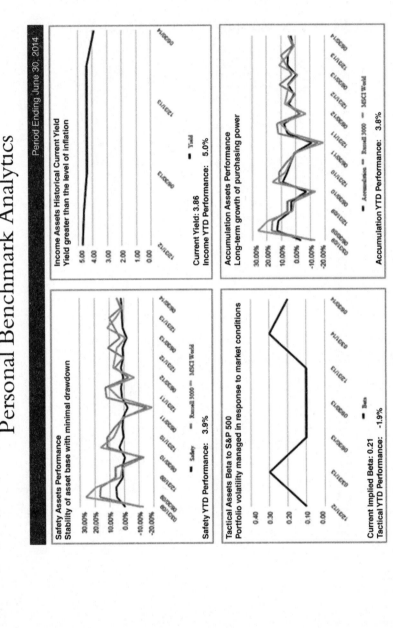

Personal Benchmark Analytics

Period Ending June 30, 2014

Income Assets Historical Current Yield
Yield greater than the level of inflation

Current Yield: 3.86
Income YTD Performance: 5.0%

■ Yield

Accumulation Assets Performance
Long-term growth of purchasing power

Accumulation YTD Performance: 3.8%

■ Accumulation   ■ Russell 3000   ■ MSCI World

Safety Assets Performance
Stability of asset base with minimal drawdown

Safety YTD Performance: 3.9%

■ Safety   ■ Russell 3000   ■ MSCI World

Tactical Assets Beta to S&P 500
Portfolio volatility managed in response to market conditions

Current Implied Beta: 0.21
Tactical YTD Performance: -1.9%

■ Beta

Source: Brinker Capital, Inc. Hypothetical example for illustrative purposes only.

FIGURE 1.14

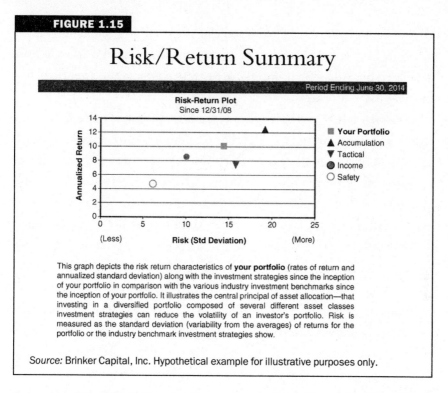

FIGURE 1.15

Risk/Return Summary

Period Ending June 30, 2014

Risk-Return Plot
Since 12/31/08

- ■ **Your Portfolio**
- ▲ Accumulation
- ▼ Tactical
- ● Income
- ○ Safety

(Y-axis: Annualized Return; X-axis: Risk (Std Deviation))

(Less)   **Risk (Std Deviation)**   (More)

This graph depicts the risk return characteristics of **your portfolio** (rates of return and annualized standard deviation) along with the investment strategies since the inception of your portfolio in comparison with the various industry investment benchmarks since the inception of your portfolio. It illustrates the central principal of asset allocation—that investing in a diversified portfolio composed of several different asset classes investment strategies can reduce the volatility of an investor's portfolio. Risk is measured as the standard deviation (variability from the averages) of returns for the portfolio or the industry benchmark investment strategies show.

Source: Brinker Capital, Inc. Hypothetical example for illustrative purposes only.

fluctuate. The black line in the upper right shows that the Income bucket's yield exceeds inflation. In the lower left, the Tactical bucket shows low Beta as a result of hedging. In the lower right, the black line illustrates accumulation is ongoing with the portfolio's risky assets.

After the first year, Brinker Capital's performance report includes a risk/return plot, as illustrated next in Figure 1.15. The square plots the performance of Jim and Jane's investment strategy. Here, the square shows that the portfolio, as anticipated, has more return than the Tactical, Income, and Safety buckets, while posting less return and less risk than the Accumulation bucket.

Summary

In the financial markets, we have great freedom, and this freedom necessitates great responsibility to identify our goals, create effective investment strategies, and weather the inevitable ups and downs en route to the goal. The behavior gap trap indicates that this mission may not be as easy or straightforward as it sounds. And, all too often, individual investors have failed to participate in the attractive capital market returns generated by America's economic growth machine in the twentieth and twenty-first centuries.

Personal Benchmark, Brinker Capital's solution, is a market-tested and elegant innovation to aid advisors in designing and communicating investment strategies that both create purchasing power and manage the investment and behavioral conflicts which surface while advising investors. This makes Personal Benchmark a game changing innovation and important tool for closing the investor behavior gap trap.

Dan Whittenburg, a Salt Lake based advisor, has built an extremely successful practice by always having a sharp focus on the investor's needs. "Serve first" is the guiding principle for many advisors who were trained at Connecticut General Life Insurance Company. (In 1981, Connecticut General merged with INA and became known as CIGNA.) Dan says all of these concerns (conflict resolution, achieving personal goals, increasing purchasing power, and managing volatility) are floating around in people's heads. Personal Benchmark organizes it. It makes it simple.

References

Center for Applied Research. *The Influential Investor: How Investor Behavior is Redefining Performance.* Boston: State Street, 2012. www.statestreet.com/centerforappliedresearch/doc/the-influential-investor.pdf.

Dalbar, Inc. *Quantitative Analysis of Investor Behavior.* Boston: Dalbar, 2014.

Frankl, Viktor E. *Man's Search for Meaning.* New York: Simon & Schuster, 1959.

Gates, Henry Louis "Skip" Jr., (2014) "Finding Your Roots." Corporation for Public Broadcasting and PBS, http://www.pbs.org/wnet/finding-your -roots.

Haver Analytics (2014). www.haver.com

Kerry, John. "Kerry's Press Briefing in Kyiv, Ukraine." U.S. Department of State. (March 4, 2014). http://iipdigital.usembassy.gov/st/english/texttrans/2014/03/20140304295372.html#axzz319yFCwaq.

Markowitz, Harry M. (March 1952). "Portfolio Selection." *The Journal of Finance,* 7(1): 77–91. doi: 10.2307/2975974.

Phelps, Edmund S. *Mass Flourishing: How Grassroots Innovation Created Jobs, Challenge, and Change*. Princeton: Princeton University Press, 2013.

Securities Industry and Financial Markets Association. (SIFMA). (2013). www .sifma.org.

Smith, Winthrop H. Jr. *Catching Lightning in a Bottle: How Merrill Lynch Revolutionized the Financial World*. Solvay: Prestige Publishing, 2013.

Thaler, Richard, and Cass Sunstein. *Nudge*. New Haven: Yale University Press, 2008.

U.S. Bureau of Economic Analysis. (2014). www.bea.gov.

Zakaria, Fareed. "Reasons for optimism in today's world." CNN World. (May 25, 2012).   http://globalpublicsquare.blogs.cnn.com/2012/05/25/reasons-for -optimism-in-todays-world.

CHAPTER 2

Investor Emotions and Financial Decisions

Dr. Daniel Crosby

Money can get rid of your financial problems, but it won't get rid of your emotional problems.

—Sonya Parker, author

To truly understand the nature of the Personal Benchmark solution, it is helpful to first understand its underlying theory. A traditional investment product typically relies on one, two, or three schools of thought. These include Investment Theory, Risk Theory, and Economic Theory. We will discuss all three in some detail in Chapter 4. But for now we will discuss something more unique. At its core, Personal Benchmark was developed with deep reliance on the multidisciplinary study we know as Behavioral Finance: The idea that our financial decisions and behaviors are not fully rational.

Behavioral finance has risen to the public consciousness through at least three primary channels: an academic spat with traditional finance, a collection of pithy anecdotes about human irrationality, and an explanatory framework for a series of recent financial catastrophes beginning with the dot.com bubble and ending with the Great Recession. This chapter provides an overview of this field, including its origins, what behavioral finance is and is not, and how these concepts are applied to the everyday work of financial advisors.

The Origins and Evolution of Behavioral Finance

Behavioral finance sits at the crossroads of finance, economics, psychology, social psychology, decision-making science and neurology, to name but a few of the disciplines that make up its strange brew. This makes behavioral finance a true mutt of the financial industry, and it continues to rapidly evolve and adapt as both popular and academic interest in the sciences increase and more and more resources are allocated to its pursuits.

Early Writings

The earliest recorded use of the term *behavioral finance* is found mere decades ago by Boulding (1958) and Johnson (1958), but unofficial adherents can be found hundreds of years earlier. One of these is Adam Smith, best known for his work, *The Wealth of Nations* (1776), in which he popularized the notion of an "invisible hand" and forever changed the formal study of economics. His lesser known and earlier work, *Theory of Moral Sentiments* (1759), can be considered the seed of behavioral finance as a true sub-discipline. "Moral Sentiments" touches on Smith's notion of economic behavior being driven by a struggle between a person's passions and his or her "impartial spectator." The battle Smith portrays mirrors the current discussion on "rational" versus "irrational" investor behavior.

By 1841, Scottish journalist Charles Mackay had published his groundbreaking work, "Extraordinary Popular Delusions and the Madness of Crowds," which covered everything from financial bubbles to the more sensational elements of herding behavior found in witch hunts, religious crusades, and fortune telling. Despite the unscientific nature of some of Mackay's work, the chapters on financial delusions remain relevant to this day.

Legendary economist John Maynard Keynes and value-investing darling Benjamin Graham both emphasized the impact of emotions on investing in their work in the early to mid-20th century. Then, Daniel Kahneman and Amos Tversky (1979) earned notoriety for Prospect Theory: An Analysis of Decision Under Risk which they published in

Econometrica. Their article was widely agreed to herald the birth of behavioral economics (which subsumes behavioral finance), as Kahneman would go on to win the Nobel Memorial Prize in Economic Sciences for his work on decision-making under uncertainty. Sadly, Amos Tversky passed away at the time of the award and Nobel Laureates are not awarded posthumously.

Three Phases of Evolution

Angner and Loewenstein (2012) have identified three distinct phases of behavioral finance:

- Phase 1 (1980s): Cataloguing behavioral phenomena inconsistent with the economic models of the day, such as asymmetrical relationship between appraisals of gain and loss. In simple terms, we are more upset with a loss than we are happy about an equivalent gain, which flies in the face of traditional economic theory.

- Phase 2 (1990s): Incorporating behavioral considerations into mathematical models of economic behavior, for example, the Black-Litterman model is a portfolio allocation model that seeks to integrate behavioral finance to overcome some of the "real world" problems seen when modern portfolio theory is put into practice.

- Phase 3 (2000s): Incorporating behavioral economics into public policy considerations. An example is the book *Nudge* (Thaler and Sunstein 2009), which discussed various approaches to persuading others to enact certain behaviors and popularized the notion of "libertarian paternalism" as a middle ground between laissez-faire and coercive societies. *Nudge* received so much acclaim that the British government established a Nudge Unit and President Obama retained the book's authors to aid in his reelection efforts.

The Next Evolution in Behavioral Finance

Almost a decade removed from the third wave of behavioral finance, we hope to initiate a fourth epoch by filling what we consider an important gap: anticipating and circumventing investor misbehaviors through carefully designed advisory practices. Doing so requires two activities: defining a universe of investor misbehaviors and designing embedded investment advisory practices that account for and reduce this misbehavior.

By outlining a universe of misbehavior, we avoid the "list of biases" approach that dominates the financial services world today. Investment advisors are not benefitted by a list of the myriad ways in which their clients might make poor decisions. Such lists are unwieldy, hard to remember, and too vast to be useful. What's more, when they are presented haphazardly in list form, they seem sometimes to contradict one another ("Are investors overconfident or risk averse?"). We aim to create a smaller, theoretically cohesive universe that will allow investment professionals to protect against a host of behavioral risks while attending to a very few simple variables that cover a great deal of ground.

We further hope to improve on existing approaches by showing how embedding behavioral fixes within an advisory model can avoid the shortcomings of more traditional methods like simple investor education. While investor awareness and education can be powerful, the very nature of stressful events is such that rational thinking and reliance are at their nadir when fear is at its peak. Through a "baked in" approach, we hope to help investors remain at their best even when financial markets are at their worst. While these are ambitious goals, we feel as though the trust with which financial professionals are entrusted warrants concentrated attention to anything that can improve the client experience, not to mention returns.

The Myths of Efficiency and Rationality

Ask five people familiar with behavioral finance what it is and you're likely to get just as many answers. However, one common thread to the answers is that they are likely to speak of behavioral finance in relation to "efficient market hypothesis," (EMH) the idea that all stocks are perfectly priced according to their inherent investment properties, the knowledge of which all market participants possess equally. The traditional finance paradigm is undergirded by a belief in markets with "rational" participants. This rationality has two primary features:

- First, rational market participants have access to information and update their beliefs immediately upon gaining access to new information.
- Second, rational market participants make decisions consistent with Subjective Expected Utility (SEU) as outlined by Savage (1964).

The appeal of this elegant, simple approach is obvious: If investor behavior can be reduced to two simple rules, the predictive power of market experts would be enormous (not to mention enormously lucrative). This concept would also make a lot of other decisions in life far easier, from which movie to see this weekend to which suitor you would like to forbid your daughter from dating.

Sadly, the lived experience of hundreds of years of observing financial markets, sitting though terrible movies, and enduring dreadful boyfriends tells us that the EMH, for all its elegance, is an oversimplified model that fails to accurately map the behavior of market participants. Let's quickly examine the two assumptions of EMH in light of actual events. The assumption that market participants are "informationally efficient," that is, that they incorporate new information into a rational decision making process, is one with which behavioral finance theorists take issue on anecdotal grounds. If investors are indeed informationally efficient, it would mean that dislocations from true value would soon be arbitraged away by investors who incorporated this new information into their reasonable preferences.

There are two problems with this notion of efficiency. The first is that the history of the stock market tells us that values can deviate wildly from true value for a protracted period of time. The second is that even when such a dislocation may occur, limits to arbitrage may exist that make correcting the dislocation impossible or undesirable.

This Time, It's Different

One of the primary reasons the market may deviate from fundamental values over time is a belief that "this time it's different," an idea that explains everything from stock bubbles to why some people choose to get married for a fourth or fifth time. In the case of marriages, the oft-tossed-about statistic about half of marriages ending in divorce is a little misleading. In reality, less than half of first marriages end in a split, but 67 percent of second marriages and 73 percent of third marriages end in divorce.

There are certainly a number of things that make second and third marriages difficult, but foremost among them is the tendency to rebound without accurately addressing the problems underlying the past failure. Dating coaches call this the "Liz Taylor Syndrome," while psychologists call it "New Era Thinking." Both involve a belief that the unique circumstances of this time will make it different than the past.

Four hundred years ago, in one of the first speculative bubbles on record, a Dutch commodity traded for 10 times the annual salary of a skilled laborer. In some cases, this commodity fetched as much as 12 acres of prime farmland and could even be traded for a single-family dwelling.

What was the commodity? A single tulip bulb. At the time, the Dutch believed these bulbs were different, 10–12 cm of wonder and promise, an investment unlike anything that came before them. The belief was that tulips would always appreciate in value and were immune to the ups and downs of comparable tradable goods. Sound familiar?

Sadly, New Era Thinking (this time, it's different) is not a relic of the past, a trick of the mind that fooled investors less savvy than ourselves. Instead, we have plenty of contemporary examples around us of our own, from the housing bubble and Great Recession of the 2000s and the tech bubble of the turn of the twenty-first century, New Era Thinking is alive and well. The advent of the Internet was greeted by Wall Street with great enthusiasm, such great enthusiasm that people lost their minds. The thought that the Web would revolutionize the way we do business was largely correct, but the notion that financial fundamentals no longer mattered was not. Consider these facts from 1998:

- eToys.com, an Internet upstart, had sales of $30 million profits of −$28.6 million and a total stock value of $8 billion.

- Toy veteran Toys "R" Us, on the other hand, had more than 40 times the sales but only 3/4 of the total stock value.

Such massive dislocations from true value over prolonged periods of time erode the EMH notion of informational efficiency. Perhaps John Maynard Keynes was right, the markets really can stay irrational longer than we, as investors, can stay solvent.

Another consideration corrosive to a belief in investor efficiency is "limits to arbitrage," or the theory that due to restrictions, traders who would typically arbitrage away pricing inefficiencies are unable to do so. The poster children for the impact of limits to arbitrage are Long-Term Capital Management (LTCM), a hedge fund set up by future Nobel laureates Myron S. Scholes and Robert C. Merton. LTCM used complex mathematical models to arbitrage away pricing inefficiencies in treasury bonds brought about by differences in liquidity. Through what is called a convergence trade, LTCM would short a more expensive bond and buy a less expensive bond and profit from the regression of their prices toward the mean over time. Since the pricing differences in the bonds were so small, the company needed to take on significant leverage to make attractive profits, as high as 25:1, at the time of their eventual demise.

In 1998, LTCM made bets on bonds that were guaranteed to converge over the long run, but acted erratically, given the East Asian debt crisis and the Russian government's default on its debt. As a result of these two circumstances, harried investors traded against LTCM, forcing them toward margin calls that eventually led them to close out their positions at catastrophic losses, even though they would have eventually resulted in large gains. Once again, we see how the shortsighted panic experienced by stressed investors can thwart the calculations of those attempting to arbitrage mispricing. As a result of the manias and panics mentioned above, all but the staunchest proponents of EMH have relinquished their belief in informational efficiency.

Avoidance of Ambiguity

A belief underlying EMH is that investors act so as to maximize Subjective Expected Utility (SEU). An intuitive understanding of SEU can be achieved by a simple dissection of the word. The "subjective utility" portion of SEU attempts to give a behavioral patina to the concept by recognizing that value is an individual consideration and that the worth of something will vary from person to person. The "expected" part of SEU means that an individual's assessment of the likelihood of an event will serve as another part of the equation. Simply put, the utility of an outcome to a person, weighted by its perceived likelihood, will determine the SEU (Karni 2006).

> ### Subjective expected utility:
> The belief that each individual calculates the value and likelihood of the return on an investment

However, one of the most consistent violations of SEU is driven by what is termed, "ambiguity aversion," or the preference for humans to make bets on known instead of unknown risks. The quintessential lab proof of ambiguity aversion is the Ellsberg Paradox (Ellsberg 1961), which suggests that people prefer placing risks when they know specific odds versus situations when the odds seem completely ambiguous. In other words, they will choose a known probability "the devil they know" over an unknown probability "the devil (or angel) they don't," even when the known probability is very low and the unknown probability could include the guarantee of a win.

The presence of ambiguity aversion is hardly limited to the lab, however. Why else would the child of an alcoholic parent marry an alcoholic herself? Why would someone gutted by the insanity of his job remain there year after year? In these cases, the behavioral preference for certainty, even a negative certainty, is shown to trump the EMH notion of people being programmed to maximize subjective utility.

The financial markets have also given us ample proof of ambiguity aversion in what is called the "equity premium puzzle." The equity premium puzzle "refers to the empirical fact that stocks have out-performed bonds over the last century by a surprisingly large margin (Benartzi and Thaler 1995), much more than we would expect from rational investors seeking to maximize utility. For example, using annual data from 1871–1993, Campbell and Cochrane (2000) report that the average log return on the S&P 500 Index is 3.9 percent higher than the average log return on short-term commercial paper. If efficient market theorists were correct, investors would notice such a pattern and begin to allocate away from bonds and toward stocks: After all, if stocks consistently provide superior risk-adjusted returns such an anomaly should be arbitraged away by informationally efficient, utility max-imizing market participants. Yet, decade after decade, the equity premium exists.

In the examples above, we have set forth the two fundamental axioms of efficient market theory and provided empirical refutations of each. While a more detailed dismantling of EMH is not useful for the purposes of our book, we hope the reader is sufficiently convinced that market participants do not always act in ways that dispassionately take advantage of all extant information for the maximization of subjective utility. While they often do act in such a way, they just as certainly act in ways that ignore important pieces of information and can be self-sabotaging in their efforts to avoid uncertainty and loss. Events as unrelated to market fundamentals as plane crashes, sunshine and soccer team performance have been reliably shown to impact markets (Benartzi 2011) and as long as we remain influenced by such external-ities, adherents to a belief in rational market participants will have some explaining to do.

A Definition and Framework for Behavioral Finance

In the previous section, we positioned behavioral finance as distinct from, and in some cases in opposition to, efficient market theory.

Although this is a necessary first step for defining behavioral finance, it is by no means sufficient. At this point, our definition is like an adolescent, having established distance from its parents, but still needing to create an identity in order to thrive as an autonomous entity and not just a rebel without a cause.

Therefore, a less oppositional definition of behavioral finance is, "a discipline that attempts to increase the explanatory and predictive power of financial theory by providing it with more psychologically plausible foundations" (Angner and Loewenstein 2012, p. 642). Put succinctly (and as suggested in the previous section), behavioral finance takes the position that financial phenomena can be better understood by realizing that some agents are not fully rational.

This is an increasingly popular idea in the wake of the recent economic catastrophes of the bubbles and recessions that have sent shockwaves through the global economies. However, behavioral finance will quickly become obsolete if it does not integrate itself into a more cohesive whole. After all, professorial fights grow tiresome after a season, as does the erosion of confidence in our ability to make rational decisions. What began as a useful critique of the flawed paradigm of EMH could quickly turn to petulant whining if behavioral finance experts do not quickly look for ways to apply their learning for the benefit of the investing public. It is just such holism and applicability that is our aim here.

One of the nagging, if not entirely unfair critiques of behavioral finance, is that it is a collection of observed biases without any sort of underlying theory. In one sense this is fair: If behavioral finance wants to hold itself up against the worst of EMH, it must also consider the best of traditional finance, which is the fact that it is undergirded by a consistent set of theoretical assumptions. In other ways, this criticism may be nothing more than a reflection of the differences between economics and psychology (see Rabin, 1998, 2002, for a detailed comparison). As we read in Whalen (2013), "the field of psychology has its roots in empirical observation, controlled experimentation, and clinical applications. From the psychological perspective, behavior is often the main object of study, and only after carefully controlled experimental measurements do psychologists attempt to make inferences about the origins of such behavior. In contrast, economists typically derive behavior axiomatically from simple principles such as expected utility maximization, resulting in sharp predictions of economic behavior that are routinely refuted empirically."

A full discussion of whether or not a discipline with roots in psychology can ever achieve the kind of theoretical parsimony (however flawed) found in finance is beyond the scope of this work. What's certain, however, is that the current system could benefit from a move in the direction of greater cohesiveness. At last count, the popular Psy-Fi Blog (2008-2014) listed 117 different behavioral biases that impact investment decision making. 117! Obviously, lists of that size are unwieldy and of limited usefulness to advisors or investors when trying to plan and make financial decisions, often under duress. In addition to the sheer difficulty of managing this quantity of information, financial professionals are suffering from what we call "bias fatigue." Simply put, bias fatigue is a weariness with being told how endlessly irrational investors are and a simultaneous hunger for applying behavioral ideas to more positive ends. Investors and financial professionals alike are telling us, "We make mistakes, we get it. Now what?"

In a 2008 paper on neuroeconomics, economist George Loewenstein said: "Whereas psychologists tend to view humans as fallible and sometimes even self-destructive, economists tend to view people as efficient maximizers of self-interest who make mistakes only when imperfectly informed about the consequences of their actions" (Loewenstein, Rick, and Cohen, 2008 p. 648).

The trick, we think, is in not oversimplifying views of human nature one way or the other to ensure that our views are both consistent with reality and able to be used in the real world. In this spirit, we present what we believe to be a simplifying framework that gathers most forms of potential investor misbehavior under three pillars—Simple, Safe and Sure. By reducing the 117 (or so) observed behavioral biases into three main categories, we provide a structure from which manageable embedded behavioral finance solutions can be created.

The Psychology of Simplicity

I'm not sure what time of day you're reading this, but whenever it is I can be sure of one thing: you've already made a lot of decisions today. First was whether to hit the snooze button. Then, what to have for breakfast? Loufa with body wash or bar soap in the shower? Grey suit or navy suit? And so on and so forth. The point is, given the myriad decisions we all face every day, it's no wonder that we end up relying on heuristics or experiential rules of thumb, even when important decisions need to be made.

Selective Recall through Heuristics and Emotional Salience

To give you a little firsthand experience with simplifying heuristics, I'd like to ask you to do the following:

Name all the words you can that begin with the letter "K." Go on, I'm not listening. How many were you able to come up with?

Now, name all of the words you can in which K is the third letter. How many could you name this time?

If you are like most people, you found it easier to generate a list of words that begin with K; the words probably came to you more quickly and were more plentiful in number. But, did you know that there are three times as many words in which K is the third letter than there are that start with K? If that's the case, why is it so much easier to create a list of words that start with K?

It turns out that our mind's retrieval process is far from perfect, and a number of biases play into our ability to retrieve data with which we'll make a decision. Psychologists call this fallibility in your memory retrieval mechanism the "availability heuristic," which simply means that we predict the likelihood of an event based on things we can easily call to mind. Unfortunately for us, the imperfections of this simplifying heuristic are hard at work as we attempt to gauge the riskiness of different financial decisions and if we are not appropriately simplifying, we can find ourselves in a great deal of trouble.

In addition to having a memory better suited to recall things at the beginning and the end of a list, we are also better able to envision things that are scary. I know this firsthand. Roughly 7 years ago, I moved to the North Shore of Hawaii along with my wife for a 6-month internship. Although our lodging was humble, we were thrilled to be together in paradise and eager to immerse ourselves in the local culture and all the natural beauty it had to offer. That is, until I watched *Shark Week*.

For the uninitiated, *Shark Week* is the Discovery Channel's seven-day documentary featuring all things finned and scary. A typical program begins by detailing sharks' predatory powers, refined over eons of evolution, as they are brought to bear on the lives of some unlucky surfers. As the show nears its end, the narrator typically makes the requisite plea for appreciating these noble beasts, a message that has inevitably been overridden by the previous 60 minutes of fear mongering.

For one week straight, I sat transfixed by the accounts of one-legged surfers undeterred by their ill fortune ("Gotta get back on the board, dude") and waders who had narrowly escaped with their lives. Heretofore an excellent swimmer and ocean lover, I resolved at the end of that week that I would not set foot in Hawaiian waters. And indeed I did not. So traumatized was I by the availability of bad news that I found myself unable to muster the courage to snorkel, dive or do any of the other activities I had so looked forward to just a week ago.

In reality, the chance of a shark attacking me was virtually nonexistent. The odds of me getting away with murder (about 1 in 2), being made a Saint (about 1 in 20 million) and having my pajamas catch fire (about 1 in 30 million), were all exponentially greater than me being bitten by a shark (about 1 in 300 million). My perception of risk was warped wildly by my choice to watch a program that played on human fear for ratings, and my actions played out accordingly. I simplified my decision making process by relying on the data that was most available to me and had the greatest emotional impact. As a result, I missed out on lots of great opportunities for fun in the sun. My simplification process, wrong-headed as it was, had impacted my behavior irrationally.

Hopefully by now the application to investment decision-making is becoming apparent. For so long, we have been sold an economic model that posited that we had perfect, uniform access to information and made decisions that weighed that information objectively. In reality, our storage and retrieval processes are limited and imperfect. It is now estimated that the Federal Reserve releases over 45,000 pieces of economic data in any given month! Given the sheer volume of information available to investors, we must necessarily simplify, deciding which information is germane to our investment goals and which is not. Moreover, the many emotionally charged economic events of recent decades lead to certain pieces of data looming larger than the rest. The glut of information and the weight we give to information of different emotional salience biases the way in which we recall and utilize knowledge.

Framing and Mental Accounting

Another way we simplify information is through framing, which means we react to information differently, depending on whether it is presented as a loss or a gain. While a rational economic agent (sometimes referred to as *homo economicus*) would weigh all decisions equally and disregard framing effects, actual behaviors indicate that the lens through which we view a decision has everything to do with the eventual outcome. Frames can take a number of shapes: it could be the physical place in which we make a decision, whether a question is positively or negatively framed, and even the way in which we mentally account for the options from which we are selecting.

Consider walking into your neighborhood Starbucks and, instead of ordering your usual, you decide to try something new. You ask the barista, "What do you recommend?" He responds, "Oh, you've got to try our new 92 percent fat free triple mocha frappucino!" Assuming you like mocha, you just may go for it.

But what if he said, "Oh, you've got to try our new 8 percent fattening triple mocha frappucino!"

Rationally, you realize that the two are equivalent. But doesn't one sound more appealing than the other? As you can see from this silly example, framing can have a profound impact on the decisions we make.

However, a study conducted by Thomas Gilovich shows that our frappucino example may not be so silly after all. Gilovich asked half of the respondents to a questionnaire whether or not they could save 20 percent of their income, to which only half said yes. The second half of the respondents were asked whether they could live on 80 percent of their income, to which 80 percent replied in the affirmative.

This may be a simple case of *To-MAY-to, to-MAH-to*, right?

So why are the responses so different?

The answer, of course, is that the way we choose to simplify information matters. The first phrasing frames it as a 20 percent loss of spending power (there is a large body of research that indicates that saving is viewed as a loss), whereas the second frames it more positively. Thus, equivalent financial realities are viewed through entirely different lenses that lead to decisions with profoundly different outcomes.

Consider a real-life framing example with a huge cost to the U.S. taxpayer. Twice in the past few years, the government has tried to stimulate the economy by offering tax rebates to the hardworking citizens of the United States. Both times, these efforts have met disappointing ends—and behavioral finance may just be able to tell us why.

Belsky and Gilovich lead us toward the answer in their excellent primer, *Why Smart People Make Big Money Mistakes* (2000). They describe a study conducted at Harvard wherein 24 students were given $25 to spend in a lab store as part of their participation in a research. Any unspent money, they were told, would be returned to them shortly via check. But wait, there's a rub (there always is when psychologists are involved!). Half of the students were told that the $25 was a "rebate" and the other half were told that it was a "bonus." Could such a minute difference in cognitive framing have a measurable impact on spending behavior? It turns out, it could.

The study mentioned above is an excellent example of the power of "mental accounting," a form of framing in which decisions are made on the basis of the mental bucket into which they are placed. For those whose earnings were mentally accounted for as a bonus, 84 percent spent some money in the lab store, a behavior mimicked by only 21 percent of those whose money was framed as a "rebate." Now consider the decision of the U.S. government to give "tax rebates" to help stimulate the economy, an action that ultimately failed, probably at least in part due to a misunderstanding of the power of mental accounting. Irrational decision makers that we are, we fail to grasp the fungible nature of dollars and account for them differently based upon how they are framed in our mind. As Nick Epley, the psychologist who conducted the Harvard study said more forcibly, "Reimbursements send people on trips to the bank. Bonuses send people on trips to the Bahamas."

Money Illusion

On a cold winter day (8 degrees!) in early 2013, I stood in Times Square and did a series of "(Wo)man on the Street" interviews to try and understand what ordinary people thought were their best and worst financial decisions historically. Dostoevsky famously said, "All happy families are alike; all unhappy families are unhappy in their own way." What Dostoevsky says of families was also true of peoples' evaluations of their financial decisions. There were myriad ways in which those we interviewed felt they had made bad decisions, but the perceived most positive decision was the same in every interview: they had bought a house.

Students of finance may find this (highly unscientific) result curious. After all, Robert Shiller of Yale, famous for forecasting the housing bubble in the U.S., has shown fairly conclusively that real estate is not the great investment so many of us suppose it to be. His research shows that middle class families have 65 percent of their wealth in their homes and that homeowners expect a 13 percent appreciation in their home value annually! However, his research shows that adjusting for inflation and other costs, housing in the U.S. has appreciated a not-so-whopping 6 percent over the last *century*. This reflects a simplification known as the "money illusion," or the tendency to think in nominal dollars rather than in terms of purchasing power. Homeowners tend to focus on nominal appreciation over time, without factoring in the 3 percent or so per year loss of purchasing power those numbers reflect. Thus, what may appear nominally to be a six-figure increase over 20 years may be a loss in absolute terms. This overly simplistic way of thinking about money can cause investors to both under save for their futures and misallocate their resources in the meantime.

Choosing Simplicity

Given the complexity of life, the enormity of the decisions we are called upon to make, and most peoples' unfamiliarity with financial principles, it is much less a question of *whether* people will simplify the information they process and recall and more a question of *how* they will simplify. Our tendency toward selective recall, framing and mental accounting, and money illusions can have disastrous consequences for our finances, but only if we are controlled by our simplification processes rather than controlling them. Properly harnessed, these simplifications can be used for good as surely as they can for ill, a process we'll describe in detail as we continue to introduce you to the concept of a personal benchmark.

The Psychology of Safety

Abraham Maslow, an American psychologist best known for hypothesizing a hierarchy of needs that motivate human behavior, believed that safety was a fundamental human need, coming into play just after our physiological needs (Maslow 1943). He argued that unless our needs for safety were met, we would fail to pursue other higher order needs such as love and belonging, self-esteem, or self actualization. That's fine, until you consider the state of our lives. Stanford researcher Robert Sapolsky in his 2008 National Geographic documentary *Stress: Portrait of a Killer* points out, "If you're a normal mammal, what stress is about is the three minutes of screaming terror on the savannah, after which either it's over with or you're over with." Sapolsky's thoughts on stress give some levity to what is a very real problem. Our stressors couldn't be more different than those of our agrarian and nomadic forebears, but the cognitive hardware with which we process them remains largely unchanged. That being the case, our physiological reaction to seeing a bear differs very little from the reaction we experience when seeing a stock plummet, although what is required of us to respond rationally to one versus the other situation is quite different.

While we are largely free of the fear of lion attacks on the savannah these days (at least here in the States), we are no more stress free as a result. In fact, the American Psychological Association, which releases figures on stress each documented in their final report for 2011 (published in 2012), states that, "More adults report that their stress is increasing than decreasing. 39 percent said their stress had increased over the past year and even more said that their stress had increased over the past five years (44 percent). Only 27 percent of adults report that their stress has decreased in the past five years and fewer than a quarter of adults report that their stress has decreased in the past year (17 percent)."

Where exactly is all of this stress and fear coming from? From the same report we read that: "Significant sources of stress include money (75 percent), work (70 percent), the economy (67 percent), relationships (58 percent), family responsibilities (57 percent), family health problems (53 percent), personal health concerns (53 percent), job stability (49 percent), housing costs (49 percent) and personal safety (32 percent)."

In a nutshell, we feel less safe than ever and money is the very thing we're most worried about. What do we do with all of this stress and how does this affect our investment decisions? Oftentimes, we look to and follow others' decisions and behaviors (known as "herd behavior") and engage in emotional decision making.

Herd Behavior

Earlier in this chapter, we discussed the tulip bulb, one of the first speculative bubbles on record, and the dot.com phenomenon, a more recent bubble. Both of these bubbles were driven by herd behavior, meaning groups of people acting together without planned direction. Robert Cialdini, the world's foremost authority on the science of influence, has discovered that following the crowd is one of the six primary ways in which we are persuaded. It is one of the ways we seek safety and we do this in many small and large ways every day.

Consider what you ate for dinner the last time you went out for an evening in a new city. You may have chosen a restaurant using a smartphone app like UrbanSpoon that gives restaurants scores based on aggregated user reviews. (Herd Behavior #1).

Once you were seated at the restaurant and asked for your order, you may have asked the waiter, "What's your most popular dish?" (Herd Behavior #2). In hundreds of ways each and every day, we are influenced by the herd, often to our benefit.

But what works well when finding a great Thai dish in a new city often fails us when making investment decisions. The greatest historical inflow of cash to equities occurred in January of 2000 when an unprecedented $44 billion flowed into markets. This massive inflow was shortly followed by the disastrous plunge of the NASDAQ ignited by the dot.com bust.

Conversely, October 2005 was the first time in history that market outflows exceeded inflows for five consecutive months. October proved to be the bottom of the market that immediately preceded a profound market hot streak that lasted years (Richards 2012). Warren Buffett's (2004) admonition to be "greedy when others are fearful and fearful when others are greedy" is some of the best but most ignored financial advice around. Instead, investors tend to take their cues from others, looking to benchmarks such as the Dow Jones Industrial Average or S&P 500 Index to heat up for clues as to when to enter the market.

This tendency to make decisions relative to the benchmark has had disastrous consequences for the portfolios of investors everywhere. Although estimates vary, experts suggest that the average disconnect between the market performance and the performance of average investors range from 6.97 percent to 7.42 percent (Dalbar 2014). That is, the tendency to wait to buy until others are buying and wait to sell until others are selling causes most of us to wildly underperform our potential. So much for safety in numbers!

Emotional Decision-Making

Stress triggers a move away from a rational and cognitive decision-making style in favor of an effective style driven by emotions. (Remember my *Shark Week* story earlier in this chapter?) Research also has suggested that we experience a 13 percent reduction in our intelligence during times of stress, as valuable psychophysiological resources are shunted away from the brain in service of our ability to fight or flee (UPI 1983). Dr. Greg B. Davies, Managing Director, Head of Behavioral and Quantitative Investment Philosophy at Barclays Wealth, characterized emotionally charged decisions and their outcomes in three ways:

- **Emotional decisions are myopic**—When under stress, we tend to privilege the now and forget about the future. Thus, we eat the pint of ice cream now despite the fact that it is in opposition to our longer-term health goals.

- **Emotional decisions are reactive**—Since our body is being signaled that something dangerous is imminent, we tend to react rather than reason. Reacting is great for swerving to miss a car, but not such a great way to invest for retirement.

- **Emotional decisions are associative**—Under pressure, we tend to make strong connections to previous events, sometimes irrationally. During the Great Recession, the media frequently drew parallels to the Great Depression (heck, look at the names), asking whether the present would be as dark as the past (and ignoring significant dissimilarities).

Davies is not alone in suggesting that excessive stress and emotionality can erode investment performance. Lo and Repin (2002) present psychophysiological evidence that even experienced traders exhibit significant emotional responses, as measured by elevated levels of skin conductance and cardiovascular variables that often occur during market events such as increased price volatility or the reversal of a trend. These results confirm and extend those of Lo and Repin (2002) and Steenbarger (2002), which find a clear link between emotional reactivity and trading performance. In specific, the data indicate that subjects whose emotional reactions were more intense on both the positive and negative side exhibited significantly worse trading performance, suggesting a negative relationship between successful trading behavior and emotional reactivity (Lo, Repin, and Steenbarger 2005).

In light of the ample research that denounces emotional decision making, it seems certain that emotion can be nothing but a hindrance to clear-eyed financial behavior, right? Well, sort of.

Gut Feeling

A CFA publication best touched on historical notions of emotion and investing by saying, "Barring a few exceptions (such as passing references to greed and fear and more extensive discussions of loss aversion), emotions have tended to be treated, in both academic and professional circles, as dangerous signs of weakness or sources of embarrassment and anxiety in an investment manager. Cold, rational calculation is idealized" (Tuckett and Taffler 2012). But modern science has led to a more nuanced understanding.

One study in particular highlighted the centrality of emotion in decision making by studying individuals whose emotion producing centers of the brain had been traumatized, for example, through accidents or war-related brain injuries, among others (Shull 2011). Far from making them rational decision makers, these emotional lesions caused paralyzing indecision. It would seem that emotion catalyzed action and that each decision we make, no matter how seemingly insignificant, has some emotional component to it.

Why the paralysis? Tuckett and Taffler explained, "Thoughts, feelings, and actions . . . are inextricably linked at both the mental and biochemical levels," meaning emotions are *central* to the way we make decisions!

Quoting LeBron James of the Miami Heat, "Warren Buffet told me once and he said always follow your gut. When you have that gut feeling, you have to go with don't go back on it." Tuckett and Taffler (2012) agreed, calling gut feelings an evolved human ability that "allows fast and frugal processing of everyday sensations and accords rapid meaning and purpose to all things." According to them, emotions and gut feeling are central to all thinking as well as reliable and accurate decision making.

We touched before on the ubiquity of stress in the modern world and financial stress in particular, citing that numerous examples of irrationality, short sightedness, and even low intelligence can be borne of excessive worry. But it also is true that some emotion is necessary to make decisions in the first place and that making decisions in a vacuum is all but impossible.

Managing Emotion

So, which is it? Are stress and emotion necessary for making financial decisions or should they be avoided? As you may suspect by now, the truth about the appropriate level of emotion for optimal decision making lies somewhere in the middle. Tuckett and Taffler (2012) encouraged, "It may, therefore, be useful to bring the feelings experienced in financial markets out into the open, discuss them frankly in an informed way, and incorporate them, where relevant, into theory and practice." Unfortunately, this sort of Zen-like balance is difficult to achieve as investors are whipsawed through the highs and lows of volatile holdings.

One important piece of managed emotion is managed volatility. As the highs and lows of investments are brought under tighter control, so too will the emotions of the investors that hold them.

Additionally, investors must learn to worry about the appropriate things, such as matters with personal significance and those that are within their personal control. Far too often, investors worry about externalities that have no direct impact on them or their wealth but which create a sort of vague anxiety that can never be truly calmed. At the same time, only a minority of Americans is prepared for retirement and over a quarter have no retirement savings at all. These individuals are not stressed enough!

By managing volatility as a means for controlling emotional extremes and by focusing on germane financial matters within personal control, investors can reap the benefits of appropriate stress without the paralyzing effects of excessive worry. The Personal Benchmark solution takes a middle path with respect to emotions; seeking to calm the extremes that lead to frantic decisions, while harnessing the positive feelings linked to achieving personal goals.

The Psychology of Surety

Since you have invested a few hours of your time in reading this book so far, I feel as though I'm getting to know you a little better. In fact, I feel like I know you well enough to make some guesses about your personality preferences. Let me give it a shot: Consider the following statements in terms of how true they are of you and let me know how I did:

> *Although others may see you as put together, inside you are worried and insecure. You want to be admired by others and you think about this when making decisions. Although you may not have done big things yet, you feel like that day will come. You feel as though you have a lot of untapped potential. You're an independent thinker who thoughtfully considers ideas before accepting them. You enjoy a certain amount of variety and change and dislike being restrained by restrictions or limitations. You know you're not perfect, but you are typically able to use your personality strengths to compensate for your weaknesses.*

So, how did I do? On a scale from 1 to 5, with 5 being the most accurate, how accurately would you say I described your personality?

If you're like most people, you probably ranked that description of you as a 4 or 5, which likely puzzled you, since we've probably never met. (Unless you're Joe from that burger joint on East 5th Street, and then I say, "Thanks and . . . you were right about the sauce.")

My amazingly accurate description of your character, even without having met you, illustrates what is called the "Fortune Cookie Effect" or the "Barnum Effect," named for P.T. Barnum, the great entertainer and circus magnate. Barnum famously proclaimed, "There's a sucker born every minute," using his knowledge to part people from their money. Barnum's understanding of "suckers," although born under the big top, undoubtedly surpasses that of many formally trained academicians. That is, our wish for certainty about our beliefs is hard to erode, even in the face of evidence that they are untrue. Philosophers, historians, and social scientists across the ages have observed and described this in various ways:

- Psychologists call this "confirmation bias," the human tendency to look for information that reinforces ideas we already hold. This occurs through self-verification, meaning our tendency to reinforce our existing beliefs, and self-enhancement, meaning we focus on information that makes us feel good about ourselves (Darley and Gross 1983).

- Thucydides, fifth century Greek historian, wrote, "it is a habit of mankind . . . to use sovereign reason to thrust aside what they do not fancy." (Thucydides 1950).

- Sir Francis Bacon observed, "The human understanding when it has once adopted an opinion . . . draws all things else to support and agree with it. And though there be a greater number and weight of instances to be found on the other side, yet these it either neglects or despises, or else by some distraction sets aside or rejects."

- Leo Tolstoy (1904), Russian writer and philosopher, wrote that even the most intelligent among us can accept "even the simplest and most obvious truth" if it requires them to discard other ideas they hold true, especially if they are proud of these ideas, have taught them to others, and/or built their lives around them.

Simply put, once we have formed an opinion, especially one central to our worldview, we cling tenaciously to that opinion, even when the facts reveal just how wrong it is. Schein (1998) added that this is not simply a conscious discarding of conflicting information; he hypothesized that we do not even *perceive* conflicting information.

We cannot be too hard on ourselves, as clinging to what we know and discarding conflicting or threatening information helps us maintain our self-esteem and feelings of confidence. In general, this is a positive; after all, who doesn't want to feel good about himself or herself? However, these dynamics work in overdrive and become problematic when it causes us to maintain the status quo in the face of disconfirmatory information or to overlook realistic, negative feedback. ("Getting $20 off this toaster oven at the Black Friday sale was *totally* worth waiting in line for 3 days!") The drive to ignore warnings and, worse yet, to hate "outsiders" is even stronger when our deeply held beliefs or our self-esteem is challenged.

The truth is, Americans tend to applaud certainty in much the same way and for many of the same reasons that we so admire innate giftedness. This is a land that cheers on confident politicians and castigates "flip-floppers." Numerous studies have shown that many of the "talking heads" we revere, notably those in financial services, are no more adept at predicting stock moves than random chance. Despite their inability to outperform a dartboard, we continue to look to them and pay them exorbitant salaries. Why? Because they are bold. Surety is baseball, red meat, and the pioneer spirit. Doubt seems wimpy and "Continental."

Desperately Seeking Experts

Hopefully I've made the case above that surety is one of our central human needs. One of the foremost ways investors seek a sense of surety about their financial decisions is by looking to the "experts." If I asked you to generate a list of such experts, say the greatest investors of the last 100 years, Warren Buffett's name is likely to be near the top of your list. The "Oracle of Omaha" has a reputation for having built a massively successful investment dynasty using common sense, fundamental ideas and presenting them in his signature folksy way.

But just how good is Buffett? The hedge fund AQR examined Buffett's portfolio from 1991 to 2011 (Frazzini, Kabiller, and Pedersen 2012) and found that the Oracle beat the S&P 500 Index by an average of 2.4 percent a year. Make no mistake, 2 percent a year over a lifetime can make someone exceedingly wealthy; but it's perhaps not as significant as we might have imagined for "The Best That Ever Lived." If Buffett averages 2 percent, what hope do the rest of us have?

Barber, Lee, Liu and Odean (2009) set out to measure trading skill in another population when they undertook a study of 360,000 Taiwanese day traders from 1992 to 2006. In an average year, they found that only 1 in 360 of the traders could outperform the market, net of fees. While hundreds of thousands are confident enough in their abilities to put their hard-earned money on the line, only a small fraction of them exhibit true skill.

But mediocre performance is hardly limited to "armchair quarterbacks" trading from discount online brokerages. It even touches some of the most well known names in the business. Each night, Jim Cramer achieves six-figure viewership on his program, "Mad Money." For the uninitiated, "Mad Money" is one part investment advice to two parts circus sideshow. Cramer yells at the camera, hits a variety of buttons linked to comical sound effects, vocally derides his critics and keeps an odd assortment of toys and other trinkets on hand just to ensure things don't get boring. To be sure, Cramer's bombast is off-putting to some. However, in a world full of disclaimers, fine print, mealy-mouthed lawyers and half-truths, the certainty with which he makes his pronouncements is oddly soothing. In an investment landscape full of hedging, Cramer is all in.

But is his confidence justified or mere hubris? Cramer underperformed the market by double-digits from 2005 to 2007 and improved to just 5 percent underperformance during the most recent economic downturn. And no mention of Cramer's track record would be complete without mentioning that he called Bear Stearns a "buy" just 12 days before its ultimate collapse and reiterated that "Bear is fine" a mere 5 days before the stock went to zero. What's more, some fund managers have actually created successful strategies based solely on shorting his picks! In what is typically seen as a meritocracy, it seems strange that the financial services profession has kept Cramer around in light of his subpar track record. But Cramer's longevity teaches us a lesson about human psychology. My guess is that if Cramer was just wrong, he'd have been let go years ago. But Jim Cramer is wrong in just the right way: He is wrong in a way that makes us feel confident.

Serenity. Now!

A second symptom of our need for surety is a tendency to operate in the short-term: We plan on the fly and choose our behaviors based on our emotions. In many ways, this makes perfectly good sense. After all, I could tell you exactly what I'm going to do today (write this chapter, go to the bank, see a movie with my wife), but I have no clue as to what May 30, five years from now holds. I couldn't tell you with any degree of confidence what I'll be doing, who I'll be with, or even where I'll be living at the time. In most endeavors, today is more certain than tomorrow and certainly many tomorrows from now.

A second reason for our "right now" focus is that we feel so well informed. Our access to data is breathtaking and is so democratic and ubiquitous that I won't spend much time trying to convince you of this. At the Techonomy conference in Lake Tahoe in 2010, Google CEO Eric Schmidt made a stunning pronouncement: He claimed that every 2 days, we now create as much information as we did from the dawn of civilization until 2003. Most of this data is user-generated content, everything from tweets about stock tips to funny cat videos. And while this sort of unprecedented access to data is breathtaking, the signal-to-noise ratio is equally noteworthy (I'm looking at you, cat videos). So, we have the illusion of being well-informed due to our access to high-speed computing and floods of data, but may not realize that so much of what is available to us is biased, useless or poorly researched.

Happily ignorant of the questionable nature of our information, we proceed, confident that the now is more predictable than the future, and so we make our investment decisions in fundamentally different ways than in decades past. Nate Silver, in his excellent work on forecasting, *The Signal and the Noise* (2012), reports that in the 1950s, the average holding period of an equity was six years. By the 2000s, holding periods had fallen exponentially, to a brief six months on average. What's more, volume is on pace to double every five years!

Through our faith in technology, information, and the certainty of the now, we are ever more confident making decisions on the fly. Day trading has proliferated and high frequency trades now make up an overwhelming majority of daily volume. But is moment-to-moment tinkering a boon to investors, or is it symptomatic of our overconfidence as a human race?

One of the reasons why investing is such a difficult art is that what is required of the successful investor flies in the face of our natural psychological proclivities. We made the case above for why the present is more forecastable than the future in most human endeavors; but the exact opposite is true of financial markets. Consider the following:

- In any given month, the stock market is down 40 percent of the time.
- In any rolling 5-year period, the stock market is down 12 percent of the time.
- In any rolling 12-year period, the stock market has never been down (Haver Analytics 2014).

Financial planning is that rarity where confidence is best affixed to something far distant. Confidence in day-to-day decision making relative to the sale and purchase of equities is hardly better than a coin flip! But, given an appropriate time horizon, you can be nearly certain that you will have been rewarded for your patience.

In culminating our introduction to confidence, it may warrant considering the term itself. The *Oxford English Dictionary* (2014) defines confidence as the "feeling or belief that one can rely on someone or something." It is impossible to be confident without a roadmap, a North Star that is guiding your actions. Moment-to-moment reactivity will never engender confidence, but strict adherence to a plan over an appropriate length of time will. Our desire for surety is natural, but the means by which we have sought financial certainty have often provided little comfort. Any good system of financial preparedness must satisfy our natural need for surety by keeping an appropriate timeline and following a plan that is deeply meaningful to the participants. It must simultaneously detract from the counterfeit certainty afforded by talking heads and trying to time markets in the short term. Therein lies true surety.

Summary

Ancient Grecians believed in geocentricity, the idea that the Earth is the center of the Universe around which all others objects orbit. In classical antiquity, it was widely supposed that the body contained four humors— blood, black bile, yellow bile, and phlegm—and that optimal health resulted from an appropriate balance of the four. Maternal Impressionists explained birth defects in children as resulting from negative thoughts from the mother during pregnancy. And phrenology, the practice of making inferences about someone's character and personality from the shape and contour of their head, was for some time thought to be a legitimate science.

Much as we laugh at these pseudo-scientific anachronisms, I am confident that the time is not far distant that we will wonder how we ever developed financial models that did not somehow seek to account for the behavior of market participants. In making such a provocative statement, I do not wish to pick on traditional financial models or necessarily to elevate what currently constitutes the burgeoning field of behavioral finance. Rather, I hope to illuminate the ways in which arriving at any sort of truth is an imperfect endeavor and discuss the way in which ideas that begin on the lunatic fringe can sometimes be welcomed into the fold of legitimate scientific inquiry.

Almost since its inception and increasingly with its popularization, proponents of behavioral finance have delighted in dismantling the efficient market machine, gleefully poking holes in this dogma with quirky anecdotes about investor irrationality. For their part, efficient market theorists have given as good as they've gotten, criticizing behavioral finance for its lack of theoretical underpinning. But all of this rhetorical jousting (while fun!), misses the point fundamentally.

Rather than hoping for the death or preeminence of one faction or the other, we ought to be working to combine the findings of both camps in applied ways that positively impacts actual investors, something Dr. Greg B. Davies calls "behavioralizing finance." Behavioral finance has a great deal to learn from efficient market theorists about building a comprehensive, rigorous framework of assumptions. Traditional finance could learn a thing or two from the behaviorists about being tentative, respecting the limits of knowledge and safeguarding others' assets accordingly.

Behavioral finance was born in the ivory tower of academia, legitimized with Daniel Kahneman's Nobel Memorial Prize in Economic Sciences popularized by Dan Ariely, Richard Thaler and others who taught us to laugh at and recognize our own financial misbehavior. Oddly enough, the next step in the progression of behavioral finance is an anonymity of sorts, the kind that comes with widespread acceptance and integration. After all, heliocentrism (the sun being the center of the universe) is not an idea anymore, it's simply the "way things are."

My daughter is 5 years old and I hope that when she attends college, there will be no behavioral finance courses offered at her university. If there are, we will still be mired in the same intellectual turf wars that can keep great ideas from exploring their points of fusion rather than their surface dissimilarities. My hope instead is that she will learn about finance, a complicated, tentative, somewhat messy discipline that her professor approaches with some mathematical precision, but would never dream of disconnecting from the people that give it life. Such is our aim with the Personal Benchmark solution. To develop a "soup to nuts" system for meeting your most important financial goals, that embeds behavioral principles so seamlessly that they are scarcely noticed.

One of the benefits of behavioral finance is that it shines a light on the little peccadilloes that make us the flawed but lovable people we are. But irrational as we may be, we can turn the tide on ourselves and use these quirks to our personal advantage. Just as surely as irrational simplifications can lead us to focus on the wrong things, an effective system for mentally accounting for our holdings can provide us with felt security. And although our tendency to follow the herd does not afford us the safety we desire, we *can* feel safe when we start measuring our actual purchasing power relative to our specific life goals. Finally, surety, so often sought through listening to so-called experts can be achieved by benchmarking to appropriate time horizons. As we hope you are now aware, you are not as logical and dispassionate as you might have guessed. Whether or not you use that irrationality to your benefit or detriment is now up to you.

References

American Psychological Association. *Stress in America: Our Health at Risk.* Washington: American Psychological Association, 2012. www .apa.org/news/press/releases/stress/2011/final-2011.pdf.

Angner, Erik, and George Loewenstein. "Behavioral Economics." *In Philosophy of Economics*, ed. by Uskali Maki. Amsterdam: Elsevier, 2012.

Barber, Brad M., Yi-Tsung Lee, Yu-Jane Liu, and Terrance Odean. "Just How Much Do Individual Investors Lose by Trading?" (2009). *The Review of Financial Studies*, 22(2): 609–632. doi: 10.1093/rfs/hh. http://faculty.haas.berkeley.edu/odean/Papers%20current%20versions/ JustHowMuchDoIndividualInvestorsLose_RFS_2009.pdf.

Belsky, Gary, and Thomas Gilovich. *Why Smart People Make Big Money Mistakes and How to Correct Them: Lessons from the New Science of Behavioral Economics.* New York: Simon & Schuster, 2000.

Benartzi, Shlomo. "Behavioral Finance in Action: Psychological Challenges in the Financial Advisor/Client Relationship, and Strategies to Solve Them." (2011). http://befi.allianzgi.com/en/Topics/Documents/behavioral-finance-in-action -white-paper.pdf.

Benartzi, Shlomo, and Richard H. Thaler. "Myopic Loss Aversion and the Equity Premium Puzzle." (1995). *The Quarterly Journal of Economics*, 110(1): 73–92. doi: 10.2307/2118511. http://qje.oxfordjournals.org/content/ 110/1/73.abstract.

Boulding, Kenneth. E. "Contemporary Economic Research." In *Trends in Social Science*, ed. by Donald P. Ray, 9–26. New York: Philosophical Library, 1958.

Buffett, Warren. "Berkshire's Corporate Performance vs. the S&P 500." (February 28, 2005). www.berkshirehathaway.com/letters/2004ltr.pdf.

Campbell, John Y., and John H. Cochrane. "Explaining the Poor Performance of Consumption-based Asset Pricing Models." (December 2000). *Journal of Finance, American Finance Association*, 55(6): 2863–2878.

Dalbar, Inc. *Quantitative Analysis of Investor Behavior*. Boston: Dalbar, 2014.

Darley, John M., and Paget H. Gross. "A Hypothesis-Confirming Bias in Labeling Effects." (January 1983). *Journal of Personality and Social Psychology*, 44 (1): 20–33.

Ellsberg, Daniel. "Risk, Ambiguity, and the Savage Axioms." (1961). *Quarterly Journal of Economics*, 75(4): 643–669.

Frazzini, Andrea, David Kabiller, and Lasse H. Pedersen, "Buffett's Alpha." (August 29, 2012). Yale Department of Economics. www.econ.yale .edu/~af227/pdf/Buffett%27s%20Alpha%20-%20Frazzini,%20Kabiller% 20and%20Pedersen.pdf.

Haver Analytics. (2014). www.haver.com.

Johnson, Harold. "Exploration in Responsible Business Behavior: An Exercise in Behavioral Economics." Georgia State College of Business Administration Research Paper No.4, 1958.

Kahneman, Daniel, and Amos Tversky. "Prospect Theory: An Analysis of Decision under Risk." (March 1979). *Econometrica*, 47(2): 263–291. doi: 10.2307/1914185. JSTOR 1914185. www.princeton.edu/~kahneman/ docs/Publications/prospect_theory.pdf.

Karni, Edi. "Subjective expected utility theory without states of the world." (June 2006). *Journal of Mathematical Economics*, 42(3): 325–342. doi: 10.1016/ j.jmateco.2005.08.007.

Lo, Andrew W., and Dmitry V. Repin. "The Psychophysiology of Real-Time Financial Risk Processing." (2002). *Journal of Cognitive Neuroscience*, 14(3): 323–339.

Lo, Andrew W., Dmitry V. Repin, and Brett N. Steenbarger. "Fear and Greed in Financial Markets: A Clinical Study of Day-Traders." (2005). *Cognitive Neuroscientific Foundations of Behavior*, 95(2): 352–359. http://web.mit.edu/ alo/www/Papers/AERPub.pdf.

Loewenstein, George, Scott Rick, and Jonathan D. Cohen. "Neuroeconomics." (2008). *Annual Review of Psychology*, 59(1): 647–672. doi: 10.1146/ annurev.psych.59.103006.093710.

Mackay, Charles. *Extraordinary Popular Delusions and the Madness of Crowds*. London: Richard Bentley, 1841.

Maslow, Abraham H. "A theory of human motivation." (1943). *Psychological Review*, 50(4): 370–396. http://dx.doi.org/10.1037/h0054346.

Oxford English Dictionary. "Confidence." Last modified 2014. www.oxforddictionaries.com/us/definition/american_english/confidence?q=confidence.

Psy-Fi Blog. "A Sideways Look at Psychology and Finance." (2008-2014). www.psyfitec.com/p/the-big-list-of-behavioral-biases.html.

Rabin, Matthew. "A Perspective on Psychology and Economics." (May 2002). *European Economic Review*, 46(4–5): 657–685. doi: 10.1016/S0014-2921 (01)00207-0.

Rabin, Matthew. "Psychology and Economics." (March 1998). *Journal of Economic Literature*, 36(1): 11–46. www.nyu.edu/econ/user/bisina/rabin_survey.pdf.

Richards, Carl. *The Behavior Gap: Simple Ways to Stop Doing Dumb Things with Money*. London: Penguin, 2012.

Sapolsky, Robert M. *Why Zebras Don't Get Ulcers* (3rd ed.). New York: Holt, 2004.

Savage, Leonard J. *The Foundations of Statistics*. New York: Wiley, 1964.

Schein, Edgar H. *Process Consultation Revisited: Building the Helping Relationship*. Englewood Cliffs: Prentice Hall, 1998.

Shull, Denise. *Market Mind Games: A Radical Psychology of Investing, Trading and Risk*. New York: McGraw-Hill, 2011.

Silver, Nate. *The Signal and the Noise*. New York: Penguin, 2012.

Smith, Adam. *The Wealth of Nations*. London: W. Strahan and T. Cadell, 1776.

Smith, Adam. *Theory of Moral Sentiments*. Edinburgh: Kincaid and Bell, 1759.

Steenbarger, Brett N. *The Psychology of Trading: Tools and Techniques for Minding the Markets*. New York: Wiley, 2002.

Thaler, Richard, and Cass Sunstein. *Nudge*. New Haven: Yale University Press, 2008.

Thucydides. *The History of the Peloponnesian War*. (trans. by Richard Crawley). New York, NY: E.P. Dutton and Co., Inc., 1950.

Tolstoy, Leo. *What is Art?* (trans. by Alymer Maude). London: Penguin, 1899.

Tuckett, David, and Richard J. Taffler. *Fund Management: An Emotional Finance Perspective*. Charlottesville: The Research Foundation of CFA Institute, 2012. www.cfapubs.org/doi/pdf/10.2470/rf.v2012.n2.1.

UPI. "Study Ties I.Q. Scores to Stress." (May 31, 1983). The New York Times. www.nytimes.com/1983/05/31/science/study-ties-iq-scores-to-stress.html.

Whalen, Charles J. *Financial Instability and Economic Security After the Great Recession*. Cheltenham: Edward Elgar, 2013.

CHAPTER 3

Risk, This Time It's Personal

Dr. Daniel Crosby

Only those who will risk going too far can possibly find out how far one can go.
—T.S. Eliot

While there are myriad differences between EMH and behavioral approaches to financial theory, nowhere are these differences more pronounced than in how they each define and think about risk. If asked to speak to the heart of the difference, this is at the core: behavioral approaches are embodied, whereas efficient market approaches are disembodied. Behavioral approaches attempt (with varying degrees of success) to couch theory in the imperfect minds and behaviors of those who play it out. In contrast, efficient market approaches opt for "dream world" scenarios wherein the messiness of behavior is removed in favor of parsimonious modeling.

As Dr. Greg B. Davies, Managing Director, Head of Behavioral and Quantitative Investment Philosophy, Barclays Wealth, says about the phenomenon of EMH and its associated approaches, "These shortcuts made it much easier to build an elegant theory. Convenience and parsimony in presentation became more valued than an accurate representation of reality" (Davies and De Servigny 2012). He goes on to explain the uncertain times in which we find ourselves in a post-EMH world by stating, "Thus we now find ourselves in a very interesting situation where the plans of the financial market architects largely have been followed, the infrastructure exists, but the foundations on which these plans were grounded have been shown to be less sound than they appeared initially." Old models of risk are dead or dying, but the sterility of the past is being replaced with an ideology that offers less simplicity, safety and surety, albeit in an effort to present a less idealized model.

Indeed, it is with some sadness that we ought to mourn the inefficiencies of efficient market theory. After all, the old paradigm was one of certainty that allowed us to coronate experts and develop risk models that gave us a deep sense of security. What's more, it gave us a (we now know) false sense of foreknowledge, as it painted a picture of risk borne of assumptions that the future would look much like the past. Best of all, EMH models, disembodied as they were, asked nothing of us, the investor. The gears of market efficiency were thought to turn, godlike, unaffected by mere mortals like you and I. In a world where people do everything from hog the armrest on airplanes to perpetrate acts of genocide against one another, one can hardly be faulted for pining for a system unbesmirched by human failings. Like a wealthy, handsome lover with an incurable case of halitosis, it was frustratingly close to perfection, but irrevocably flawed.

The two components of a useful scientific hypothesis are that it ought to be predictive and explanatory. There is no denying the explanatory thoroughness of the efficient school of thought; it is utterly comprehensive. Predictive power too, is of use during times of limited emotionality in the financial markets. However, "when the risk hits the fan" as my co-author is fond of saying, efficient approaches simply come undone and are unable to predict or even account for wild fluctuations that seem to defy logic. Recall the cautionary tale of Long Term Capital Management, whose strategy worked perfectly . . . until it didn't. It is for this reason that James Montier, author of *The Little Book of Behavioral Investing* (2010), refers to traditional approaches to measuring risk as being akin to airbags that work until you get in a wreck.

In this chapter, we examine three fallacies of traditional approaches to risk measurement and management, along with our own behavioral refutations. (We've got our own mythbusters in-house, although with no beards, goatees, or berets. Take that, Discovery Channel!). In addition, we'll suggest improvements that can be made to these three that reflect a more current, embodied approach to measuring risk that accounts for investment and investor behavior simultaneously.

Fallacy 1: Risk and Return Are Systematically Correlated

America is a land in love with risk. What do you expect from a fledgling upstart, still only a few hundred years old, which had the audacity to topple a globe-spanning empire on the way to becoming the world's greatest economic superpower? One of our most popular sports involves drivers racing at breakneck speeds for 500 laps, risking life and limb. Our business heroes are the ones brought to the precipice of poverty who chose to go "all in" despite the odds and emerged triumphant. And one can scarcely attend any rah-rah corporate teambuilding event without hearing a quote by someone famous about the virtues of risk in the workplace (not that you asked, but my favorite is the one at the start of this chapter). Is it any wonder then that the traditional notion of a perfect, positive relationship between risk and return was so readily incorporated into our collective consciousness? It seems fair and just to us that with great risk should come the opportunity for great reward.

To understand how EMH espouses a "no pain, no gain" attitude toward risk, we need only to revisit its two fundamental assumptions. First, remember that it is believed by EMH proponents that rational market participants have comprehensive access to information and update their beliefs immediately upon gaining access to new information. Second, market participants are thought to make decisions that maximize their subjective utility. Given these two assumptions, if a rational market participant became aware of a less risky way to make an equivalent return, they would jump on it. In this model, risk and return are constantly being evaluated so that an individual participant never takes on more risk than she ought to, given the return characteristics of the investment. To do otherwise would be, well, irrational. Conversely, if an investor is earning outsized returns, it can be taken as an article of faith that they are also taking outsized risks. Let's take a look at this concept from the lens of behavioral approaches.

Behavioral Mythbuster #1-1: We Don't Want Skin in the Game

The Capital Asset Pricing Model (CAPM, as it is more frequently abbreviated) is one of the keystones of traditional financial modeling. The CAPM is used to determine the appropriate rate of return for a given amount of systematic risk and is used in determining the suitability of adding an investment to an existing portfolio. Like so much of traditional finance, the CAPM is intuitive in its layout. The formula is simply:

Discount Rate = Risk Free Rate + Investment Beta (Market Rate−Risk Free Rate)

Or, expressed formulaically:

$r = rf + B(rm-rf)$

Consistent with the two basic tenets of market efficiency, CAPM assumes that investors must be compensated for the time value of money as well as for bearing risk (Investopedia 2014). The risk-free rate serves as a proxy for the time value of money and Beta, a measure of volatility relative to the benchmark, is a stand in for risk-taking.

The logic behind using CAPM is that if a given investment does not appropriately reward an investor for his or her time and risk, it should not be undertaken. Inasmuch as investors are thought to maximize risk-adjusted utility seeking, it makes sense that rational investors would not consistently choose investments that were either too risky for the returns or not rewarding enough for the risk. Makes sense, but how does it play out empirically?

In their 1985 paper by the same name, Rajnish Mehra and Edward C. Prescott introduced the world to what they called the "equity premium puzzle." Mehra and Prescott found that, "historically the average return on equity has far exceeded the average return on short-term virtually default free debt. Over the 90-year period from 1889–1978, the average real annual yield on the S&P 500 Index was 7 percent, while the average yield on short-term debt was 1 percent." The two went on to test whether liquidity constraints or transaction costs might have accounted for the substantial differences. They concluded that these costs and constraints did not. The "puzzle" portion of the equity premium puzzle refers to the lack of consensus as to why there should be any demand for government bonds, whose risk/return characteristics are so much worse than equities. If a true systematic relationship existed between risk and return, investors ought to have left short-term debt behind years ago, but yet, they have not.

We know intuitively that stocks are riskier than government bonds; therefore, we would expect higher returns for bearing additional risk. However, the differences in return characteristics are so great that choosing government bonds never makes sense, given the assumptions of the CAPM. Investors in government bonds are simply not adequately rewarded. The "equity risk premium," meaning the reward for sticking with the riskier option, varies by return period but is generally thought to be in the 3–7 percent range. Dimson, Marsh and Staunton (2006) calculated the return to be "around 3–3.5 percent on a geometric mean basis."

As we leave the ivory tower of academia and cast our gaze down to the level of empirical observation, we do not see investors who maximize risk-adjusted returns. Rather, we see that investors demand an outsized premium for bearing barely discernible risk and are often content to enjoy very little return if it helps them sleep more soundly. The equity premium puzzle is a strong refutation of the systematic relationship between risk and return posited by CAPM and traditional finance.

Behavioral Mythbuster #1-2: Volatility is a Heartless Beast

As you're now well aware, the operationalization process that provides beautiful formulas such as CAPM requires an observable measurement to stand in for a larger construct. In the case of CAPM, volatility is what stands in for the bigger idea of "risk." The chosen measure of volatility, Beta, is simply a measure of the fluctuation of a security relative to a benchmark, most commonly a market index like the Dow Jones Industrial Average or the S&P 500 Index (Dreman 2012). This is worth mentioning since, as Dreman points out, the EMH, along with "the great preponderance of modern risk theory, used by investors, their advisors, and their mutual funds, believe that risk is solely volatility. EMH argues that the greater the risk taken, the higher the perceived rewards will be."

Given that most investment professionals are steeped in CAPM and efficient market notions, it is natural to believe that they would advocate for more volatile approaches for clients seeking higher returns. If risk (volatility) and returns are so inextricably connected, this makes sense. But are they?

To answer this question, we'll begin by examining volatility as a theoretical measure of risk and conclude by empirically considering the relationship between volatility and returns.

While Beta provides a simple measurement proxy for risk, it is easy to criticize the measure on at least two theoretical grounds. Beta is symmetric (positive and negative variance contribute to Beta computation), while felt risk is asymmetric. Moreover, Beta is relative, whereas felt risk is more absolute. Obviously, volatility is a useful approximation of risk only insofar as it accurately models how humans perceive risk in their own investment lives. Volatility is a symmetric measure that includes both positive and negative fluctuations as "risky."

Perhaps we differ in this regard, but I never see financial *gains* as risky, while I see every loss as a threat to my financial wellbeing. That the traditional methods treat gains and losses as theoretically equivalent is a huge black eye on the model. Our lived experience of risk is asymmetric, so ought to be our measures of it.

A second philosophical criticism of volatility as a risk proxy is that it is measured relative to a benchmark. Beta, the volatility measure found in CAPM, is a measurement of variance typically relative to a broad market index. Thus, a Beta of:

- One would suggest a perfect correlation with the market (volatility would increase and decrease in lockstep with the market).

- Zero would imply no correlation with the market (movements of volatility seem to have no relation at all to the movements of the market).
- Less than zero would mean movement in the opposite direction of the market (as volatility increases, the market goes down, and vice versa).

Thus, an investment portfolio with a Beta of one would be considered appropriate for most investors thought to have a moderate overall risk tolerance. It is easy to see why this relative measure makes sense from a pragmatic standpoint. After all, if we are going to say something is volatile, the logical follow-up question is "relative to what?"

But as we are learning, lived experience and mathematical reductionism don't always blend so nicely. After all, someone in an "average risk" equity portfolio lost nearly 34 percent in 2008. I bet if you ask them if seeing their life savings cut by a third felt risky, they'd answer in the affirmative, even if their exposure to volatility and, by association, "risk" was not greater than average. So, on theoretical grounds, we have exposed two weaknesses of volatility as a measure of risk: it sometimes treats gains as risky but counts monstrous losses as par for the course, insomuch as they are part of a correlated collapse.

Behavioral Mythbuster #1-3: Can't Buy Me Love (or a Return, It Turns Out)

"Enough!" you say. "Theoretical criticisms of esoteric mathematical formulas are for dullards who attended too much college. I just want to make money." Fair enough. In this utilitarian frame of mind, let's examine the hypothesized versus realized returns, relative to volatility. If rational investors will only take on more risk if they are appropriately rewarded and if volatility is a valid stand-in for risk, then we would hypothesize a positive correlation between volatility and returns. That is, those willing to hold securities that fluctuate more should be justly rewarded for their sleepless nights.

One of the first indictments of this idea was a 1975 paper by Haugen and Heins that concluded with, "the results of our empirical effort do not support the conventional hypothesis that risk (volatility)—systematic or otherwise—generates a special reward." The second slug to the gut of risk as a predictor of return came in the form of a 1977 article in the *Journal of Portfolio Management* written by J. Michael Murphy. Citing a handful of studies, Murphy concludes that, "realized returns often tend to be higher than expected for low-risk securities and lower than expected for high-risk securities . . . or that the (risk–reward) relationship was far weaker than expected." More damning still, Murphy goes on to say, "Other important studies have concluded that there is not necessarily any stable long-term relationship between return achieved and risk taken; and that high volatility unit trusts were not compensated by greater returns."

This foundational gutting of traditional finance led some of the foremost adherents to EMH dogma to respond personally. In 1992, Eugene Fama, considered by many to be the father of EMH, released his own work that examined the relationship between volatility and returns. Fama, who had published a paper in 1973 indicating that higher Beta lead to higher returns (Fama and MacBeth 1973), was forced to recant. After looking at 9,500 stocks from 1963 to 1990 (Dreman 2012), Fama (Fama and French 1992) arrived at the conclusion that risk, as measured by Beta, was not a reliable predictor of performance. Fama and French found that stocks with high and low Betas had roughly equivalent performance and went on to say, "Beta, as the sole variable in explaining returns on stocks, is dead" (Dreman 2012). A noted contrarian, Dreman said (one imagines, with some sense of self-satisfaction), "The risk-return paradigm must exist, or EMH will be remembered in history much like the Ptolemaic system, a theory widely popular for a long time that ultimately failed and was discarded."

Fallacy 2: Investors Have a Single, Static Level of Risk Tolerance

Consider the following statement, taken from the risk tolerance questionnaire of a prominent index fund (The Vanguard Group, 1995–2010):

"Generally, I prefer investments with little or no fluctuation in value, and I'm willing to accept the lower return associated with these investments."

☐ Strongly disagree

☐ Disagree

☐ Somewhat agree

☐ Agree

☐ Strongly agree

Consider the question in light of your current financial realities. How would you rate yourself along this continuum?

Now consider the following:

- How might your response change if you answered this three months after the passing of your spouse?

- What might differ had you just received a large inheritance?

- How would you respond after having witnessed a 40 percent decline in your portfolio, following an unexpected period of national crisis?

If you are honest and self-reflective, I think you will realize that, far from having a single, immutable risk preference, your appraisal of risk is colored greatly by your current situation.

Dr. Greg B. Davies has this to say about the wrongheaded notion of a single and static appetite for risk: "Classical economics assumes that all investors have a stable and well-defined degree of risk aversion. However, there is also considerable evidence that we make decisions on the fly, constructing preferences as we go and straying from any sort of constant, unifying ideas about stress and risk. All of this casts doubt on our ability to represent the aggregate risk attitudes of investors or individuals and that it's stable" (Davies and De Servigny 2012). Davies buttresses his argument by showing that most investors tend to ascribe lower risk to assets that are familiar to them (known as "hometown bias"), so different people view the same asset as having variable risk characteristics. To an

American engineer, an investment in Lockheed Martin is commonplace, but to a Taiwanese psychologist, it might seem strange and risky.

Efficient market notions of complete information assume that everybody should have similar expectations of risks, but this simple example shows how one man's backyard is another man's "scary and unknown." Clearly, such simpleminded notions of risk fail to account for the complexity of the human family.

It turns out that our ideas about risk as a stable personality trait are a by-product of a deep-seated and little understood cultural bias. Far from being the dogma as we might view it, static notions of a personality seem to be a uniquely Western notion. Slife and Williams (1995) have this to say about the origins of this idea:

> Western conceptions of personality vary greatly from Eastern conceptions. Westerners tend to endow people with traits and attributes that remain the same, even when the person is in differing situations. Most Asians, however, tend to identify people with their situations and do not consider them to carry around their traits from situation to situation. In Western culture, for instance, John's honesty is thought to be a trait that John has in numerous, if not all, situations. In many Eastern cultures, by contrast, John's honesty is linked to his situation, such as "John's honesty at the bank." It is more accepted in Eastern cultures for such personality characteristics to vary from situation to situation.

So, falling back on our unexamined ideas about personality, we have mistakenly sold investors a bill of goods when trying to create what we thought were their unchanging feelings about risk. Now let's look at the behavioral mythbusting facts.

Behavioral Mythbuster #2-1: Our Risk Tolerance Is A-Changing

Having hopefully convinced you that risk tolerance changes, it is now worth considering some of the psychological variables contributing to its dynamism. One such variable is what is commonly known as recency bias, the tendency for recent events to weigh heavily on the mind. Grable, Lytton, O'Neill, Joo and Klock (2006) demonstrated the impact of recent market events when they found a positive correlation between stock market activity and risk score. But recent historical realities aren't the only determinant, so is the imagined future. Davies and De Servigny (2012) point out that expectations of future returns are also correlated with greater risk taking.

Affect is another huge determinant of risk perception (and any parent of a 5-year-old knows how fleeting affective states can be). For instance, greater risk taking is associated with negatively framed situations versus those positively framed. Happy moods have been shown to lead to risk aversion (Why mess with a good thing?). When positive moods are induced, losses are reported as greater than in a flat affective state. Research has also shown clear relationships between mood and gambling behavior, as well as in the specific context of real-time financial decision making (Lo, Repin and Steenbarger 2005). Simply put, when your mood changes (and boy oh boy, does it!), your risk tolerance goes with it.

While an exhaustive coverage of all relevant factors influencing risk tolerance would be a book unto itself, research has also shown that familiarity, salience, vividness, frequency and a host of other variables impact how "available" a risk is to a client (remember how the danger of sharks was made available to me via the Discovery Channel?). Clients who are able to recall personal stories or family members affected by a given risk are likely to evaluate it as being more risky, whereas risks experienced less directly are, sometimes erroneously, perceived as being more distant. Therefore, personal experience has everything to do with whether or not a client believes the risk in question to be a threat to "people like me" (Olson and Riepe 2010). In turn, our experiences and our attitudes toward risk are as unique as human experience itself. The work of a financial advisor then becomes helping his or her clients accurately understand the probability of various risks independent of the distortions that can be caused by personal experience.

Further supporting the argument for risk tolerance as dynamic is the failure of research to establish it as a reliable psychological characteristic with roots in biology. Economists and biologists alike have failed in these efforts; no group has yet been able to develop a single questionnaire that predicts risk taking across domains. Indeed, it is somewhat puzzling why some individuals may be risk-seeking in one endeavor (e.g., skydiving) and extremely risk-averse in another (e.g., investing). Heraclitus famously opined, "You could not step twice into the same river, for other waters are ever flowing on to you." Perhaps something similar could be said of our risk preferences as they relate to our personal finances. We are constantly being changed and reformed by our moods, experiences and visions for the future.

Behavioral Mythbuster #2-2: We Have Multiple, Simultaneous Risk Preferences

Have you ever purchased a lottery ticket? I have. Have you ever experienced the sinking feeling that goes along with knowing that your number was not picked? I have.

Although we both (I hope) understood that the odds of winning were very slim, we hoped against hope that today would be our lucky day, and we are hardly alone. A recent Mega Millions jackpot sold $1.5 billion tickets in the week before the grand prize drawing. That's roughly 4.5 tickets for every man, woman, and child in America.

This all seems harmless enough, until you consider that lottery sales disproportionately impact those who can least afford it. For example, per capita lottery sales are highest in North Carolina's poorest counties. Those who make less than $40,000 account for 28 percent of the population but make up 54 percent of lottery players. Lottery play is also inversely related to educational attainment—manual laborers with less than a high school diploma are most likely to play and those with advanced degrees are least likely. Imitating the "someday my prince will come" fairy tales of our youth, we are a nation waiting on a financial panacea, no matter how slim the odds.

Lest you think me an arbitrary detractor of wishing on a star, let's consider the probability of a white knight parking his horse in your driveway. You are 24 times as likely to be put to death by your state as win Mega Millions and 3 times as likely to be on death row and receive a last minute pardon. You are 9 times as likely to be crushed to death by a TV but if I asked you to bet on any of the aforementioned calamities, you would laugh at me. If we were rational economic decision makers, we'd similarly laugh if asked to gamble away our hard earned funds on something as improbable as a lottery ticket, and yet, they continue to exist (and thrive).

Odds are, you had no misgivings about your chances of winning the lottery and didn't have your feelings hurt unduly when I pointed out how irrational it is to play. Now let me ask you a second question: Do you own any insurance policies? Odds are, if you are interested in a topic like behavioral finance, you have a couple. "Ok, so what's with the weird questions, Doc?" you ask. The reason I ask is that buying lottery tickets and buying insurance are seemingly incompatible behaviors considered in terms of traditional risk tolerance methodologies. After all, one is extremely risky and hinges its bet on amassing wealth. The other is very conservative and is focused on wealth preservation. According to classical economics, which draws a single risk preference by maximizing risk-adjusted return expectations along an "efficient frontier," these two preferences cannot exist in the same person. And yet, there they are.

The truth is, there is nothing simple about human motivation or the threats we perceive to the things we want. At any given moment, we have the desire to protect the wealth we have accumulated but also to "strike it rich" by taking gambles. So, in addition to having shifting preferences, we also have multiple, simultaneous preferences. Much financial misbehavior is brought about when our multiple, moving preferences conflict with the single, static risk category in which we've been placed by our financial advisor. For instance, an investor identified as "conservative" may grow restless at having been placed in fixed income products while equities are on a tear. Seeing friends get rich, they may approach their advisor, upset that they are missing out and request a more aggressive approach. Inevitably, when equities fall, as they always do for a time, they will angrily return to their advisor and berate them for having been so cavalier. After all, the investor is not "conservative," as identified by that blasted risk tolerance assessment they were forced to take.

We will discuss potential solutions in great detail in subsequent chapters, but suffice it to say that an appropriate system for behavioral management is one that can sate both the risk-seeking and risk-averse preferences of a client at any given time and keep him or her from the herd following and disengagement that are the undoing of so many.

Fallacy 3: One Man's Risk Is Another Man's Reasonable Probability

By definition, risk is comprised of two elements: (a) the likelihood of a negative occurrence and (b) the scope of the personal impact of the negative occurrence. Therefore, for the average middle-class American (does such a thing still exist?), buying one lottery ticket a year carries considerable "probability risk" but very little "impact risk." Sure you're down a buck, but it's unlikely to sink your ability to meet your financial goals. Conversely, betting $50,000 on a hand of blackjack may have high probability and high impact risk on most Americans, but would have little impact risk on say, George Soros. Even down a few hands, he is likely to be able to keep the lights on.

You likely nodded your head in knowing agreement to the previous example, but this highly intuitive notion of risk is not the one best integrated into most financial models. If I asked you to define portfolio risk in real terms, you would likely give me an answer that was something like, "the likelihood of me not reaching my personal financial goals, including . . ." Risk is not an abstraction and it is certainly not just the erratic movement of securities. Risk is not being able to pursue your dreams. Volatility as a measure of risk speaks only to the probability component of risk, ignoring entirely the subjective, goal-based elements. As Dr. Greg B. Davies says, "Two individuals may have different subjective perceptions of the overall risk of an investment while still agreeing completely on the shape of the returns distribution" (Davies and De Servigny 2012). Classical economic approaches chose probability risk to stand in for all types of risk for this very reason: It is objective and not up for debate. However objective it may be, though, it only paints half of the picture, for something can only be risky if it is risky to somebody.

Behavioral Mythbuster #3-1: It's Not the Bogeyman, It's Just Volatility-Based Risk

Like so much else in our current approach to finance, risk is a concept that was bastardized to serve a computational end. But a closer look at the roots of the word "finance" show that a personal, goals-based approach is highly consonant with the original understanding of the term. The word "finance" actually comes from the Latin "finis," meaning objective or goal. Finance then, truly considered, is the management of money to meet personal objectives. Risk management, by extension, is the safe-guarding of money so as to minimize the potential that those goals will not be met. Real risk, as humans experience it, is not portfolio volatility; rather, it is the likelihood that they will fail to reach their goals. This goals-based definition of risk does two things: it embodies it within a subjective human context and it lengthens the timeline against which risk is measured. The embodied portion is fairly intuitive, it is easy to understand how my financial goal risk is different than that, of say, Warren Buffett.

Turning our attention now to the time element of risk, let me ask a personal question: "What matters most to you in the world?" While we've never met, I can't say for certain. But if you are like most people with whom I speak, you probably said something like, "provide ade-quately for my family" or "leave a philanthropic legacy" or "be a great mother" or "go back to school to finish my degree." My point is, whatever your answer, it seems unlikely that the finish line is this afternoon or even 3 months from now. Meaningful goals tend to exist along a time horizon that is a few years, if not a few decades, in the future. Ok, Ok you say, but what does that have to do with financial risk?

Volatility, the disembodied if wholly objective measure of risk previously privileged by the financial establishment, is measured over a specified period, typically 30 or 90 days. While this sort of short-term horizon works well for mathematical formulas, it is not the horizon against which we measure most of our most meaningful financial objectives, which typically exist further in the distance. By taking a myopic view of probability, we may mistakenly view an investment vehicle as more dangerous than it really is. In any given month, average stock returns suggest that an investor will have a 60/40 chance of a positive return. A 40 percent chance of loss is more than most investors can stomach, so considered on a 30-day timeline, equity investing seems risky indeed! But let's lift our view and lengthen our horizon a bit, this time to 5 years. Over 5-year rolling periods, the stock market has only produced negative returns 12 percent of the time (Haver Analytics 2014). Looking out further still, the stock market has not, so far, returned a nominal loss in any 12-year rolling period, a time horizon more likely to be consistent with your personal investment goals anyway. A volatility-based view of risk, myopic as it is, paints a picture of stocks as scary, which they certainly can be over the short term. A goals-based view of risk, couched in timelines more consistent with most major personal goals, paints a different picture entirely.

Behavioral Mythbuster #3-2: Okay, This is the Bogeyman—Variance Drain and Risk

As discussed, volatility-based models of risk posit a linear relationship between risk and reward, meaning that more volatility must be taken on if greater financial rewards are to be achieved. Many investors seeking exposure to the returns to be had from Beta investing turn to index funds as a means of increasing their exposure to volatility. While there is much to suggest index funds in many regards, "buying the market" also means that you are buying market volatility, which can have a profound impact on returns. This is a fact that is seldom considered. The technical term for the phenomenon by which volatility can actually rob rather than drive returns is "variance drain."

Variance drain:

The difference between mean return and compound return over a period of time, owing to the variance of periodic returns. The greater the variance of periodic returns, the more likely the compound return will fall below the mean. Typically, the compound return will lag the mean return by about one-half of the variance (definition from IFCI Risk Institute).

While this idea may seem esoteric at first, it is actually very simple: investors will achieve lower total returns with increased variance because positive returns will compound off lower lows. In other words, not all 10 percent average annual returns are created equal!

Gregory Curtis gives an intuitive and humorous example of the damaging power of variance drain on pages 84–86 of his excellent book, *The Stewardship of Wealth* (2012). Curtis presents us with a fictitious pair of twins whom he has named, cleverly enough, Dick and Jane. Dick and Jane are bequeathed a million dollar windfall on their 21st birthday, with instructions that neither principal nor interest would be paid out until 10 years later. Their strange benefactor, intent on thickening the plot, has also stipulated that over the course of 10 years, the twins must invest their inheritance, and that a winner will be chosen according to who has accumulated the greatest dollar figure at the end of the decade-long investment period.

Dick, a John Bogle devotee focused on controlling costs, sticks the lion's share of his million dollars in a Vanguard index fund. Jane, on the other hand, works closely with an advisor on a portfolio spanning eight asset classes, allocating 15 percent to core bonds. At the unveiling 10 years on, Dick and Jane learn that their portfolios have both achieved an arithmetic annual return of 9 percent. Despite the seeming dead heat, however, Dick has a final account balance of $1,936,412 and Jane's account sits at $2,387,938. How is it that equivalent returns have yielded such different returns? Enter variance drain.

TABLE 3.1

Volatility and the Growth of Wealth						
	Scenario 1	Scenario 2	Scenario 3	Scenario 4	Scenario 5	Scenario 6
Arithmetic Annual Return	10%	10%	10%	10%	10%	10%
Standard Deviation	0%	10%	20%	30%	40%	50%
Geometric Annual Return	10%	9.6%	8.3%	6.03%	2.58%	−2.42%
Starting Funds	$1,000,000	$1,000,000	$1,000,000	$1,000,000	$1,000,000	$1,000,000
Ending Funds	$2,593,742	$2,501,561	$2,219,353	$1,796,293	$1,290,725	$782,784
Total Period Return	159%	150%	122%	80%	29%	−22%
Source: Greycourt.						

While Dick had been wise to account for costs, he had borne the brunt of market volatility in his passive fund, which, in this example, was 19 percent over the 10 years (average market volatility is roughly 16 percent). Jane, on the other hand, had worked closely with an advisor to keep volatility in check, understanding that not only could volatility lead to behavioral miscues, it would also lead to compounding off of lower valleys, ending in a lower final figure. Table 3.1 provides further evidence of this, showing that a healthy double-digit return might even lead to substantial losses if volatility is great enough.

Now that you understand the concept of variance drain, let's return to our discussion of risk. Traditional notions of risk would suggest that rational market participants will only accept more volatility if it ends in higher returns, symmetrically trading risk and return. Thus, the uninitiated might invest in volatile products in an effort to reach their personal financial goals, with little understanding of the ways in which they might sleep better at night and generate greater returns by pursuing a low volatility strategy. Is there a relationship between risk and reward? Certainly. Cash, bonds, and equities all have return characteristics that are roughly related to the risk associated with them over the short term. However, investors using a personal benchmark strategy know that risk is so much more than variance and that taking on greater volatility in an undisciplined manner can lead to both behavioral and return threats that endanger their ability to hit the only benchmark that matters.

Behavioral Mythbuster #3-3: Abandon Hope, All Ye Who Focus on Volatility-Based Notions of Risk

Relying on probability-only, volatility-based notions of risk are far from just an academic problem. It currently pervades the investing collective consciousness and may cause investors to miss their personal goals in the pursuit of some illusory safety. If I asked you if stocks or bonds were riskier, you'd almost certainly say "stocks." If I then required you to prove your point, you could easily produce data showing that stocks are, in general, more volatile and you would have won the day, right?

John Spears (1993), in a paper titled, "The Road to Wealth: Long Term Investment in Stocks," compared the returns of stocks and bonds from 1871 to 1992. Over 10-year periods, consistent with medium-term goals like paying for a child's college, stocks beat bonds 80 percent of the time. Over rolling 30-year periods, consistent perhaps with a larger goal like saving for retirement, stocks beat bonds 100 percent of the time. Pre-tax stock returns were shown to beat inflation in each rolling 20-year period measured, whereas bonds and bills beat inflation 31 percent and 59 percent of the time, respectively. This work reinforces that of authors Wernder De Bondt and Richard Thaler (1994), who found in their research that the real rate of return on bonds over a nearly 70-year period was 1 percent, while stocks returned 7 percent. Bonds, the "safer" option in light of a volatility-based model of risk, had not even kept up with inflation. I know very few investors who could reach even their least extravagant investment goals by following such a "safe" pattern of investing.

If, by some miracle, I were given the ability to excise one phrase from the financial vernacular, it would surely be "flight to safety" (sometimes, "flight to quality"). A flight to safety, so called, is the tendency of investors to run to the comfort of cash or treasuries, often when equities are at their most handsome prices. Treasuries, cash, gold and bonds all have their place in a balanced portfolio and I am not criticizing these assets, per se. What I am critical of, however, is the notion that risk is tantamount to the last 30 days price volatility. It is just this idea that leads investors to flee to what they perceive as safe holdings, only to find out too late that they are unable to provide the life of which they dreamed as a result. Risk is not an abstraction. Risk is not underperforming a market index, not doing as well in the markets as your golf buddy, or losing money on paper in any given month. Real risk is the likelihood of not being able to do what matters most to you over a lifetime, nothing more—nothing less.

This discussion of risk is perhaps the most important conversation a financial advisor can have with his clients and prospects. Unfortunately, the client or prospect probably comes to the meeting with the notion that bonds are safer than stocks. Most likely they do not know why. The client or prospect may know that bonds are legal contracts for the debtor to pay interest and principal to the creditor. And that stocks are a call on residual profits of a company. Thus bonds are safer than stocks because bonds are senior obligations to stocks. Most likely they do not know such legal detail. Never the less, a sensible financial advisor will educate them. So doing gives the financial advisor a wonderful opportunity to frame risk beyond the legal virtues of debt obligations. Yes, the legal structure of a bond makes them safer in terms of interest and principal repayment. But no, they are not safer in terms of preserving purchasing power, building wealth for retirement, and intergenerational planning.

Behavioral Risk and You

In what you, intrepid reader, are undoubtedly starting to recognize as a theme, we have been sold an idea of risk that had more to do with creating pretty models than creating good lives. As Nobel Laureate Paul Krugman said of this, "As I see it, the economic profession went astray because economists, as a group, mistook beauty, clad in impressive looking mathematics, for truth" (Dreman 2012). As much as we'd like to believe the truth was "out there," ready to be mined and used to personal advantage, the hard truth is that we are both the problem and the solution.

I mention at the outset of this chapter that the defining difference between EMH and behavioral notice of risks was embodiment. Please make no mistake that the body in which this embodiment resides is your own. Far more predictive of your ability to meet your personal financial goals than volatility risk is what we might call, "behavioral risk," or the likelihood that your own decisions will stand in the way. Will you maximize your own human capital sufficiently to have a remunerative career that will help you retire in style? Will you stick to your personal benchmark and avoid the mania induced by following the herd? Will you remain mired in the minute-to-minute unpredictability of the markets or will you affix your gaze to your goals, thereby minimizing the risk of negative returns?

Dalbar, the nation's leading financial services research firm, has for the last 30 years, conducted a study to determine the "behavior gap" between market returns and investor returns. For the 30 years ending on December 31, 2013 the numbers looked like this:

S&P 500 Index Returns—11.11 percent

Average Equity Mutual Fund Investor—3.69 percent

This 7.42 percent "behavior gap," greater than any other measure of risk, is what threatens your ability to live your financial dreams. The bad news? Our subpar returns are at least partially our fault. The good news? Since the blame lies with us, so does the potential fix. Sure, it's a bummer that you can't judge the risk of an investment solely by looking at a single number. But what you can do is personally impact your returns by an impressive magnitude, simply by following a few best practices.

In the summer of 2009, in the throes of the worst economy in nearly a century, I did something wholly risky: I quit a lucrative consulting job and started my own business without a single client or a surplus dollar in my bank account. Oh yes, and as my wife likes to remind me, we also had a 6-month-old baby, on whose account she had recently quit her own job.

So, was my decision to quit my job a risky one? Looked at in traditional, probabilistic terms, the answer is a resounding yes. Consider the following:

- Only 40 percent of small business are profitable, while 30 percent master only the art of losing money.
- 50 percent of small businesses fail within the first year.
- Those with fewer than 20 employees have a 9 percent chance of lasting a decade.

But, as I hope you're convinced now, probability (typically measured by volatility in finance) is only half of the equation. The other half is life. I was miserable at my job, no matter how well I was being compensated. My health, both mental and physical, was suffering as a result of my dissatisfaction. I was meeting some of my goals (e.g., keeping food on the table), but other goals (e.g., living a happy life, creating something of lasting value professionally) were fallow and unrealized. Had I tried to "flee to safety" to manage some of my basic risks, I might have thwarted any chance of meeting other goals that were of equal importance to me, and so it goes in finance.

Summary

This chapter presented three fallacies of risk from the minds that brought you EMH and busted these myths with the home truths of behavioral approaches to financial theory. The heart of the difference is that behavioral approaches allow for the imperfect minds and behaviors of investors who play it out. In contrast, efficient market approaches opt for "dream world" scenarios wherein the messiness of behavior is removed in favor of parsimonious modeling.

The bottom line is that we can hedge against volatility risk by holding "sure things" like treasuries and cash. But another thing we can be equally sure of is that following such a strategy will not allow us to meet most of our personal financial goals: We are simply buying security for one-half of the risk equation at the expense of the more important piece, our goals.

Consider the most meaningful thing you have ever done. I would wager it took a measure of risk, uncertainty and hard work to achieve. In this, as with all risk, comes a valuable lesson: To strive for certainty is to doom oneself to mediocrity. Consider the person who remains committed to avoiding the risk of heartache and only finds loneliness in the process. Or the would-be entrepreneur who never makes the leap of faith and wastes a career working at jobs they hate. The irony of obsessive loss aversion is that our worst fears become realized in our attempts to manage them.

References

Curtis, Gregory. *The Stewardship of Wealth.* New York: Wiley, 2012.

Dalbar, Inc. *Quantitative Analysis of Investor Behavior.* Boston: Dalbar, 2014.

Davies, Greg B., and Arnaud De Servigny. *Behavioral Investment Management: An Efficient Alternative to Modern Portfolio Theory.* New York: McGraw-Hill Professional, 2012.

De Bondt, Wernder, and Richard Thaler "Financial Decision Making in Markets and Firms: A Behavioral Perspective." (1994 NBER Working Paper No. 4777). (June 1994). Cambridge: National Bureau of Economic Research. http://www.nber.org/papers/w4777.pdf.

Dimson, Elroy, Paul Marsh, and Mike Staunton. "The Worldwide Equity Premium: A Smaller Puzzle." Paper presented at the EFA 2006 Zurich Meetings, Zurich, April 7, 2006. http://dx.doi.org/10.2139/ssrn.891620.

Dreman, David. *Contrarian Investment Strategies: The Psychological Edge.* New York: Free Press, 2012.

Fama, Eugene F., and James D. MacBeth. "Risk, Return, and Equilibrium: Empirical Tests." (1973). *Journal of Political Economy,* 81(3): 607–636. doi: 10.1086/260061.

Fama, Eugene F., and Kenneth R. French. "The Cross-Section of Expected Stock Returns." (June 1992). *The Journal of Finance,* 47(2): 427–465. doi: 10.2307/2329112 www.business.unr.edu/faculty/liuc/files/badm742/fama_french_1992.pdf.

Grable, John, Ruth H. Lytton, Barbara O'Neill, So-Hyun Joo, and Derek Klock. "Risk Tolerance, Projection Bias, Vividness, and Equity Prices." (Summer 2006). *The Journal of Investing,* 15(2), 68–74. doi: 10.3905/joi.2006.635632.

Haugen, Robert A., and A. James Heins. "Risk and the Rate of Return on Financial Assets: Some Old Wine in New Bottles." (December 1975). *Journal of Financial and Quantitative Analysis*, 10(5): 775–784. www.jstor.org/stable/2330270.

Haver Analytics. (2014). www.haver.com.

Investopedia. "Capital Asset Pricing Model—CAPM." (2014). www.investopedia.com/terms/i/international-capm.asp.

Lo, Andrew W., Dmitry V. Repin, and Brett N. Steenbarger. "Fear and Greed in Financial Markets: A Clinical Study of Day-Traders." (2005). *Cognitive Neuroscientific Foundations of Behavior*, 95(2): 352–359. http://web.mit.edu/alo/www/Papers/AERPub.pdf.

Mehra, Rajnish, and Edward C. Prescott. "Equity Premium Puzzle." (March 1985). *Journal of Monetary Economics*, 15(2): 145–161. doi: 10.1016/0304-3932(85)90061-3. www.academicwebpages.com/preview/mehra/pdf/The%20Equity%20Premium%20A%20Puzzle.pdf.

Montier, James. *The Little Book of Behavioral Investing*. Hoboken: John Wiley & Sons, 2010.

Murphy, J. Michael. "Efficient Markets, Index Funds, Illusion, and Reality." (Fall 1977). *Journal of Portfolio Management*, 4(1): 5–20. doi: 10.3905/jpm.1977.408620.

Olson, Bryan, and Mark W. Riepe. "Using Behavioral Finance to Improve the Adviser–Client Relationship." (December 2010). *Research Foundation Publications*, 9(2): 125–154. doi: 10.2470/rf.v2010.n2.9. www.cfapubs.org/doi/pdf/10.2470/rf.v2010.n2.9.

Slife, Brent Donald, and Richard N. Williams. *What's Behind the Research?: Discovering Hidden Assumptions in the Behavioral Sciences*. Thousand Oaks: Sage, 1995.

Spears, John. *The Road to Wealth: Long Term Investment in Stocks*. Unpublished manuscript, 1993.

The Vanguard Group. "Investor Questionnaire." (1995–2010). https://personal.vanguard.com/us/FundsInvQuestionnaire.

PART 2

What Is the Personal Benchmark Approach?

CHAPTER 4

Brinker Capital's Multi-Asset Class Investment Philosophy

Chuck Widger

There is nothing so practical as a good theory.

—Lewin 1951

Picture yourself moving very slowly in stop-and-go traffic on an expressway. You're listening to the radio and thinking through the agenda for an upcoming meeting. You've come to a stop and are looking ahead at the lanes of stopped traffic ahead of you.

Wham! Another vehicle has slammed into you from behind. You jerk forward against your seatbelt. Coffee sears you and coats your console. Your back seizes.

You get out of your car and survey the damage. The rear end of your car is badly contorted. Your back hurts. You feel frustrated, angry, and anxious about all the tasks that now lie ahead for you.

After logging a claim with your insurance company, you consult a famous plaintiff's counsel for advice. After listening to your recitation of the facts, counsel says that to proceed with a lawsuit, you have to have a legal theory that applies to the situation. She explains that a theory is a statement of the legal principles tested in litigation and formalized through appeals over hundreds of years in our and other legal systems that describe both (a) a pattern of behavior and (b) the legal outcome resulting from that behavior.

Counsel quickly summarizes the facts in your case: It was a sunny day, early in the morning, with stop-and-go traffic. You were stopped and were hit from behind. Counsel then advises that the relevant legal theory is negligence. In this theory, the pattern of behavior concerns someone not being careful under given circumstances and the outcome is liability for damages and injuries caused by the carelessness. Thus, when applied to the facts and implemented through a court of law, your theory of negligence produces a predictable outcome: damages.

This short example shows how a talented lawyer (a) identifies legal principles, (b) applies them to your situation to predict outcomes— liability and damages, and (c) implements or tests the applications as a practitioner in a court of law. Steve Carlotti, a very bright and talented attorney at Hinckley Allen law firm notes that to prevail, "you always have to have a theory." Theories turn our experiences into concepts and principles that, in turn, lead to useful applications (Lewin 1951).

Similarly to prevail as an investor, you need a talented investment manager who has mastered a meaningful array of investing principles so that you can apply them to your situation, take appropriate action and, in turn, achieve the outcome you seek: generating returns to meet real-world goals. In other words, you invest to grow your money, and this money is used to pay for college, take a trip, pay for retirement, or achieve any other tangible goal you may have.

This chapter begins by providing a brief history of investing as a backdrop to explaining Brinker Capital's multi-asset class investment philosophy. The remainder of the chapter describes our philosophy, including its underlying principles and theories; how it is applied; and how it is implemented.

A Brief History of Investing

Diversifying one's investments is plainly an ancient concept. Solomon, who ruled Israel from 970–931 B.C.E. and reportedly led the nation to unprecedented prosperity (1 Kings 10:14–29, New International Version), advised people to spread their wealth and belongings across eight buckets to hedge against disaster (Ecclesiastes 11:2, New International Version). More recently, the English proverb tells us, "Don't put all your eggs in one basket" and the German proverb tell us, "Make sure you have a lot of legs to stand on." Thus, investors have been diversifying or allocating their capital into different investments for centuries.

However, the full range of possible investments were not always given equal attention. The 1920s featured a broader participation of ordinary Americans in the stock market, especially as the glamorous lives and impressive returns of some successful stock speculators were publicized and buying stocks was made easy by brokerage firms. Stock prices steadily rose of the 1920s during America's post–World War I boom and many investors thought that buying stocks, even on margin, was safe speculation.

The Wall Street Crash of 1929 and ensuing 10-year Great Depression changed all of that. Fortunes were lost and investors were deeply spooked. For the most part, they stayed out of equities.

Through the early 1940s, bonds became popular in individual retail markets, as the sale of government bonds took hold as a means to finance the $300 billion World War II. So when the war ended in 1945, individual investors as well as institutional investors were already conditioned to emphasize bonds in their portfolios.

In particular, endowments were guided by the Prudent Man Rule, in place since 1830, which required that investments be judged in isolation on their own merits and with a strong bias toward safety of capital. This meant that investors who favored fixed income securities—which represent loans to other entities that are paid back over time—can generate stable cash flows and offer low volatility compared to other asset classes.

Equity Investing Redux

But not everyone simply continued with bonds. Insightful business leaders like Charlie Merrill of Merrill Lynch believed it was possible to bring Wall Street back to Main Street. He held two prescient but radical (for the time) ideas. First, he believed that although Americans were bruised by the crash and depression, millions of them had again experienced successful investing through the war bond effort. Merrill also predicted that America would experience a significant economic post-war boom. Subsequently, under Charlie Merrill's leadership, Merrill Lynch played a significant role in persuading and helping the American public embrace equity investing. The 1950s and 1960s were a time of great prosperity and success for talented equity investors.

The success was rather short-lived, however. In the 1970s, the American economy succumbed to stagflation and excessive deficits in the wake of expansive money printing intended to finance war and huge increases in domestic spending. Inflation was high and economic growth was poor. Equities do poorly in such slow-growth, high-inflation economies.

In 1981, Federal Reserve Chairman Paul Volcker led the assault on stagflation. Federal Reserve monetary policy pushed short-term interest rates to over 12 percent and squashed inflation by creating a severe recession during 1981–1982. With the inflation genie returned to the bottle, the economy returned to robust growth and equity markets soared. Individual investors, served by a large nationwide network of financial service firms, again embraced equity investing. Pensions and endowments also embraced equity investing to meet the return goals needed to provide pension retirees with distributions and to satisfy the established endowment spending rates to support university and college operations.

Modern Portfolio Theory

Another profound change in the world of investments, which began in the 1950s and 1960s, came from an unknown 25-year-old graduate student at the University of Chicago. That student was Harry Markowitz, who later earned the Nobel Memorial Prize in Economic Sciences in 1990 for his paper entitled "Portfolio Selection," which he submitted in 1952 for publication in the *Journal of Finance*.

In it, Markowitz defined risk mathematically for the first time. It is hard to believe, but before Markowitz, risk was gut, experience, or instinct. "Throughout most of the history of stock markets—about 200 years in the United States and even longer in some European countries—it never occurred to anyone to define risk with a number." Markowitz did, and that idea quickly produced a dominant theory.

The aim of investors operating according to the theory is to produce an efficient portfolio, meaning one that produces maximum portfolio returns for a given amount of portfolio risk as measured by the standard deviation. Moreover, by plotting all combinations of efficient portfolios whose return is the highest per unit of risk, one can construct an efficient frontier (see Figure 4.1). The efficient frontier presents the optimal combination of risk and return, and those portfolios closest to the efficient frontier are expected to produce the best risk–reward ratio.

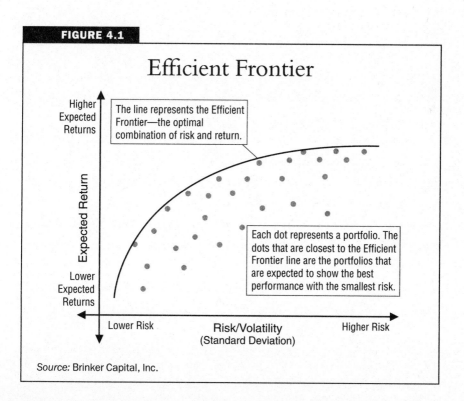

FIGURE 4.1

Efficient Frontier

The line represents the Efficient Frontier—the optimal combination of risk and return.

Each dot represents a portfolio. The dots that are closest to the Efficient Frontier line are the portfolios that are expected to show the best performance with the smallest risk.

Higher Expected Returns

Lower Expected Returns

Expected Return

Lower Risk

Risk/Volatility (Standard Deviation)

Higher Risk

Source: Brinker Capital, Inc.

Modern Portfolio Theory operates upon a number of critical assumptions:

- All investors are rational: they hold mean–variance efficient portfolios (i.e., portfolios with the highest expected return for a given level of risk).
- All investors are well-informed: They hold the same, correct beliefs about means, variances, and covariances of securities.
- Markets are efficient: Every investor can lend or borrow any desired amount at the risk-free rate. Investors also can sell short without limit and use the proceeds of the sale to buy long positions.
- Returns follow a normal distribution.
- Correlations between asset classes are fixed.

Although these assumptions may be appropriate for modeling purposes, a variety of empirical studies suggests that they do not likely hold for practical purposes. Since the original framework was developed, investors have had nearly three decades and a financial crisis to better understand the effectiveness and limitations of Modern Portfolio Theory (Kobar 2006). Empirically, we now know that not all segments of the capital markets are efficient. We also know that not all investor decisions are well informed and rational (see Chapter 2 for a more comprehensive discussion). Markets are difficult to forecast and not perfectly efficient. The 2008 financial crisis also highlights that assumptions of "normal distributions" of volatility and constant correlations between asset classes may also be flawed. Rather, experience suggests that fat tails and ever changing correlations are more likely to be experienced. Harry Markowitz's quotation from a 1998 Money Magazine article is most illustrative when he says, "I should have computed the historical covariance of the asset classes and drawn an efficient frontier. Instead I visualized my grief if the stock market went way up and I wasn't in it—or if it went way down and I was completely in it. My intention was to minimize my future regret, so I split my contributions 50/50 between bonds and equities" (Zweig 1998).

Thus over time, aided by the advent of cheap computing and technological advancements, Markowitz's mean-variance analysis has transformed into mean-variance optimization, whereby computer algorithms solve for the efficient portfolio given estimated returns, standard deviations, and correlations. Understanding of the concepts of Modern Portfolio Theory, tempered by awareness of the theory's limitations, has influenced Brinker Capital's overall investment theory of multi-asset class investing. The next section discusses how Brinker Capital applies its philosophy.

Diversification and the Rise of Multi-Asset Class Investing

Despite its limitations, Modern Portfolio Theory has contributed substantial value to investors in terms of underscoring the benefits of diversification. In fact, in the area of fiduciary duty of trustees, the original 1830 version of the Prudent Man Rule was updated in 1992 as the Uniform Prudent Investor Act with an emphasis on Modern Portfolio Theory and total return.

Thus inspired by the concept of diversification, individual investors in the 1980s, diversified their portfolios through investments of cash, stocks, and bonds (so-called balanced portfolios). Until the mid-1990s, this was the basic diversification model for individual investors.

Meanwhile, institutions, pensions, and endowments were guided in shaping their investment policies by consultants like AG Becker, which relied on decades of data that provided risk and return information. Institutional investors thus were advised to diversify their portfolios into bonds, stocks, real estate and commodities on a global basis achieved through public and private vehicles. This sophisticated approach to diversification is called multi-asset class diversification. In our view, the most prominent institutional investor in developing the multi-asset class investment model was, and remains, David Swensen, chief investment officer of the Yale University Investment Office.

The popularity of multi-asset class investing rests in its ability to produce equity-like returns while managing volatility. This type of investing has been practiced on a global basis by most institutional investors since the 1980s. Thus, pension plans, insurance companies, banks, and endowments alike invest in traditional asset classes such as domestic and international equity and bonds as well as non-traditional asset classes such as absolute return, real assets, and private equity.

In the 1990s, multi-asset class investing, the next evolution of balanced fund investing, also took hold among individual investors. Whereas balanced funds invest in stocks and bonds, multi-asset class portfolios invest in real estate, commodities, absolute return strategies, venture capital, and private equity, as well as stocks and bonds.

Despite their foray into multi-asset class investing, individual investors typically did not experience the same benefits as institutional investors. Their shortfall was because investment advisors emphasized index-oriented or relative return investing, where one's investments are benchmarked to indices such as the S&P 500 Index; Barclays Aggregate Bond Index; MSCI EAFE Index; or others. The problem with index benchmarking is that if you design your portfolio to compete with or beat the S&P 500 Index, you also take on the risk of the S&P 500 Index. Few institutional or individual investors actually want and can handle the more than 50 percent drawdown that most equity indexes incurred in 2008–2009.

Since the 2008–2009 financial panic and Great Recession, the number of investment products based on a multi-asset class philosophy has greatly expanded throughout individual markets domestically and internationally. Subsequently, investment strategies focused on controlling downside volatility while providing a competitive return have been increasingly in demand.

Based on the strength of this idea, we expect the popularity only to grow. One recent research study indicated that capital investment among 43 percent of European investment management firms is going into the development of multi-asset class products (Cerulli Research Report 2013). Also indicative of expansion in individual multi-asset class

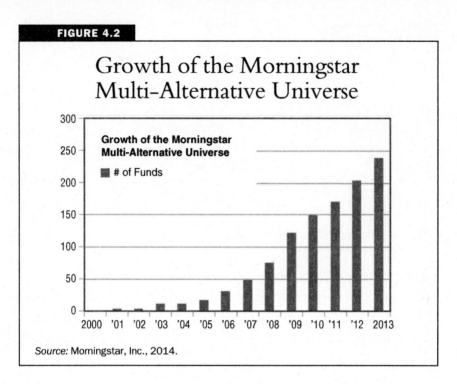

FIGURE 4.2

Growth of the Morningstar Multi-Alternative Universe

Source: Morningstar, Inc., 2014.

products is the rapidly increasingly number of mutual funds in Morningstar's multi-alternative universe (see Figure 4.2).

The continued embrace of multi-asset class investing by institutional investors and the ongoing expansion of individual multi-asset class and absolute return offerings constitute proof that it works. Multi-asset class investing seeks to deliver equity-like returns and manage volatility. It is a theory that works and is therefore a practical solution for achieving the outcomes many investors seek.

Multi-Asset Classifications

Today, multi-asset class investing means different things to different people. Bloomberg's most recent *Fund Classifications*, published on September 2, 2013, described eight asset classes: equity, fixed income, mixed allocation, specialty, real estate, money market, commodity, and alternative, as shown in Figure 4.3. This report was Bloomberg's first to include the alternative classification for mutual funds, clear evidence of a

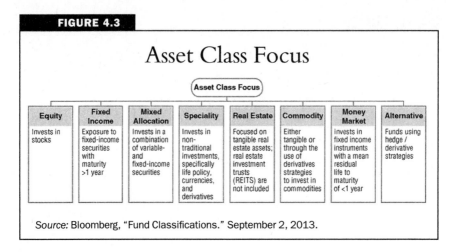

FIGURE 4.3

Asset Class Focus

Source: Bloomberg, "Fund Classifications." September 2, 2013.

recent phenomenon. However, we note that Bloomberg's mixed allocation asset class only includes mutual funds that invest in stocks, bonds, and cash. Someday, we expect Bloomberg will expand the mixed allocation category to span funds that invest in all asset classes, including real estate, commodity, and alternative, as well as stocks, bonds, and cash. This broader definition will better reflect the current trends in practice.

Morningstar updated its asset class definitions in a July 31, 2012, paper titled, "The Morningstar Category Classifications" (for portfolios available for sale in the United States). In that paper, Morningstar highlighted its recent changes. We note that it added "alternative" as a classification on July 31, 2008, and "multialternative" as a classification on April 30, 2011.

Unfortunately, similar to Bloomberg, Morningstar uses a narrow group of traditional asset classes when describing multi–asset class investing, describing "balanced funds" as only investing in three asset classes (stocks, bonds and cash). The reality is that more and more balanced, allocation, and multi–asset class funds have progressed to invest in real estate, commodities, and alternatives, as well as stocks, bonds, and cash. In addition to showing a lag in reflecting the most advanced portfolio theory through their category labeling, Bloomberg and Morningstar also leave the user confused about the distinction between fund category and asset class. Specifically, mixed allocation/multi–asset is not a distinct asset class, but rather a blend of other existing asset classes.

Swensen (2009) noted that market participants disagree about the appropriate number of asset classes to use. When carried to an extreme, the number of classes can be so voluminous that the sheer multiplicity of alternatives is unmanageable. He advised that the number of asset classes be selected so that the subsequent allocations make a difference, but not too much of a difference. He explained, "Committing less than 5 percent or 10 percent of a fund to a particular type of investment makes little sense; the small allocation holds no potential to influence overall portfolio results. Committing more than 25 percent or 30 percent to an asset class poses danger of overconcentration. Most portfolios work well with around a half a dozen of asset classes." As a result, he uses seven distinct asset classes: domestic equity, foreign equity, fixed income, absolute return, natural resources, real estate, and private equity.

Swensen (2009) further advised that investors operate according to an overarching investment philosophy, defined as an articulated, intentional approach to generating returns. In other words, it rises to the level of professional conviction. An investing philosophy, in turn, is comprised of a body of investment principles that have been studied, tested, and formalized over long periods of time. These principles explain how investing works or why things happens. These principles are rooted in and refined based on real-world observations, insights, and research. The next section presents Brinker Capital's investment philosophy.

Our Multi-Asset Class Investment Philosophy

Since its founding in 1987, Brinker Capital's purpose has been to deliver an institutional quality investment experience to its individual investor clients. Knowing that multi-asset class investing has been practiced on a global basis by most institutional investors since the 1980s, since 1994, we have offered our clients multi-asset class products that have delivered attractive risk-adjusted returns. Thus, multi-asset class investing constitutes our investment philosophy. We believe that sensible investors build portfolios with the broadest group of asset classes available to them. Underlying our philosophy are four core principles: diversification, innovation, active management and equity-like bias.

Fortunately, history is full of rich theory supporting our core principles. Here we will highlight some examples from risk theory, investment theory, and economic theory. Diversification is key to the risk statistic tools and law of large numbers presented by Jakob Bernoulli in 1689 (and published posthumously in 1713), both important parts of risk theory. Even economic theory, which calls for specialization production, advocates diversity in your trading partners to allow the maximum overall utility for the group as a whole. As discussed, diversification has been a hallmark of investment theory since Harry Markowitz's paper "Portfolio Selection" was published in 1952, wherein he defined risk mathematically for the first time (before Markowitz, risk was gut, experience, or instinct!). Markowitz further explained that because of the mathematics of diversification, the return on a diversified portfolio would be equal to the average of the rates of return on its individual holdings, but the risk would be *less than* the average volatility of its individual holdings. Bernstein (2009) summed it up by saying, "diversification is kind of a free lunch at which you can combine a group of risky securities with high expected returns into a relatively low-risk portfolio," as long as the individual securities are not highly correlated.

Innovation can be seen clearly across various disciplines as advances in knowledge and technique improve our collective understanding. Fibonacci's innovation of bringing Arabic numerals to Italy in 1202 changed the way calculations were performed, allowing for further innovations in mathematics and risk theory. The advent of the Black-Scholes model in investment theory provided the ability to better price options and hedge portfolios. Some of the greatest advocates of innovation are found in economic theory, led by Joseph Schumpeter's creative destruction and the Solow-Swan model of economic growth which cites technology advances and innovation as one of the three major variables of growth.

Active management, referring to the ability to adjust probabilities to new information in risk theory, is the focus of Thomas Bayes' "An Essay Toward Solving a Problem in the Doctrine of Chances" of 1763. Whether it be Graham and Dodd's "Security Analysis" in 1934 that discussed how to conduct fundamental analysis and make gains when the market offers mispriced securities or, more recently, Fama and French's (1992) three-factor model that notes the advantages of investing in high book-to-price and small cap equities, active management in investments continues to make sense. Economic thought also has been dominated by theories on how to better manage economies. Marx argued for full active control. Keynes argued for government intervention to help during periods of demand shortages. Friedman's government intervention is through money supply. Even the economic liberalism of Hayek calls for the government to help manage externalities in the markets. The message across the various disciplines is clear: Don't take your hand off the wheel.

An equity-like bias is adopted for all but our most conservative investor clients. We have this bias because people invest to fund current and future activities. Financing future activities requires increased purchasing power. Equity ownership provides far greater returns than the nominal returns offered by bonds—5.7 percent more, to be exact, according to historical return data for stocks and bonds (see Table 4.1). This difference is the equity risk premium, meaning the premium in the return paid to equity investors in exchange for taking more risk. This is, equity investors have a residual claim on corporate assets, meaning they get paid last when things go bad. Finance theory holds that if an investor takes more risk, the investor should get more return. Moreover, capital markets would not function without the equity risk premium.

TABLE 4.1	
Equities Generate Superior Returns in the Long Run	
Wealth Multiples for U.S. Asset Classes and Inflation, December 1925–December 2005	
Asset Class	**Multiple**
Inflation	11 times
Treasury bills	18 times
Treasury bonds	71 times
Corporate bonds	100 times
Large capitalization stocks	2,658 times
Small capitalization stocks	13,706 times

Source: Ibbotson Associates, Stocks, Bonds, Bills, and Inflation, 2006 Year Book.

Who would agree to the risks of equity investing if there was no possibility of a greater return? It follows that equity-like diversification generally produces more purchasing power (Swensen 2009). Thus, over the last 75 years, stocks have achieved an annualized return of 10.9 percent (FactSet 2013). This is a notable return. It follows that stocks drive portfolio growth. Over longer periods, stocks also provide a hedge against inflation because operating companies will increase prices over time to maintain margins and pass along the increased cost of inputs. Finally, stocks trade in broad, deep liquid markets, allowing investors to enter and exit the market easily.

The principles of diversification, innovation, active management and equity-like bias are well-supported by several schools of academic thought, including investment theory, risk theory, and economic theory. Figure 4.4 plots key developments in each of these schools of thought. For example, investment theory, despite findings of reasonable efficiencies in markets, continues to note the benefits of active management.

Applying Our Philosophy

Application means translating your investment theory and underlying principles into a long-term, strategic plan that produces your desired outcomes. At Brinker Capital, this means using the principles of diversification, innovation, active management, and equity-like bias to create specific investing plans. For years, Brinker Capital has identified, applied, and enhanced the principles of multi-asset class investing.

Our Six Asset Classes

The foundation of our investment approach is broad diversification across and within six major asset classes, including traditional asset classes (domestic equity, international equity, fixed income) and non-traditional, or alternative, asset classes (absolute return, real assets, private equity). Each of these classes plays a role within a client's portfolio, such as growth, inflation protection, and uncorrelated returns or stability. Our sophisticated diversification approach provides us with great flexibility in

FIGURE 4.4

Key Developments in Investment Theory, Risk Theory and Economic Theory

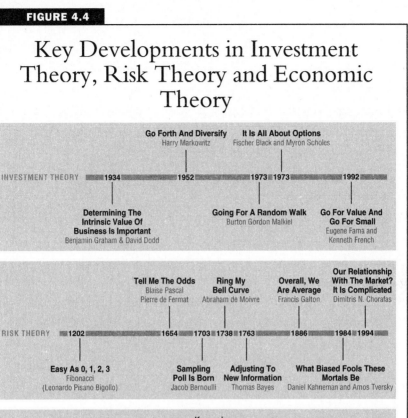

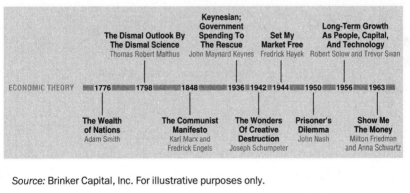

Source: Brinker Capital, Inc. For illustrative purposes only.

building portfolios using combinations of the various major and sub-asset classes, resulting in a suite of investment solutions that can meet a multitude of investor goals and objectives.

Notably, we utilize Swensen's (2009) original six asset classes of domestic equity, international equity and fixed income (considered traditional asset classes) as well as absolute return, real assets and private equity (considered non-traditional asset classes). Swensen (2009) later divided real assets into natural resources and real estate. We prefer his original six asset classes because we don't mind heterogeneous structural and legal characteristics as long as the functional attributes are similar. In the case of real assets, we want to diversify against unexpected inflation; natural resources and real estate both do that.

Domestic Equity

Domestic equities represent ownership of a piece of a U.S.-based corporation and provide a direct link to growth of the economy. Over the long term, the driver of domestic equity returns is growth in company earnings. An equity investor can participate in the growth in company earnings and cash flow over time. However, over the short term, investor sentiment as well as the market multiple (how much investors are willing to pay for the company's earnings) can affect the price of an equity security. The higher expected return characteristics of equity-oriented assets fit with the need to generate substantial portfolio growth over time. However, these higher expected returns come with a higher level of risk, or volatility, from the asset class.

The domestic equity asset class can be sliced by market capitalization. Market capitalization is a measure of the size of the company and is calculated by multiplying the share price by the number of outstanding shares. Larger capitalization companies are more liquid and have more research coverage; therefore, the sub-asset class tends to be more efficient. The opposite is true for those that are smaller. As a result, the small cap space is less efficient. Small cap companies also can have higher price volatility and therefore higher risk.

Equity investors can also target a specific type of company. Investors in growth-oriented companies are seeking a higher growth rate for a company's earnings stream than the overall market would deliver. A growth investor may seek companies that are growing earnings at a level of 15 percent or higher. Investors in value-oriented companies are looking for companies trading at discounts to their intrinsic value.

Companies may trade at a discount for various reasons, such as membership in an out-of-favor industry. Investors can also target companies that pay a dividend. Historically, dividend-paying stocks have offered attractive downside protection to equity investors.

International Equity

The characteristics of domestic equities described earlier equally apply to international equities. An important distinction between domestic and international equities is that being domiciled in different regions means they are subject to different economic exposures. It follows that differing return patterns are generated, thereby creating greater diversification.

For example, international equity investment creates exposure to foreign currencies. Currency exposure is a generally accepted risk. Realistic investors understand that over time, currency fluctuations offset one another and therefore do not speculate in currencies. Moreover, finance theory argues that currency exposure increases portfolio diversification, provided foreign currency exposure is no more than 20–25 percent of portfolio assets.

The international equity asset class can be further broken down into developed economies and emerging economies. Developed international equities include companies based in economies like Japan, Western Europe, Canada and Australia. Developed economies are comparable to the United States in terms of economic infrastructure and drivers of economic performance. For the period 1976–2007, the MSCI Developed Markets Index revealed an annualized return of +10.8 percent for North America, Europe, and Asia. In comparison, the S&P 500 Index was up +11.2 percent for the same period. However, investors in foreign developed markets should be aware that periodic structural changes, shifts in national policies, and differing economic forces in foreign regions can lead to differentiated returns.

Emerging economies include companies based in countries like Asia, Latin America and Eastern Europe. Emerging economies continue to represent a growing share of the global economy and increasingly participate in the global economy through world-class companies. These faster growing economies have become like developed markets and should play a central role in a portfolio because emerging market equities can provide higher expected returns than developed equities. Investors need to proceed with caution, however, because despite their attractive growth prospects, their immature economies, capital markets, and regulatory environments mean they involve less stability and higher levels of risk.

As with domestic equities, the long-term driver of international equity returns is growth in company earnings. However, during short periods of time, investor sentiment and factors influencing the price an investor is willing to pay for the company's earnings stream can affect equity prices.

Fixed Income

Fixed income securities, which represent loans to other entities that are paid back over time, can generate stable cash flows for investors and offer low volatility compared to other asset classes. Additionally, they offer the opportunity for price appreciation as bond prices and interest rates have an inverse relationship: When interest rates fall, bond prices rise, and when interest rates rise, bond prices fall. To capture this price sensitivity, duration is a measure of the price sensitivity of a bond to changes in interest rates. Longer duration bonds exhibit greater price sensitivity to interest rate moves than shorter duration bonds. If an investor holds a bond until it matures, he or she will have received coupon payments over the life of the bond and the principal would have been returned at par value. However, over the short term, movements in interest rates and credit spreads can have a significant impact on bond prices.

Additionally, a key role for U.S. Treasury securities is as deflationary protection. Given the lack of credit risk due to the implicit guarantee of the U.S. government and the fixed payment present in the majority of debt instruments, Treasuries should increase in value as rates drop in response to an economy in decline.

Investors in the fixed income market can target multiple sectors, some of which offer significant depth and liquidity, and others that are less efficient and offer less liquidity. Debt issued by the U.S. government (U.S. Treasury securities) or debt that offers an implicit guarantee of the U.S. government, like government agency debt and agency mortgage-backed securities, are large, highly liquid sectors of the fixed income market. Investors can also allocate to debt issued by corporations, debt issued by international and emerging market sovereigns, and debt issued by U.S. state and local municipalities that currently enjoy tax-exempt status.

In addition to allocation to specific sectors of the market, fixed income investors can target allocations to securities with a specific duration mandate (short, intermediate, or long) or with a specific credit quality mandate (high quality or high yield). Brinker Capital employs a core-satellite approach when constructing our allocations to the fixed income asset class, where allocations to passive and/or active broad market strategies are bolstered by meaningful allocations to various fixed income sectors. This approach provides maximum flexibility to use our active management style to capture market opportunities across and within sectors.

Absolute Return

Absolute return strategies are actively managed strategies that seek to exploit market inefficiencies to generate attractive risk-adjusted returns. Absolute return strategies typically rely on manager skill to deliver alpha, or outperformance versus traditional asset classes. Strategies considered absolute return may have little or no Beta, or market sensitivity, to traditional asset classes or may simply have a key driver of performance that is independent of traditional equity and fixed income strategies. Because their return stream is wholly or partially independent of overall market returns, absolute return strategies provide meaningful diversification benefits.

Types of absolute return strategies include, but are not limited to, long/short equity, market neutral, relative value, event driven, and global macro. Investors can allocate to specific absolute return strategies that complement their overall portfolio. Over the long term, the return of absolute return strategies should be alpha-driven by active manager skill since these strategies should have low correlation to traditional asset classes. Over the short term, returns can be driven by market fluctuations and asset cross-correlations.

Historically, absolute return strategies have been offered in a limited partnership structure. However, today there is an expanding universe of absolute return strategies structured as mutual funds. Brinker Capital prefers accessing absolute return strategies through mutual fund vehicles because of the attractiveness of daily liquidity, daily pricing, and greater transparency. Absolute return strategies accessed through separate account vehicles are also attractive for those reasons.

The selection of absolute return managers requires significant resources and expertise. Casual manager selection will almost certainly lead to disappointment given that absolute return manager success is all about skill in exploiting inefficiencies based on serious, in-depth research and expertise.

Real Assets

Real assets exhibit a higher correlation to inflation, most notably unexpected short-term inflation spikes, and thus help protect against a loss of purchasing power. Inflation means that it takes more dollars to purchase the same basket of goods and services; therefore, inflation erodes an investor's purchasing power over time and clients will need more money in the future to maintain the same standard of living they enjoy today. Investors can combat this loss of purchasing power with an allocation to real assets, such as real estate investments, commodities, natural resources, and Treasury Inflation Protected Securities (TIPS).

Real estate investments involve owning office properties, apartment complexes, industrial warehouses, and retail establishments across the globe along with exposure to the benefits and risks of these investments. For example, real estate investments also provide a cash flow component. Investors can access real estate through private investments or through publicly traded real estate investment trusts (REITs). Typically, all but large, sophisticated institutional and large family wealth offices prefer public investment vehicles. Our experience indicates that during periods of financial system stress or economic duress, accredited investors do not want to own illiquid investments. In other words, private investments sound good at the outset. However, the inevitable bumps during the holding period trigger an uncomfortable awareness of risk and a demand for unavailable liquidity. Thus, Brinker Capital does not offer private investments. Rather, it provides access to these asset class strategies through public vehicles. Notably, real estate is highly correlated to inflation because the labor and materials used to construct buildings rise in cost with inflation. Key to a positive correlation is equilibrium in supply and demand. Additionally, investment properties that can adjust their rents in response to inflation can pass these increases directly on to their investors.

Commodities are basic goods of value, of uniform quality, produced in large numbers by many producers. In addition to protection against rising inflation, historically, commodities have offered diversification benefits because of their lower correlations to traditional asset classes.

Natural resources equities provide exposure to commodity prices, but also can benefit from the operating leverage of the company. Through equities, an investor can also gain exposure to certain commodities that are not traded on futures exchanges.

TIPS are securities issued by the U.S. government that are indexed to inflation. In addition to coupon payments, investors in TIPS will receive a semi-annual adjustment in their principal value depending on the level of the consumer price index (CPI). Investors in TIPS will directly participate in periods of rising inflation; if the CPI increases, the principal of the bond will increase. Because TIPS are fixed income instruments, they do have duration risk and will be affected by movements in interest rates.

As suggested by the earlier discussion, individual real asset strategies can react differently to changes in inflation; therefore, it is important to diversify within the asset class. Supply and demand factors are key drivers of value for real assets. Moreover, allocations to real assets can be shifted over time in response to the economic environment. For example, the allocation to real assets may be higher in a high-inflation environment but lower during periods of falling inflation.

Private Equity

Private equity is equity capital that is not quoted on a public exchange. Private equity investors make investments directly into private companies or conduct buyouts of public companies. Private equity funds, which raise capital from investors, will then try to improve the financial and operational results of a company with the intent to sell the company at a later date for a profit. Private equity strategies are often categorized as leveraged buyouts, venture capital, and special situations, such as mezzanine and distressed deals.

Private equity is most commonly accessed through limited partnerships, where a long holding period is required and investor access is limited. Investors can also gain exposure to private equity through publicly traded companies that have underlying private equity investments. These listed private equity companies are relatively new in the United States, although global markets have broadly accepted the vehicles for decades. The public markets serve as a constant investment pool for private equity managers and, in most structures, public investors can gain access to the same deals as investors in the limited partnership. Although limited partnerships require long lock-up periods, listed private equity companies offer daily valuation and liquidity.

Private equity investments seek to generate higher returns relative to other equity strategies, but with greater levels of risk. Private equity is viewed as less of a diversifier and more as a way to enhance overall portfolio returns. Over the short term, prices of listed private equity companies are affected by market sentiment and the credit markets; however, over the long term, investors should benefit from higher exit values due to operating improvements in underlying portfolio companies.

Brinker Capital has found ways to access the expected potential higher returns from private equity through the careful selection of specific "liquid private equity" opportunities. Brinker Capital's skills and research resources dedicated to thorough due diligence identify and select for inclusion in certain client portfolios small capitalization securities where managements are focused on enhancing operations and growing the business. In addition, active management of investment in publicly traded affiliates of large private equity firms presents meaningful opportunities to augment the equity returns in client portfolios. Brinker Capital has identified such a strategy and included it in client portfolios.

Because access to top-tier active managers is difficult, private equity makes little sense for most casual investors. However, for investors like Brinker Capital, with the resources and expertise to conduct careful due diligence, "liquid private equity" opportunities can enhance return.

Asset Class Summary

In Table 4.2, the basic characteristics of these six asset classes are summarized.

Today, using our investment philosophy as our foundation, we build broadly diversified strategies that span the risk–return spectrum. As we move further out on the risk spectrum, greater emphasis is placed on equity-oriented asset classes that possess a higher expected return, but also higher levels of volatility.

While the first section of this chapter focused on our investment philosophy, the remainder of the chapter discusses and illustrates the application and implementation of the principles and concepts which constitute our investment philosophy. The application phase consists of applying our principles to construct strategic or long term model

TABLE 4.2

Summary of the Six Asset Classes

Asset Class	Return	Risk	Key Portfolio Role
Domestic equity	High	High	Mature economic growth exposure
International equity	High	High	International economic growth exposure
Fixed income	Low	Low	Stability and income
Absolute return	Various	Various	Returns with low correlation to the markets
Real assets	High	High	Short-term inflation hedge
Private equity	Very high	Very high	Young business growth exposure

Source: Brinker Capital, Inc. For illustrative purposes only.

portfolios with neutral asset classes and ranges and risk controls. The implementation phase involves an assessment of the investment and macroeconomic environment and the selection of strategies to execute the strategic model portfolios in the current environment. Figure 4.5 depicts the application and implementation process.

FIGURE 4.5

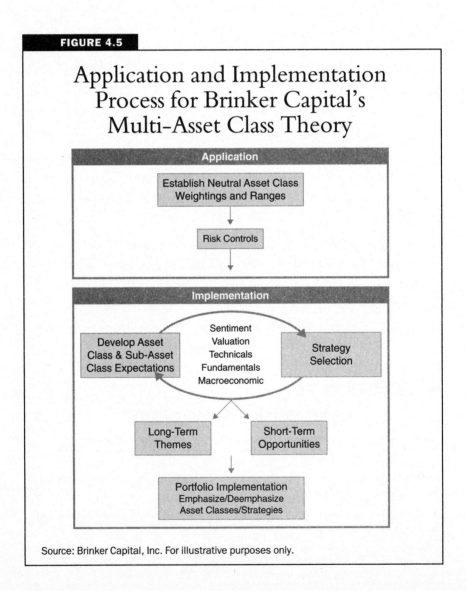

Application and Implementation Process for Brinker Capital's Multi-Asset Class Theory

Source: Brinker Capital, Inc. For illustrative purposes only.

Application Process for Multi-Asset Class Theory

Portfolio creation and selection requires attention to three activities: assessing investor risk tolerance, establishing neutral asset class weightings and ranges and determining the neutral weight models.

Investor Risk Tolerance

An investor's risk tolerance can be measured as the level of variability in returns an investor is willing to accept in his or her portfolio. This tolerance also is expressed as the level of capital loss (drawdown) an investor is willing to withstand. The longer an investor's time horizon, the more willing he or she should be to take on additional risk in order to maximize returns over the long term.

Offering a variety of strategies enables clients to select the one that best fits their risk tolerance and time horizon. For example, conservative investors are more sensitive to short-term losses and thus are willing to accept lower returns to better protect on the downside. Moderate investors can accept more risk than a conservative investor but balance the importance of both safety and return. Aggressive investors are willing to accept large fluctuations in value, in exchange for higher returns.

Neutral Asset Class Weightings and Ranges

Brinker Capital uses a combination of strategic asset allocation and tactical asset allocation to plan and implement investor portfolios. Strategic asset allocation traditionally means setting target allocations for each class and then periodically rebalancing the portfolio back to those targets as investment returns skew the original asset allocation percentages. After setting these targets, we use active management to make shorter term tactical asset allocation decisions that allow us to take advantage of specific market opportunities. Tactical asset allocation allows for a range of percentages in each asset class (such as domestic equities comprise 40–50 percent of the portfolio). Tactical asset allocation decisions can be long-term (expressed for 12+ months) or short term (expressed for less than 12 months).

To guide our strategic asset allocation process, we create neutral asset class weightings, meaning the baseline allocation for each asset class given certain risk-reward scenarios. In other words, these weightings constitute a sensible, static, and strategic mix of asset allocations for a hypothetical long-term investor at each risk tolerance.

In addition to determining neutral asset class weightings, we also determine asset class minimum and maximum allocation ranges for each of our portfolios. Our ranges provide flexibility for active management, but also ensure that our portfolios remain true to their target risk level and objective. The neutral allocations and ranges for our moderate portfolio provided in Table 4.3 illustrate one of Brinker Capital's model portfolios. Compliance within these ranges is continually monitored, as is the reasonableness of the ranges.

The three traditional asset classes of domestic equity, international equity and fixed income have return and risk data going back 20 years (see Table 4.4), which constitutes a much longer track record than what is available for the three non-traditional asset classes of absolute return, real assets and private equity. While the past is not always a prologue, it is

TABLE 4.3		
Neutral Weights and Ranges for Brinker Capital's Moderate Portfolios		
Asset Class	**Neutral Weight**	**Range**
Traditional		
Domestic Equity	42%	30–55%
International Equity	18%	11–27%
Fixed Income	40%	25–45%
Non-traditional		
Absolute Return	0%	0–20%
Real Assets	0%	0–10%
Private Equity	0%	0–10%
Source: Brinker Capital, Inc. For illustrative purposes only.		

TABLE 4.4

Historical Data for Traditional Asset Classes

Asset Class	20-Year Annual Return*	20-Year Annual Standard Deviation*	Representative Market Index
Domestic Equity	9.3%	15.5%	Russell 3000
International Equity	6.7%	17.3%	MSCI All Country World ex USA
Fixed Income	5.8%	3.7%	Barclays Aggregate

*20-year period ending November 30, 2013.
Source: FactSet and Brinker Capital, Inc. For illustrative purposes only.

common practice for professional investors to seek the longest streams of historical data when building neutral models along the risk-return continuum. Longer streams of data create greater predictability. Thus, for simplicity, integrity and familiarity, we use the three traditional asset classes to formulate our neutral asset class weightings.

When determining the appropriate split of our equity allocation between domestic equity and international equity, several factors come into play. International equity markets are gaining a greater percentage of global equity market capitalization, and international markets could offer diversification benefits, both of which argue for a higher allocation. However, we believe our investors prefer a home country bias, as they need to spend U.S. dollars. Therefore, we have settled on a neutral global equity allocation of 70 percent U.S. and 30 percent non-U.S. We increased this allocation from 20 percent to 30 percent of total equity in 2008 and will continue to monitor the appropriate mix going forward.

While our neutral asset class weightings are represented only by traditional asset classes, in practice we also allocate to non-traditional, or alternative, asset classes in all of our portfolios. We add the non-traditional, or alternative, asset classes (including absolute return, real assets, and private equity) to the neutral weight models in the implementation step.

Neutral Weight Models

Brinker Capital offers portfolios across the risk-return spectrum, and each of these portfolios is managed to a desired risk or volatility level as determined by the investor client. To reach that desired risk level, we build the portfolios using an appropriate blend of our six major asset classes, combining lower volatility asset classes like fixed income with equity-oriented asset classes that offer a greater expected return, but with a higher level of volatility.

Risk-return scenarios and accompanying portfolios are created by examining the broad market indices associated with each asset class (see Table 4.4), although it is important to note that these indices are not inclusive of all of the sub-asset classes in our opportunity set. Using the long-term risk and return characteristics for these market indices displayed in Table 4.4, we determine the appropriate asset mix that results in the desired risk level, measured by standard deviation, for each of the portfolios.

Our resulting six target risk portfolios (see Table 4.5) have neutral equity exposures ranging from 30 percent to 98 percent and standard

TABLE 4.5

Neutral Weight Models				
Neutral Target Risk Portfolio	Neutral Equity Exposure	Neutral Fixed Income Exposure	20-Year Annual Return*	20-Year Annual Standard Deviation*
Conservative	30%	70%	6.7%	5.2%
Moderately Conservative	40%	60%	7.0%	6.5%
Moderate	60%	40%	7.7%	9.4%
Moderately Aggressive	70%	30%	8.0%	10.9%
Aggressive	80%	20%	8.2%	12.4%
Aggressive Equity	98%	2%	8.6%	15.2%

*20-year period ending November 30, 2013.
Source: FactSet and Brinker Capital, Inc. For illustrative purposes only.

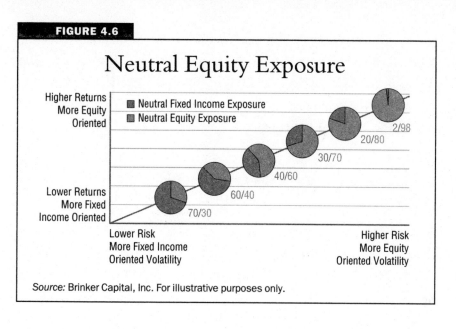

FIGURE 4.6

Neutral Equity Exposure

Higher Returns / More Equity Oriented

- ■ Neutral Fixed Income Exposure
- ■ Neutral Equity Exposure

2/98
20/80
30/70
40/60
60/40

Lower Returns / More Fixed Income Oriented

70/30

Lower Risk / More Fixed Income Oriented Volatility

Higher Risk / More Equity Oriented Volatility

Source: Brinker Capital, Inc. For illustrative purposes only.

deviation targets that range from 5 percent to 15 percent. The portfolios are spaced along the risk–return spectrum to assure that each portfolio possesses its own unique set of risk characteristics (see Figure 4.6).

Implementing Our Philosophy

Implementation is the busy crossroads where theory and application meet practice. At this important intersection, a financial advisor knowledgeable in theory and skilled in its application helps investors meet their goals, such as generating income for spending requirements and protecting the purchasing power of their savings. Investors expect their advisors to act as a fiduciary with independence and objectivity.

Implementation builds upon the neutral asset class weightings and ranges determined during the application phase to develop asset class and sub-asset class expectations. Implementation is accomplished through the selection of strategies that execute the asset classes and sub asset classes (see Figure 4.3). In order to select the most effective or efficient strategies, Brinker Capital builds a mosaic out of a number of market- and economic-related factors. These factors include sentiment, valuation, technicals, fundamentals, and macroeconomic considerations. Once the mosaic is built then it is interpreted to identify long-term themes, pick short-term opportunities, and determine risk controls. Having built and interpreted the mosaic, strategies are selected and executed as the final step in the portfolio implementation process.

Develop Asset Class and Sub-Asset Class Expectations

Brinker Capital's framework for developing return, risk, and correlation expectations for major asset classes and sub-asset classes centers on the consideration of market and economic-related factors of sentiment, valuation, technicals, and the macroeconomic environment. These various factors allow us to determine the relative favorableness or unfavorableness of the various asset classes and sub-asset classes. These components are described in greater detail in the sections that follow. Insights about how mean–variance analysis and other tools of Modern Portfolio Theory factors into this process are also addressed.

Sentiment

Investor sentiment measures how positive (bullish) or negative (bearish) groups of investors are about the equity markets at any given point in time. Sentiment is a contrarian indicator, so when sentiment is negative, meaning investors are extremely pessimistic about the equity markets, it is often a great entry point. And when sentiment is elevated and investors are exhibiting excessive optimism in equity market prospects, it often signals a market top. Sentiment is typically measured by survey, as shown in Figure 4.7, but it can also be measured by examining flows into various asset classes of mutual funds. If investors are moving significant amounts of capital into domestic equity funds, for example, this could be a sign that sentiment is elevated. However, sentiment can remain elevated for some time, so it is important to consider sentiment in the context of the other factors in the mosaic.

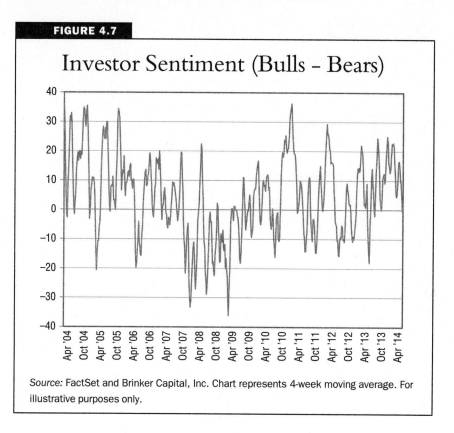

FIGURE 4.7

Investor Sentiment (Bulls – Bears)

Source: FactSet and Brinker Capital, Inc. Chart represents 4-week moving average. For illustrative purposes only.

Valuation

Valuation measures the estimated worth of an asset. Financial assets can be valued using absolute measures that determine the present value of the asset's future cash flows or relative measures that determine value based on similar assets or history. A number of commonly used relative valuation metrics exists, including price–to–earnings (using both historical and expected future earnings), price–to–book value, price–to–cash flow, enterprise value to earnings before interest, taxes, depreciation, and amortization (EBITDA), enterprise value to sales, price/earnings (P/E) to growth, and the Shiller cyclically adjusted P/E ratio (see Figure 4.8). It is important to incorporate a number of different valuation metrics into the mosaic and compare current valuation to historical valuations for context. Similar to sentiment, both elevated and compressed valuations can persist for an extended period. With that said, elevated valuations

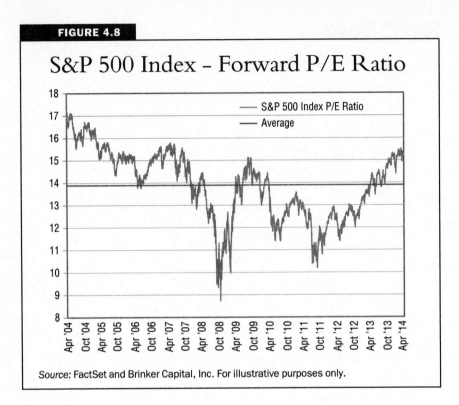

FIGURE 4.8

S&P 500 Index – Forward P/E Ratio

Source: FactSet and Brinker Capital, Inc. For illustrative purposes only.

relative to history should prompt caution when determining a view on an asset class; however, low valuations are good entry points for investors as we saw in the equity markets following the 2008 financial crisis.

Technicals

Technical analysis is a security analysis discipline for forecasting the direction of prices through the study of past market data, primarily price and volume. Technical analysis relies on the basic dynamic of supply and demand. Momentum can be a very strong factor driving asset prices (see Figure 4.9). We look at the price trends of various asset classes and sub-asset classes compared to their shorter term (50-day) and longer term (200-day) moving averages. Should an asset class fall below its 200-day moving average, this may be cause for concern.

FIGURE 4.9

Momentum – U.S. Large Cap

Source: FactSet and Brinker Capital, Inc. For illustrative purposes only.

Macroeconomic Environment

The macroeconomic environment can affect all asset classes and strategies in various ways, so it is important to understand the sensitivity of those asset classes to changes in the macro environment (see Figure 4.10). The macroeconomic environment includes an assessment of the global economy, including growth and inflation measures, interest rates, and global monetary and fiscal policy, which can have a significant effect on economic growth and confidence as we experienced after the 2008 financial crisis. For example, a weaker global growth profile will weigh on company earnings and could push valuation metrics lower.

When determining our short-term (<12 months) and longer-term (>12 months) views on major and sub-asset classes, we interpret the mosaic created by sentiment, valuation, technical, and macroeconomic

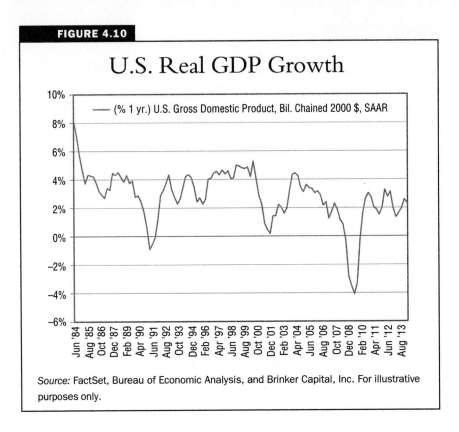

FIGURE 4.10

U.S. Real GDP Growth

— (% 1 yr.) U.S. Gross Domestic Product, Bil. Chained 2000 $, SAAR

Source: FactSet, Bureau of Economic Analysis, and Brinker Capital, Inc. For illustrative purposes only.

factors. We determine both a short-term and a longer-term view on the asset classes, determining return and risk expectations, as well on how an asset class will behave relative to other asset classes given the mosaic. The resulting portfolio allocations will be weighted based on how favorably or unfavorably we view the asset classes.

Apply Mean-Variance Analysis and Other Tools

Brinker Capital's overall investment process incorporates mean-variance analysis and other tools of Modern Portfolio Theory. Mean-variance analysis is a mathematical optimization of portfolio construction using expected returns, standard deviations and correlations. It is a quantitative tool which can confirm if your strategic portfolio construction is directionally correct. However, it is important to note that flawed assumptions of Modern Portfolio Theory and uncertainties around its input variables

TABLE 4.6			
Sample Moderate Portfolio			
Asset Class	**Current Allocation**	**Neutral Weight**	**Range**
Traditional Asset Classes			
Domestic Equity	40%	42%	30–55%
International Equity	12%	18%	11–27%
Fixed Income	29%	40%	25–45%
Non-traditional Asset Classes			
Absolute Return	15%	0%	0–20%
Real Assets	2%	0%	0–10%
Private Equity	2%	0%	0–10%
Source: Brinker Capital, Inc. For illustrative purposes only.			

have prompted investors (ourselves included) to place heavy constraints on models based on this theory. As David Swensen wrote, "unconstrained mean-variance [optimization] usually provide[s] solutions unrecognizable as reasonable portfolios . . . Because the process involves material simplifying assumptions, adopting the unconstrained asset allocation point estimates provided by mean-variance optimization makes little sense" (Swensen 2009).

Whereas a pure Modern Portfolio Theory framework would rely entirely on precise estimates of returns, standard deviations and correlations, our approach places greater emphasis on relative areas of outperformance, asset classes with higher risks, and a strong understanding of links among asset classes and strategies. Consider the portfolio presented in Table 4.6 which has allocations in each asset class that align with our asset class neutral weightings and ranges.

Moving into 2014, we began by generating forecasts for each of the six asset classes in our client allocations, often using historical correlations (see Table 4.7). This task is performed by Brinker Capital's investment team in January and July each year.

When these expectations were fed into a portfolio optimizer based on Modern Portfolio Theory, the recommended portfolio shown in Table 4.8 was produced. The optimized recommendation involved

TABLE 4.7		
Anticipated Asset Class Performance		
Asset Class	**Forecasted Return**	**Expected Risk**
Traditional Asset Classes		
Domestic Equity	6.48%	15.44%
International Equity	6.72%	16.78%
Fixed Income	−0.01%	4.79%
Non-traditional Asset Classes		
Absolute Return	4.11%	7.53%
Real Assets	5.73%	14.78%
Private Equity	9.89%	19.44%

Source: Brinker Capital, Inc. For illustrative purposes only. Forecasted returns from July 1, 2014 through June 30, 2015. All forecasts are reasonably held at the time of this writing but are subject to change without notice by Brinker Capital, Inc.

allocations to only three asset classes: 14 percent to domestic equities, 56 percent to absolute return, and 30 percent to private equity.

Implementing the optimized recommendation would mean liquidating the investor's current allocations in the international equity, fixed income, and real asset classes. This provides an example of how optimized

TABLE 4.8				
Optimized Portfolio Based on Modern Portfolio Theory				
Asset Class	**Forecasted Return**	**Expected Risk**	**Optimized Recommendation**	**Current Allocation**
Traditional Asset Classes				
Domestic Equity	6.48%	15.44%	14%	40%
International Equity	6.72%	16.78%	0%	12%
Fixed Income	−0.01%	4.79%	0%	29%
Non-traditional Asset Classes				
Absolute Return	4.11%	7.53%	56%	15%
Real Assets	5.73%	14.78%	0%	2%
Private Equity	9.89%	19.44%	30%	2%

Source: Brinker Capital, Inc. For illustrative purposes only.

recommendations can become inadvisable. Namely, exiting three asset classes in this case is not rational for four important reasons:

- Trading costs: Wholesale movements in and out of assets produce unwanted trading costs.

- Taxes: Investors are taxpayers, unless the assets are held in a qualified account such as a retirement plan. Movements in and out of assets can incur premature capital gains taxes.

- Humility: It is wise to be humble in the face of uncertainty because our forecasts are not always correct.

- Diversification: Multi-asset class investing commits both the investment professional and the client to the principles of diversification.

Strategy Selection

Once we have determined our views on the asset and sub-asset classes, we decide how best to implement those views, which is where we begin our strategy selection. Strategy selection discussions are often concurrent with asset allocation discussions. We often receive input from our underlying managers that helps in building the mosaic for the asset classes.

Selecting a Passive or Active Management Strategy

A major decision for strategy selection is whether to express the asset class view as a passively or actively managed strategy. Passive strategies allocate to a Beta-oriented position using a passive exchange-traded product or index fund. These strategies are appropriate when we seek pure asset class exposure, as a passive vehicle will deliver the exposure in a cost-effective manner without the worry of style drift. Passive vehicles also allow for more specificity in implementing the asset class view, as these vehicles, primarily exchange-traded funds (ETFs), can offer very granular exposures.

We prefer active management when we are targeting inefficient segments of the market and when performance across active managers varies greatly. In such cases, an active manager can add significant value

TABLE 4.9				
Dispersion of Active Manager Returns				
Dispersion of Active Manager Returns (%)				
Asset Class	**First Quartile**	**Median**	**Third Quartile**	**Range**
International Equity	10.5	9.0	4.0	6.5
Fixed Income	7.4	7.1	0.5	6.9
Real Estate	17.6	12.0	9.2	8.4
Absolute Return	15.6	12.5	7.1	8.5
U.S. Equity	12.1	11.2	1.9	10.2
U.S. Small Cap Equity	16.1	14.0	4.8	11.3
Leveraged Buyouts	13.3	8.0	−0.4	13.7
Venture Capital	28.7	−1.4	−14.5	43.2

Source: Pioneering Portfolio Management, David Swensen. Data represents the ten-year period ending June 30, 2005.

when that manager has a significant competitive advantage or when a desired exposure cannot effectively be replicated passively. Moreover, active management makes sense in asset classes where there is a high level of dispersion between the returns of a first quartile manager and a third quartile manager (see Table 4.9 and Figure 4.11, for example). An investor will be rewarded for selecting a top-performing manager.

Active management requires attention to asset class and strategy. Effective active management is iterative. Often, the best active managers are generalists. For example, specialists in manager due diligence and selection often are blind to asset allocation considerations such as which asset class is favored. The specialist knows only best manager performance and capability. On the other hand, an asset allocation specialist is familiar with trends in each asset class but unfamiliar with the best managers in each asset class. Brinker Capital's investment managers are skilled in both asset allocation and manager selection.

Selecting an active manager suitable for your needs is an important step in implementing your investment plan. A manager search may be conducted for a number of reasons: to gain exposure to a new asset class or investment strategy, to gain additional manager depth, or to replace an

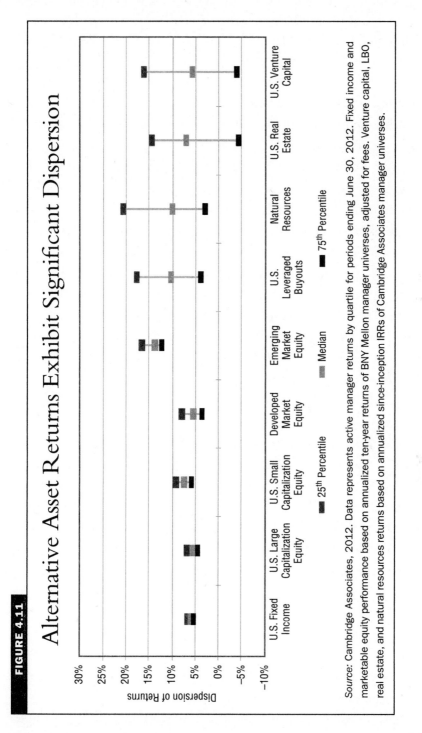

FIGURE 4.11

Alternative Asset Returns Exhibit Significant Dispersion

Source: Cambridge Associates, 2012. Data represents active manager returns by quartile for periods ending June 30, 2012. Fixed income and marketable equity performance based on annualized ten-year returns of BNY Mellon manager universes, adjusted for fees. Venture capital, LBO, real estate, and natural resources returns based on annualized since-inception IRRs of Cambridge Associates manager universes.

existing manager. The next section outlines how Brinker Capital selects active managers.

Selecting an Active Manager

The first step in our manager selection process is to identify a group of candidates to include in the search process. This process may begin by screening funds in a database to identify potential managers. The quantitative screening process varies depending on the specific investment strategy. For example, the screening process is more uniform when looking at traditional asset classes (e.g., domestic equities), which have a well-developed opportunity set. Some factors used in a more traditional screening may include performance rankings within a peer group, expense ratio, assets under management, and manager tenure, among others. The screening process may be less formalized with more esoteric sub-asset classes, as the opportunity set is often smaller. Managers also can be identified using industry contacts, existing manager contacts, referrals and publications. It is common that the number of candidates found will vary depending upon the asset class and purpose of the search.

After a workable group of search candidates is identified, further due diligence must be performed using technical and non-technical considerations. Technical performance metrics may include total returns, risk-adjusted returns, peer universe comparisons, downside risk, performance consistency, up- and down-market capture ratios and number of holdings, among others. Non-technical indicators of performance may include expense ratio, portfolio manager tenure and strategy assets under management, among others. These forms of data can be used to produce some initial impressions and rankings of the active managers.

Candidates then undergo a telephone interview to get a better understanding of their investment philosophy, team and process. After the interviews are completed, the candidates are narrowed down further to a group of finalists.

Finalists are required to complete a detailed New Manager Questionnaire. We also visit finalists' sites to gain a deeper understanding of the key drivers of their performance, including their people, process, and philosophy. We seek to gain a good understanding of what drives their strategies, whether it is a key portfolio manager or a team of analysts, a sound and repeatable process or the passion of the team to unite under a single philosophy. This understanding will help in setting expectations for the strategy and monitoring the strategy once it has been added to our portfolios.

Once the onsite visit is completed and the questionnaire is reviewed, we complete a quantitative manager scorecard as well as a more qualitative investment summary memo that describes the key aspects of each manager's strategy. The portfolio managers will discuss the merits of each strategy and make the final manager selection decision.

It is important to note that we are not simply looking for the best manager in isolation. Instead, we are looking to build a portfolio of managers and strategies that accomplish our goal of generating consistent returns over time. This is in keeping with the principles of diversification: Just as Markowitz urged us to focus on the portfolios in aggregate rather than assets in isolation when making a final decision, we too always look for the best manager to complement our existing portfolio.

Before adding a manager to our portfolio, we determine the drivers of performance and set expectations for that strategy's behavior in various market environments. While we understand that a manager's strategy can fall in and out of favor, we do not want all of our managers in a specific asset class to have similar performance characteristics across all market environments. We seek a group of managers that complement each other during various market environments, which as a whole delivers consistent returns over time.

The manager evaluation process does not end once they are added to our portfolio. Instead, we continue to monitor advisors' strategy characteristics, so that we can identify when fundamental changes should result in a termination before it shows up in poor manager performance. We typically remove managers from our portfolios only if there has been a fundamental change in personnel, investment philosophy, or process that we believe will negatively affect future performance, result in performance that does not meet our expectations, indicating the team is not executing as we would like, or change significantly the fund characteristics or structure, including excessive growth in assets under management.

We believe our extensive manager due diligence process enables us to select first-rate managers. Through our manager interview and questionnaire process, we can identify the most important characteristics that have made the strategy work in the past. We have found that many mutual fund investors don't have the knowledge or resources to analyze fund data that typically thought to give advisors an edge, including tracking fund flows, using linked track records to secure more complete data, and analyzing how fund candidates interact with other funds in our portfolio. Finally, our flexible selection process allows us to consider smaller and newer funds, which in turn allows us to take advantage of attractive opportunities before they are recognized by the broader universe of mutual fund investors.

Themes and Opportunities

With neutral asset class weightings and ranges set, asset and sub-asset class expectations determined, and our strategies selected, it is time to implement long-term themes (typically longer than 12 months in duration) and seize short-term opportunities (up to 12 months in duration). Within these themes and opportunities, asset class views are framed relative to our neutral asset class weightings and we over- or underweight specific major and sub-asset classes to express our views.

It is important to note that our strategic portfolio construction process includes and is bolstered by a number of risk controls, the most important of which is our very broad diversification across and within asset classes and sub-asset classes. In addition, in the implementation phase we size positions to mitigate specific manager or strategy risk. Finally, even after implementing our tactical views, our asset class exposures for each portfolio must remain within their stated ranges, as depicted in Figure 4.12.

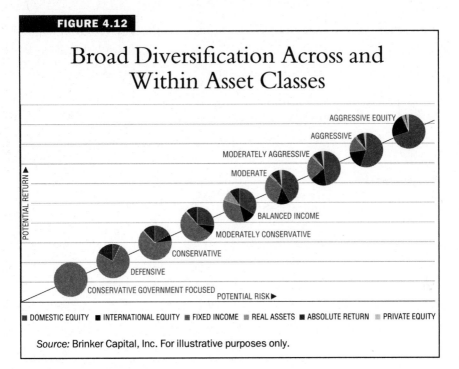

FIGURE 4.12

Broad Diversification Across and Within Asset Classes

POTENTIAL RETURN ▲

AGGRESSIVE EQUITY

AGGRESSIVE

MODERATELY AGGRESSIVE

MODERATE

BALANCED INCOME

MODERATELY CONSERVATIVE

CONSERVATIVE

DEFENSIVE

CONSERVATIVE GOVERNMENT FOCUSED

POTENTIAL RISK ▶

■ DOMESTIC EQUITY   ■ INTERNATIONAL EQUITY   ■ FIXED INCOME   ■ REAL ASSETS   ■ ABSOLUTE RETURN   ■ PRIVATE EQUITY

Source: Brinker Capital, Inc. For illustrative purposes only.

Summary

To compound return, an investment firm must know investment theory and be skilled in its application and implementation; the firm must be creative in discovering enhancements to its theory and committed to ongoing improvements in its implementation.

An investor's philosophy is a comprehensive statement of the principles that make up the investor's investment theory. The philosophy is an articulated, intentional approach to generating returns. It is made up of a body of studied, tested, and formalized principles in which the investor's belief is so strong it rises to the level of professional conviction. Brinker Capital's investment philosophy is multi-asset class, involving allocations across and within six asset classes. This philosophy is guided by these four fundamental principles: diversification, innovation, active management and equity-like bias.

Based upon consideration of market and economic conditions, we set neutral asset class weightings and ranges and asset and sub-asset class expectations, followed by implementation of long-term themes and short-term opportunities and institution of risk controls. The entire process is made possible through active management, which adds significant value to the investor experience.

References

Bayes, Thomas. *An Essay Toward Solving a Problem in the Doctrine of Chances.* (1763). www.stat.ucla.edu/history/essay.pdf.

Bernoulli, Jakob. *Ars conjectandi, opus posthumum. Accedit Tractatus de seriebus infinitis, et epistola gallicé scripta de ludo pilae reticularis*, Basel: Thurneysen Brothers, 1713. www.kubkou.se/pdf/mh/jacobB.pdf.

Bernstein, Peter L. *Capital Ideas Evolving.* Hoboken: John Wiley & Sons, 2009.

Cerulli Research Report. *Managed Accounts 2013.* Boston: Cerulli Associates, 2013. www.cerulli.com/vapi/public/getcerullifile?filecid=F0002IG.

Fama, Eugene F., and Kenneth R. French. "The Cross-Section of Expected Stock Returns." (June 1992). *The Journal of Finance*, 47(2): 427–465. doi: 10.2307/2329112 www.business.unr.edu/faculty/liuc/files/badm742/fama_french_1992.pdf.

Graham, Benjamin, and David Dodd. *Security Analysis.* New York: Whittlesey House, 1934.

Kobor, Adam. *A Note on Harry M. Markowitz's "Market Efficiency: A Theoretical Distinction and So What?"* Charlottesville: CFA Institute, 2006.

Lewin, Kurt. *Field Theory in Social Science: Selected Theoretical Papers* (ed. by D. Cartwright). New York: Harper & Row, 1951.

Markowitz, Harry M. "Portfolio Selection." (March 1952). *The Journal of Finance*, 7(1): 77–91. doi: 10.2307/2975974.

Morningstar. "The Morningstar Category Classifications." (July 31, 2012). Working paper. https://corporate.morningstar.com/us/documents/Meth odologyDocuments/ResearchPapers/MorningstarCategory_Classifications .pdf.

Swensen, David F. *Pioneering Portfolio Management: An Unconventional Approach to Institutional Investment.* New York: Free Press, 2009.

Zweig, Jason. Interview Harry Markowitz. (January 1998). *Money Magazine*.

CHAPTER 5

The Power of Buckets

Dr. Daniel Crosby

It is always the simple that produces the marvelous.

—Amelia Barr

Given the seeming complexity of the problems that beset investors, it has made some intuitive sense that the proposed solutions to what ails us have been equally convoluted. But as Dhirendra Kumar (2012), CEO of Value Research points out in his piece for the *Economic Times*, part of the answer may lie in something to which we are naturally prone. He says of this tendency,

> *So what's the solution? Some sophisticated analytical tool that will give us an insight? No, actually, it's something that someone in your family probably already practices, or at least used to in the decades gone by.*
>
> *The solution is bags. I had this aunt who used to have a set of little bags which would close with a string around their necks. When her husband's salary would arrive, she would divide up the money into heads like vegetables, milk, dhobi, etc . . . and put each in a bag. Curiously, as a principle of budgeting, this is known to most of us, but few apply it to financial investments."*

The phenomenon to which Mr. Kumar is referring is formally known as "mental accounting" and was first documented by Dr. Richard Thaler of the University of Chicago. Mental accounting "refers to the tendency for people to separate their money into separate accounts based on a variety of subjective criteria, like the source of the money and intent for each account" (Phung 2014). More simply, the way in which we label and mentally subdivide our funds is a key determinant of how they will be used.

Mental accounting is, in the strictest sense, irrational behavior. After all, money is fungible and a dollar is a dollar is a dollar, no matter how it is labeled. One green likeness of our first President can buy you one hundred pennies worth of candy, as surely as it can pay down a similar amount of your student loan debt.

Since mental accounting is an irrational behavior, much of the historical focus on mental accounting has been on the ways in which it thwarts good financial behavior. For example, some people will keep a large pile of cash that is mentally labeled as the "Trip to the Bahamas" fund, but will fail to pay down credit card debt that carries exorbitant fees. Consumers also tend to spend more with credit or debit cards than they do when using cash, as greenbacks are accounted for as more mentally "real" and "present" than the more ethereal notion of credit. Interestingly, Dan Ariely (2009) of Duke University has also documented that people who would never steal an actual dollar bill from a register will gladly siphon off millions of them virtually through fraudulent activities. Clearly, poor mental accounting can lead us to misallocate resources and even act unethically.

Irrationalities notwithstanding, mental accounting is simply not going away. Meir Statman gives two humorous examples of mental accounting and the underworld in his book, *What Investors Really Want* (2010). He relates a study on prostitutes in Norway who also had "day jobs" where they obtained money through more legitimate means. These "ladies of ill repute" placed funds received from wages, welfare or health benefits into practical mental accounts that were used for rent and groceries. "Trick money," on the other hand, was used more recklessly, on things like drugs, alcohol and clothing. Statman also provides the example of Marty, a Philly gang member who separated his money into "good money" and "bad money," depending on whether it was honestly or ill-gotten. A complicated character to be sure, Marty would tithe to his local church using "good money," but reserved his "bad money" for reinvestment in his criminal pursuits.

But we needn't suppose that "bucketing" is limited to ne'er-do-wells; it is something in which each of us engages daily. Most broadly, each of us has mental accounts for "don't go broke" and "hopefully get rich," as epitomized by the previously mentioned tendency to buy both insurance and lottery tickets. Between and within these two extremes exists a series of predictable strata that correspond remarkably well with the way we actually develop as individuals.

Abraham Maslow first proposed his hierarchy of needs in a 1943 paper titled, "A Theory of Human Motivation." Although Maslow himself never represented his hierarchy in a triangle, the pyramid you see in Figure 5.1 has become the most common representation of his ideas. Maslow felt as though individuals must satisfy their most basic needs for hunger, thirst, sexual desire, and safety before they could move on to the esteem and self-actualization considerations that move life from the banal to the transcendent. Gandhi summed up this idea concisely when he said,

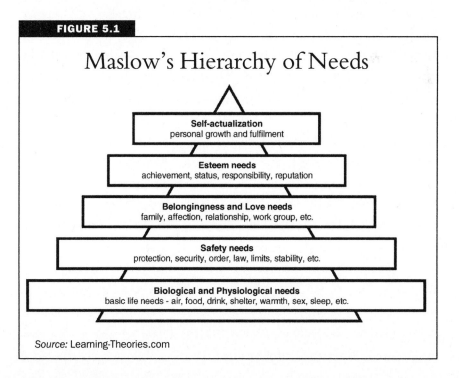

FIGURE 5.1

Maslow's Hierarchy of Needs

Self-actualization
personal growth and fulfilment

Esteem needs
achievement, status, responsibility, reputation

Belongingness and Love needs
family, affection, relationship, work group, etc.

Safety needs
protection, security, order, law, limits, stability, etc.

Biological and Physiological needs
basic life needs - air, food, drink, shelter, warmth, sex, sleep, etc.

Source: Learning-Theories.com

in effect, to a poor man: bread is God. Until we have tamed our most elemental needs, it is difficult to climb that ladder toward meaningful existence.

What we now call purpose-driven investing is drawn from an intellectual heritage rooted in the financial application of Maslow's ideas by Lola Lopes (1987) and later Hersh Shefrin and Meir Statman (2000). Lopes' breakthrough theory is known as SP/A theory, where the S stands for "Security," the P for "Potential" and the A for "Aspiration." Security, much like the bottom-most rungs of Maslow's hierarchy, represents the most primal financial needs and is rooted in the emotion of fear. If we are able to provide and account for the Security bucket, we will be less fear-based and better able to make rational financial decisions. Behavioral economists have demonstrated time and again that investors are loss averse: They are twice as unhappy about a given loss as they are a comparable gain. Until the fear of such a loss can be meaningfully brushed aside, it will dominate and hamper all higher-level wealth-planning considerations.

Potential, in Lopes' (1987) model, relates to the general wish for high degrees of wealth, and Aspiration reflects the desire to work toward specific financial goals. As opposed to the fear-based emotions underlying Security, Lopes posits that Potential and Aspiration are driven by a hopeful outlook. In her 1987 paper on SP/A theory, Lopes demonstrates the applicability of her ideas by using the example of crops chosen by farmers. Lopes tells us that subsistence farmers must make a decision about how to allocate their limited field space, just as investors must make choices with their limited financial resources. Farmers must allocate between food crops that have low but stable prices and cash crops that have volatile but potentially high valuations. Depending on how hopeful or fearful they feel, farmers will allot more or less of their valuable land to cash versus food crops. For this group from humble circumstances, cash crops represent the possibility of a better life, but food crops promise the safety of not totally going broke. Just as very few investors "go for broke" on risky assets, all but the most fearful and most cavalier farmers plant a blend of food and cash crops, thereby balancing these two mental accounts and the accompanying emotions they hold simultaneously.

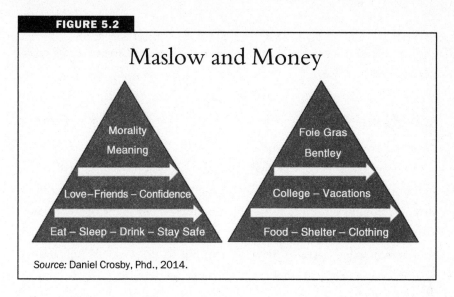

Maslow and Money

Morality
Meaning

Love – Friends – Confidence

Eat – Sleep – Drink – Stay Safe

Foie Gras
Bentley

College – Vacations

Food – Shelter – Clothing

Source: Daniel Crosby, Phd., 2014.

Shefrin and Statman's (2000) Behavioral Portfolio Theory introduced in a paper of the same name, combines elements of Lopes' SP/A theory with Kahneman and Tversky's insights into mental accounts. Behavioral Portfolio Theory suggests a counterpoint to the EMH notion that the greatest desire of investors is to maximize the value of their portfolio at any cost. Instead, it suggests that investors have simultaneous and varied aims designed to meet a range of goals. Just as with Lopes' (1987) model, the base of the pyramid presented in Figure 5.2 is to avoid financial woe, while the top of the pyramid focuses on loftier attainments. Sound familiar?

This brief overview of Behavioral Portfolio Theory and SP/A theory is not reflective of a desire on my part for you to become an expert in goal-based theory. Rather, my hope is to provide evidence that mental accounting is a value neutral fact of life that is as damaging or helpful as its application. Everyone from farmers to hookers, to gangbangers and schoolteachers engages in mental accounts. We all have buckets for the money we need to eat today as well as the money we hope will provide a brighter tomorrow. Segmentation will happen, as will the varied risk profiles that accompany each stratum. If we are thoughtful and intentional, we can use these irrational accounts to our benefit, by taming the fear-based risk bucket en route to more clear-eyed financial decision-making.

Intentional Framing

"For the cost of a cup of coffee per day . . ."

If you have ever watched daytime television (guilty), the mere mention of that phrase probably conjures up images of hungry children in a developing country, stomachs distended from want of sustenance. Charity organizations, who often exist entirely on the kindness of strangers, learned early to leverage framing to do good. When framed relative to the cost of a single cup of coffee, something many Americans purchase 365 days a year, the price of helping seems small indeed. This is what is called "narrow framing," or viewing a purchase as disconnected from the aggregate pot of money from which it is drawn (remember, since money is fungible it all comes from the same big bucket).

Using a broader frame, let's step back and examine the true cost of such a charitable gift. Some Starbucks coffees cost more than $5 for a Venti size (that's a "large" if you're from Alabama like me), but let's assume some greater moderation on your part and say the average cup of joe costs $3. Buying just such a cup of coffee each day would land you with an annual coffee tab of $1,095. As of 2011, the average, pre-tax American household income was $50,054, meaning that your coffee habit is costing you a little more than 2 percent of your gross pay. So, let's try the same commercial again!

"For just 2 percent of your gross household pay, you can help a child in need."

Not so appealing is it?

Another stunning example of framing effects was shared by communication expert George Lakoff (2010) on Truthout.org: "In NYT/CBS Don't-Ask-Don't-Tell poll on whether 'homosexuals' or 'gay men and lesbians' should be allowed to serve openly in the military: 79 percent of Democrats said they support permitting gay men and lesbians to serve openly. Fewer Democrats, however, just 43 percent, said they were in favor of allowing homosexuals to serve openly."

My intent here is certainly not to dissuade you from giving to charity nor is to opine on who should and should not serve in a war. I want only to demonstrate the sweeping power of a frame using wholly common-place examples. It is frankly a little discomfiting to think that something so important as our attitudes toward giving and equality could be influenced by something as seemingly minute as semantics. This realiza-tion undermines our sense of being in control and erodes our notion of agentiveness.

But take heart gentle reader, all is not lost and we can and ought to take advantage of our heuristics through what we call "intentional framing." Says George Loewenstein (as cited by Thaler and Sunstein 2010) of this concept, "The process of mentally bucketing money in multiple accounts is often combined with earmarking the accounts for specific goals. While it seems like an inconsequential process, earmarking can have a dramatic effect on retirement saving. Cheema and Soman (2009) found that earmarking savings in an envelope labeled with a picture of a couple's children nearly doubled the savings rate of very low income parents."

Sensing the power of intentional framing, ING Direct rolled out a new initiative in 2012 that explicitly makes use of this concept (Financial Brand 2012). The customer creates a bucket in a tool called "My Savings Goals" that corresponds with a particular desired outcome. For instance, a poor but proud psychologist might create a personalized goal called "My New Benz" and establish a corresponding budget and timeline. As the customer reaches savings milestones, emails are sent congratulating them on their success and encouraging further goal-focused behavior.

According to consultant Bri Williams (2012), there are at least three reasons why the sort of programs just mentioned work well:

- Vividness—We've previously discussed the "availability heuristic," which says that our behavior will be affected by the ease with which we can imagine a given outcome. Driving a new Mercedes? Utterly imaginable! Achieving some vague notion of "financial security?" Nebulous and hard to experience. The lesson here is, the more vivid a goal, the greater the power to catalyze behavior.

- Hedonic Framing—"Hedonism" is a fancy word for the pursuit of pleasure. Hedonic framing refers to the rush investors and savers get as they get to chip away at multiple, smaller goals simultaneously. In a sense, you have increased the surface area of their financial lives, providing greater opportunities for having a sense of achievement.

- Hyperbolic Discounting—This is a term that means that investors prefer to realize gains sooner rather than later. Hyperbolic discounting is what accounts for much of the crisis in retirement savings; we'd rather spend on today's fun than save for a hard to imagine future existence. A big goal like "have enough money to retire comfortably" can seem daunting, but more manageable goals, appropriately framed can combat this tendency to procrastinate.

Framing with Purpose

By sub-dividing and labeling our financial goals at all, we avail ourselves of the benefits of hedonic framing and mitigating the ill effects of hyperbolic discounting. The vividness of our label and its intended power to motivate good behavior remains within our control. That being the case, the logical follow-up question becomes, "What constitutes a vivid frame?"

The psychological term for what we have previously called vividness is "salience." A simple way of thinking about salience is something that stands out from other things competing for one's attention. In a visual field, a salient object might be a single red dot in a sea of white dots. In an overwhelmingly confusing investment landscape, a vivid goal is one that burns hot with purpose, even when the promise of easy money might lure us elsewhere. The first, and perhaps most obvious hallmark of a salient frame is that it must be directionally aligned with our goals. Someone with a penchant for overspending might do well to choose meaningful goals that encourage thrift, while the opposite might be true of the miserly or risk averse. Investors would do well to follow the inscription in the ancient Temple of Apollo at Delphi, "Know thyself" and frame their goals accordingly.

A second hallmark of an effective frame is that it has some positive emotional valence. There is a reason why the examples above utilized the consumers' children as the focus of their goal setting: Good parents will do almost anything to ensure that their children are well taken care of. While doing something for personal gain may provide insufficient incentive, something with positive emotional resonance—especially something that is "other focused"—can go a long way toward providing intrinsic motivation. The aforementioned example also leveraged availability, the third best practice in increasing salience. The researchers connected the mental accounts to actual pictures of the subjects' children, thereby solidifying the link between something they saw everyday and their desired goal. Having thus embedded an "available" reminder of the financial path they should be pursuing, the parents were kept on course.

A final element of salience is constancy. We have all had the experience of wanting something intensely in the short term, only to find that desire evanesce and be replaced by some new bobble. For children, it is the toys that are hocked to them through advertising. Adults, no less susceptible, might succumb to a wish for everything from a new pair of jeans to a coveted sports car. While these hoped for goodies may have incredible salience in the short term, they are not an effective backdrop against which to plan a financial life. Certain things, like a grandchild's education, a philanthropic gift, or even a wish to leave dynastic wealth, have greater staying power and make more meaningful frames. Impulse buys have salience aplenty, and the savvy investor knows as much. If your goal won't last the year, you might consider ditching it altogether.

Mental Accounting for Increased Rationality

You are likely now convinced that mental accounting and the accompanying labels we apply to these accounts are a fact of life. What may be less clear is the ways in which these tendencies can be used to make and save you money, all while keeping you on your best money managing behavior. At the outset of this book, we introduced the three S's of irrational behavior (simple, safe, sure), but also intimated that they could be turned on their head for investor benefit. In the following paragraphs, we will revisit the three S's and discuss how an embedded program of well-framed mental accounts can keep you on the straight and narrow.

Simple, the first S, refers to our need to simplify our financial lives, given the sheer volume of data available. The process of mental accounting is itself a form of simplification. We have already touched on how mental accounting and framing can increase salience, improve our ability to take a longer-term view and derive more pleasure from working toward multiple, smaller goals. But by applying mental accounts and frames consistent with our goals, we can also increase our ability to stay on budget. Meir Statman (2010) relates the story of women who were given the choice between (a) a spa package valued at $80, or (b) $85 dollars in cash. Which would you choose?

If you are trying to make rational financial decisions, the answer to that question should have everything to do with whether you are more prone to overspending or over-thrift (yes, there is such a thing!). Most chose the spa package, explaining that they were afraid that they would spend the cash on practical household items if given the option. By opting for the gift certificate, they were "forced" to treat themselves, nevermind that they could rationally have done the same with the cash and had money left over. By understanding your personal proclivities and choosing to account for and label your money in ways that help you reach your goal, you will be subconsciously programming yourself for success.

Safe, the second S, refers to our tendency to seek safety, given that we are loss averse and have a pronounced need to protect against poverty and loss. Just as human beings must satisfy their hunger pangs before they can learn to dance or paint, so too must investors conquer their fear and need for safety before they can hope to gain real financial freedom. Meir Statman (2010) has the following to say about how a stratified, goal-based approach led one family to "bend but not break" following the disastrous NASDAQ crash.

Statman recounts the story of Gena and John Lovett, who were in their late 50s at the time of the bust following the run up of the late 1990s. One of the layers of their portfolio, devoted to bequests for their children, is completely empty. Another safety layer, however, remains intact and keeps them clear of the "freedom from poverty" worries that exist in all of us. While spending your children's inheritance is far from optimal, their layered approach allowed them to keep their heads in a time of financial crisis and remain a remarkable level of composure.

SEI Investments, who had clients in both goal-based and traditional strategies at the time of the 2008 financial crisis, was well positioned to observe the calming effects of a bucketed strategy (Rayer 2008). They found the following distinctions between the two crowds:

Of those in a single, traditional investment portfolio:

- 50 percent chose to fully liquidate their portfolios or at least their equity portfolios, including many high net worth clients who had no immediate need for cash.

- 10 percent made significant changes in their equity allocation, reducing it by 25 percent or more.

Of those clients in a goals-based investment strategy:

- 75 percent made no changes.
- 20 percent decided to increase the size of their immediate needs pool but left their longer-term assets fully invested.

SEI's key finding? "Goals-based investors are less likely to panic and make ill-informed changes to their portfolios." It is philosophically intuitive that goals-based approaches would reduce panic, but seeing such dramatic results play out empirically is satisfying indeed.

The third and final S, Sure, speaks to our desire for certainty as well as the human tendency toward overconfidence. Disdaining certainty as we do, one of the first places we turn for a sense of our bearings is the financial media. There are at least two problems with trying to attain personal assurances in this manner. First, they speak to averages but no investor in particular. Second, they revel in fabricated drama as it is directly correlated with their bottom line. Real surety comes from knowing where you stand, not relative to the yield of Greek bonds, but in terms of your ability to live the life of which you've dreamed. Where there are no goals, there can be no certainty and investors are left to react emotionally to the ways in which they suppose some abstraction might impact their loose idea of a desired future state.

Goals-Based Mental Accounts: A Case Study

While it may be cliché, there seems to be some truth in the folksy aphorism that "every cloud has a silver lining." If there is any consolation in the trillions destroyed in the wake of 2008, it is surely that the world of investment management returned to a saner, more client-centric model with a focus on goals as a natural extension of that. As Jean Brunel says in his excellent article, "Goals Based Wealth Management in Practice" (Brunel 2012), "Our industry was created by institutional investors who tended to have one goal: to meet their liability stream. . . . But individuals are different. Individuals have assets for a variety of purposes, and managing their financial wealth is only one of those purposes. Wealth management clients expect their financial managers to think beyond simple dollars and cents. I have met few wealthy people who say, 'Get me the highest possible return with the lowest possible risk, and everything will be fine.' " He goes on to say that he has ceased speaking to his clients in terms of risk and return, and begun framing their initial conversations in terms of "dreams and nightmares."

At Brinker Capital, we have observed that most investors will have four basic goals. The goals correspond nicely with both the tenets of Maslowian and Behavioral Portfolio Theory previously discussed (see Figure 5.2). They are:

1. Safety: to preserve principal and reduce overall portfolio volatility. Corresponds with "Safety" needs in Behavioral Portfolio Theory.

2. Income: to generate cash flow while limiting volatility.

3. Tactical: to manage volatility and focus on opportunity for appreciation. Corresponds with "Aspiration" needs in Behavioral Portfolio Theory.

4. Accumulation: appreciation and acceptance of greater volatility for the purpose of increasing future purchasing power. Corresponds with "Potential" in Behavioral Portfolio Theory.

Each goal is comprised of each of the four buckets in Figure 5.3 in some permutation.

The level of risk taken for a given goal is dependent upon two criteria, contingency and importance. Contingency simply refers to the inevitably (or lack) of an occurrence. Having money to buy food for tomorrow is not at all contingent, but having enough money to leave an endowment to your alma mater is. The endowment may be of great

FIGURE 5.3

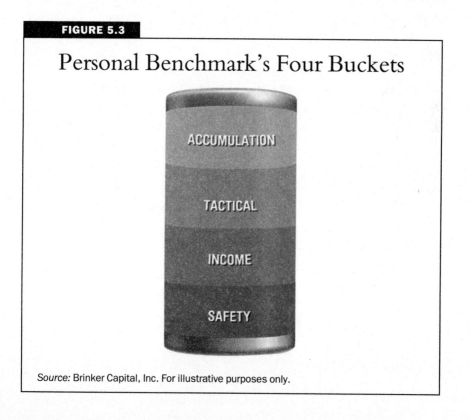

Personal Benchmark's Four Buckets

Source: Brinker Capital, Inc. For illustrative purposes only.

importance to you, but inasmuch as it is contingent, it is of less immediate importance than, say, having a passable base for retirement. The goals that are of greatest importance, that is the least contingent and most important, are the ones for which failure is unacceptable. Accordingly, very little risk will be taken here. Conversely, goals that are highly contingent and/or less important can be riskier.

Summary

This chapter revisited the concept of mental accounting and described Brinker Capital's approach to helping investors reach their important personal goals by allocating funds to four buckets (Safety, Income, Tactical, Accumulation) that align both with Maslow's hierarchy of needs and Behavioral Portfolio Theory. Intentionally framing one's investments in this way helps increase the vividness of their goals, provide greater opportunities for having a sense of achievement in investing, and inspire action today.

References

Ariely, Dan. "Our buggy moral code." TED Talk, February 2009. www.ted
     .com/talks/dan_ariely_on_our_buggy_moral_code.
Brunel, Jean L. P. "Goals-Based Wealth Management in Practice." (March
     2012). *CFA Institute Conference Proceedings Quarterly*, 29(1): 57–65. doi:
     10.2469/cp.v29.n1.7. www.cfapubs.org/doi/pdf/10.2469/cp.v29.n1.7.
Financial Brand. "My Savings Goals: Mental Accounting Trick Or Practical
     PFM?" (June 12, 2012). http://thefinancialbrand.com/24279/ing-direct
     -automatic-saving-account-application.
Kumar, Dhirendra. "Divide your investments in goal-oriented portfolios." The
     Economic Times. (October 15, 2012). http://articles.economictimes.india
     times.com/2012-10-15/news/34473263_1_investment-portfolio-long
     -term-investments-equity-funds.
Lakoff, George. "The Poll Democrats Need to Know About." TruthOut. (April
     15, 2010). http://archive.truthout.org/framing-value-shifting-california
     -budget-crisis58593.

Lopes, L. "Between Hope and Fear: The Psychology of Risk." In *Advances in Experimental Social Psychology*, (vol. 20), ed. by Leonard Berkowitz, 255–295. San Diego: Academic Press, 1987.

Maslow, Abraham H. "A Theory of Human Motivation." (1943). *Psychological Review*, 50(4): 370–396. http://dx.doi.org/10.1037/h0054346.

Phung, Albert. "Behavioral Finance: Key Concepts—Mental Accounting." Investopedia. (2014). www.investopedia.com/university/behavioral_ finance/ behavioral5.asp.

Rayer, Melissa Doran. *Goal-Based Investing Saves Investors from Rash Decisions*. Oaks: SEI Wealth Network, 2008. www.seic.com/docs/Wealth/SEI-GBI_ Saves_Investors.pdf.

Shefrin, Hersh, and Meir Statman. "Behavior Portfolio Theory." (2000). *Journal of Financial and Quantitative Analysis*, 35(2): 127–151. doi: 10.2307/2676187 www.scu.edu/business/finance/research/upload/bpt.pdf.

Statman, Meir. *What Investors Really Want: Know What Drives Investor Behavior and Make Smarter Financial Decisions*. New York: McGraw-Hill, 2010.

Thaler, Richard H., and Cass R. Sunstein. "All bank accounts have numbers. What if they had names too?" (May 27, 2010). http://nudges.org/2010/ 05/27/all-bank-accounts-have-numbers-what-if-they-had-names-too/ #sthash.RgxgILYw.dpuf.

Williams, Bri. (2012). "Delivering client advantage with Behavioural Economics." Presentation at The NewMR Behaviour Economics Event, April 19, 2012. http://b219de03d4fa586d9adb-0e04f025bcde650ce6d504251ebbc914.r60 .cf3.rackcdn.com/Bri%20Williams%20-%20Behavioural%20Economics% 20-%202012.pdf.

CHAPTER 6

Selection of an Active Investment Manager

Chuck Widger

Sensible investors seeking to engage an active manager focus on 'people, people, people.'
Nothing matters more than high quality partners.

—David F. Swensen

The Zambezi River is the fourth largest river in Africa. Beginning in northwest Zambia, it carves its way through six countries for 1,670 miles, ultimately spilling into the Indian Ocean on Mozambique's coast. The river is marked by several beautiful waterfalls and hundreds of thrill-seekers each year endeavor to navigate its rough waters by raft. Almost half the rapids on the Zambezi rafting route are classed at Grade 5, defined as having "extremely difficult, long and violent rapids, steep gradients, big drops and pressure areas." In short, Grade 5 rapids are the most difficult and violent rapids anyone should attempt in a raft. As you go down the rapids, making the right choices—to paddle hard or not at all, to paddle right or paddle left, to paddle forward or paddle back—can mean the difference between riding high and dry in the raft or plunging into the water, your body bouncing down the rocks, hoping that the next time your head pierces above the water line, you stay above it. Helping you make those vital decisions is what you hope to be a highly experienced and professional whitewater rafting guide. Therefore, it is essential to select a qualified rafting company and guide for the trip. Investing is not terribly different from rafting (although you usually stay a little drier). And some investments bear too close a resemblance to a Grade 5 route. Thus, in investing as in rafting, selection of the right partners and guides is critical.

Investors seek attractive risk adjusted returns that will finance their long-term financial goals. This means generating future purchasing power rather than focusing on beating market indices. Many investors rely on investment managers to achieve these aims. Simply put, their job is to make money.

However, not all investment managers are created equally. How can investors be certain they are hiring investment managers who execute strategies that create value?

At Brinker Capital, we spend a great deal of time getting to know the investment managers we select, both professionally and personally. Over time, we develop varying levels of confidence in particular managers as well as the strategies being executed. Our level of conviction in a manager, combined with our short and long-term views on asset classes and sub-asset classes, will determine a manager allocation within our portfolios.

In this chapter we share the logic behind whom we select and why we select them. We begin by reviewing two basic approaches to investment management, then proceed to describing the characteristics we believe to be essential in any firm and any manager investors select to manage their capital. Finally, we offer a framework for assuring that the investment management process proceeds smoothly and effectively.

Passive versus Active Management

A fundamental question to consider, even before an investment firm or investment manager is selected, is to consider whether the investor wants to take advantage of passive or active management of their investments.

Passive management, defined as simply investing through indices, does not even require the use of an investment manager and also allows for easy performance assessment. For example, if we want pure asset class exposure, we would utilize a passive exchange traded product or index fund (see more complete discussion in Chapter 4). Passive investing provides for low cost and certainty of return without the worry of style drift. Passive vehicles also allow more specificity in implementing the asset class view, as these vehicles, primarily ETFs, can offer very granular exposures. A limitation of passive management (index investing) is that it is generally limited to large, well-established, and traditional asset classes. Investable indices are not available for many niche sub-asset classes of the traditional asset classes; nor are indices generally available for the non-traditional asset classes.

Active management, in contrast, requires that someone (typically, the investment manager) is continually monitoring and adjusting (e.g., actively managing) the investments. Involvement of an investment manager is necessary to "employ a broader set of asset class alternatives in service of market beating strategies" (Swensen 2009). For example, Brinker Capital portfolios use strategies offered by the largest asset managers, along with a great number of niche strategies offered by smaller, boutique firms.

Proponents of active investing highlight the following two benefits of this approach:

1. Increased investing opportunities and reduced risk or volatility. Use of niche sub-asset classes and non-traditional asset classes both enhance the opportunity set for return and offer increased diversification, which reduces risk or volatility.

2. Enhanced performance in inefficient or otherwise challenging market segments. A high performing asset manager can add significant value when selecting niche sub-asset classes and non-traditional asset classes. Brinker Capital prefers active management in a number of situations, including when we are targeting inefficient segments of the market, when a manager has a significant competitive advantage, or when a desired exposure cannot be effectively replicated passively.

Brinker Capital's active investment approach embraces the view that it can select active managers who outperform specialized benchmarks in non-traditional asset classes and niche strategies, while using passive strategies where pure Beta exposure is desired. This combined active/passive strategy produces competitive returns and significant risk management.

Brinker Capital enacts active management during the initial execution by overweighting and underweighting asset classes and sub-asset classes and during performance monitoring by periodically reallocating across and between asset classes and sub-asset classes. Additionally, Brinker Capital selects active managers that can add value over time above index returns for less efficient asset classes.

The Successful Investment Firm

Now that you have an idea about whether you want active management, passive management, or some combined approach to managing your investments, it is time to select an investment firm. This is not a decision to take lightly. A Google search, Yelp review, or even a tip from a friend will not cut it. Top performing firms share certain characteristics that promote successful investment outcomes. Consider how your firm or the firms you are considering stack up against the following eight criteria we've used over time to detect those firms to which we would entrust our capital:

1. Size. At present, for example, Brinker Capital has relationships with more than 80 investment management firms. Some of these firms are quite large and some are quite small. Size influences such things as leadership style, culture, organizational behaviors, performance monitoring, and speed and agility of operations and availability of resources, among others. For example, larger firms can be bureaucratic and more focused on marketing than investing, whereas smaller firms can be under resourced and poorly managed. When selecting a firm, consider its size and what implications this has for its operations.

2. Leadership. Talented people are unlikely to be successful in an investment firm that does not get its leadership and management right. Leadership in successful active management firms tend to be independent and entrepreneurial in that they encourage unconventional

choices by its members. These firms are run by people who are ethical, energetic, and who provide strong intellectual leadership (Swensen 2009). Entrepreneurs who start investment management firms may be very good investors but not so good at the management of a business. When selecting a firm, get to know who is at the helm by learning about their educational and professional background, their leadership philosophy, and what they value. Then consider how this may affect the investment managers working for the firm as well as overall firm performance.

3. Employee development and mentoring. Investment management principles are, in the main, learned from experience. As such, it takes time to develop the knowledge, skill and expertise to become a masterful active manager. Top investment firms recognize this and, therefore, facilitate mentorships between senior and junior members of the team.

4. Culture. Organization culture refers to the pattern of core beliefs, values, and behaviors shared by organization members (Schein 2010). As you might imagine, culture has an enormous impact on how the firm relates to and serves it investors. For example, a firm with a sales-driven culture is more apt to push the "investment of the week" product, regardless of the investment's merits. You can find investment products run by people that don't truly believe in them, and often with insufficient resources. On the other hand, a firm with an investment-driven culture may struggle to understand and meet the needs of their clients. Successful investment firms have found a way to balance these competing drives.

5. Client focus. Firms must have a commitment to managing client relationships. At the end of the day, this relationship is about you, the investor; therefore, the investment manager needs to have the aim of creating returns on your investment at heart rather than focus on their own fee income (Swensen 2009). Consider your interactions with the firm and reflect on what you have learned about how it operates and makes decisions. Is concern for the client at the center?

6. Entrepreneurial spirit. Entrepreneurial cultures prize employee innovation, ownership, and adaptation to market challenges. Firms that are entrepreneurial encourage employees' creative and even contrarian views. Often, this encouragement is reflected in financial incentives, such as reinvesting profits in the investment management group and assuring that investment executives maintain ownership and direction over investment management business decisions. The underlying orientation in firms enables investment managers to serve their own interests while serving those of their clients. These types of environments enable organization members to transcend the binds of bureaucracy and structure. In turn, they tend to execute faster, exhibit greater agility (particularly with regard to the unexpected), attract other talent, and produce greater returns. Learn about the firm you are considering and examine the degree to which innovation, ownership and adaptation are evident in its practices.

7. Incentives for advisor performance. At firms of all sizes, portfolio managers need to be incentivized for investment performance. Frequently, the investment team will also hold equity in the firm, providing further incentives and alignment of interest with clients. Find out how the investment firm you are considering evaluates and rewards advisor performance. The right kinds of incentives for advisors can help promote the right kind of performance you desire.

8. Clear, ongoing communication. As an investor, you need to know how your assets are being managed and why they performed the way they did. You need to have confidence in your investment manager, and that confidence is built through ready access and visibility of your accounts through an intuitive, easy-to-use and technologically up-to-date interface. Straight through processing, intuitive and comprehensive websites and automated trading are a must. If these conditions aren't met, the relationship between the investor, advisor, and investment firm often falters and you will eventually move on. Well-trained advisor and investor service teams also need to be available. After all, it is the investment experience that attracts

advisors and investors, and the communication infrastructure is the meat and potatoes. Before you select a firm, make sure that it will be able to provide you with the access, information, and intuitive experience you need.

Once you have selected the investment firm who meets these criteria for your success and which you believe is suitable for you and your needs, it is time to consider the characteristics of the individual who will actually manage your investments and produce the returns.

The Successful Investment Manager

You may have thought that selecting the right investment firm was difficult; however, you were only getting started. Warren Buffet noted the challenge in his 2007 annual letter to Berkshire Hathaway investors: "It's not hard, of course, to find smart people, among them individuals who have impressive track records. But there is far more to successful long term investing than brains and performance that has recently been good." He further noted, "I've seen a lot of very smart people who lacked [the] virtues necessary for success."

At Brinker Capital, we spend a great deal of time with the investment managers we select in order to get to know them both professionally and personally. In addition to possessing needed qualitative and quantitative skills, intelligence, and a global perspective, we have identified four key traits we believe successful investment managers possess.

First, people who are active managers have a passion for the markets. It is all they do. They think about investing in the shower, during the day, and before they fall asleep at night. Find a talented person with a passion for their professional role and you will have a successful relationship.

Second, a person with passion for the markets can quickly run amok without a guiding sense of integrity. Regardless of whether an investor is a public or private pension, an endowment, an institution or an individual the investment manager will at some point have an actual or perceived conflict. The potential for conflict is why there are so many disclosures involved in investing. Interests simply don't perfectly align all the time. Ethical managers pay careful attention to investor goals when resolving conflicts.

Third, just as it is important for the firm to support and encourage entrepreneurial spirit, the investment managers themselves need to be independent and innovative in their thinking. Independent thinking leads to imagination, which can mean the difference between average and exceptional service.

Last but certainly not least, investment managers must be able to manage risk well, "seek[ing] to know as much as can be known, [and] limiting uncertainty to an irreducible minimum" (Swensen 2009). Swensen explained, "Even the most carefully researched decisions ultimately face the vicissitudes of market forces" and Buffet added, "Over time, markets will do extraordinary, even bizarre, things. A single, big mistake would wipe out a long string of successes."

Because of these harsh conditions, Buffet (2007) asserted, "We therefore need someone genetically programmed to recognize and avoid serious risks, including those never before encountered." Fortunately, it may not be so much genetic programming as traits and abilities that can be cultivated. Namely, successful investment managers must practice absolute detachment in analyzing winning and losing positions, without discouraging risk taking. They must have emotional stability and a keen understanding of both human and institutional behavior through the inevitable ups and downs of the market. They also must faithfully attend to their investors' long-term goals. When they are able to manage risk in this way, the power of investors' behavior biases can be neutralized, enabling investors to stick with an investment strategy that meets their long-term purchasing power goals.

An Effective Investment Management Process

Up to this point in the chapter, we have stressed the characteristics of successful investment firms and investment managers. Yet, even these two critical elements are just the start. An effective investment management process needs to be in place to enable investors to reach their goals. Implementing the process requires attention to five key factors:

1. Assembling a Talented Staff. A key part of managing the investment process is selecting a talented investment team. Among the team's core responsibilities is to identify investment strategies that actually add value. Talented staff is especially required in the management of the non-traditional asset classes, as these asset classes, absolute return in particular, rely heavily on the skill of the active manager.

2. Establishing Appropriate Governance. An independent investment committee should be established to provide oversight of the investment group, including both advisor clients and investor clients. Specifically, the committee monitors and provides feedback on the investment initiatives presented and performance provided by the investment group. The committee should be staffed by senior organization members who are knowledgeable in the firm's business and investment philosophy.

3. Instituting a Rigorous Decision-Making Process. Swensen (2009) urged firms to institute disciplined processes for developing and implementing investment, asset allocation, and manager selection recommendations and decisions. Ellis (2013) phrased these important topics as policy decisions, which involve setting and reviewing asset allocation targets; strategic decisions, which guide intermediate-term actions consistent with longer term policies and current market opportunities; and tactical and trading decisions, which involve the short-term execution of portfolio strategies and policies. Additionally, rigorous due diligence should be practiced (e.g., by producing written summaries or assuring that key decisions are made by small groups of 3–4 people). Establishing decision framework and due diligence processes help increase clarity and quality in decision making.

4. Holding Scheduled Meetings with Focused Agendas. Holding regularly scheduled meetings can support the decision making and oversight processes. For example, at Brinker Capital, we schedule an annual onsite meeting with each of our investment managers (see Table 6.1).

TABLE 6.1

Suggested Meetings during the Investment Management Process

Meeting Focus	Frequency	Purpose	Activities
Capital Market Assumptions	Semi-Annually	Determine return and risk forecasts for asset classes	• Investment team members provide return and risk forecasts for each major and sub-asset class • Investment team members communicate and debate forecasts • Determine relative attractiveness of asset classes and sub-asset classes • Determine the "wisdom of the crowd" forecasts • Review mean variance optimization output
Asset Allocation Meetings	As needed	Determine portfolio asset allocation	• Portfolio team members discuss shorter-term views on asset classes, as well as longer-term themes • Put together the mosaic using multiple factors—technical, sentiment, valuation, macroeconomic • Determine relative attractiveness of asset classes and sub-asset classes • Set portfolio weights • Determine next areas of focus (asset class, strategy)
Portfolio Manager Meetings	Bi-monthly	Review various portfolios	• Portfolio management teams share their mosaic and asset class views • Cross-pollination of investment ideas across portfolio management teams
Investment Manager Meetings	Various	Initial and ongoing manager due diligence; build relationships	• Initial meetings with managers prior to inclusion in portfolio • Periodic meetings with managers as part of our ongoing due diligence process, including annual on-site visits • Review and assess team, philosophy, process, performance and current positioning • Determine relative attractiveness of strategy
Investment Committee	Quarterly	Sets overarching policy	• Review and ensure adherence to product objectives • Ensure portfolio management teams have resources in place to execute effectively

Source: Brinker Capital, Inc. For illustrative purposes only.

A well-designed meeting schedule with clear agendas provides a structure for effective decision-making, which is an important characteristic of an effective multi-asset class investor. We also believe that an annual face-to-face meeting at each investment manager's office with all individuals key to the investment process, such as portfolio managers, analysts, strategists, traders, and/or operations staff. We find this meeting to be an important part of ongoing relationship management and a tool for generating improved understanding, transparency, and predictions about the future (Swensen 2009). Our goal in this meeting is to be inquisitive but not intrusive.

5. Monitoring Performance. Selecting a successful investment firm, a successful investment manager, and instituting an effective investment management process become exercises in futility without this final step of monitoring and enhancing performance. Importantly, we at Brinker Capital believe that monitoring individual underlying manager performance can be evaluated relative to market indices and peer groups.

Monitoring and Assessing Performance

As we know, investments (and indices) have two fundamental features: return and risk. Most investors want the return and not the risk. However, risk is inevitable and many investors have been discovering and rediscovering its harsh reality since 2001. In this section, we review some common ways to monitor and assess performance, consider the caveats involved in quantitative measures of performance, and when to terminate an investment manager. This section closes with a look at Brinker Capital's performance.

Benchmark Comparisons

One way to evaluate the performance is through comparison to a fair benchmark, as follows:

- Traditional asset classes trade in mature, liquid markets which have well-structured benchmarks like the S&P 500 Index for the largest publicly traded U.S. companies and the Barclays U.S. Aggregate Bond Index for a diverse mix of fixed income securities.

- Non-traditional asset classes often have less well-defined market related performance benchmarks. For non-traditional asset classes, Brinker Capital selects specialty benchmarks.

- For both traditional and non-traditional asset classes, a benchmark must embrace the entire opportunity set from which a manager chooses. And, in general, specialized benchmarks should create an apples-to-apples comparison. For example, small cap managers should not be compared to the S&P 500 Index (Swensen 2009).

Moreover, in comparing the asset class and sub-asset class performance in the portfolio to selected specialized indices it is vital to also compare risk results in the actual portfolio to the risk in the specialized benchmark. The investment objective is to not only achieve competitive returns. It is also to achieve competitive returns at less risk. Competitive returns at less risk produce more purchasing power over time. This is the heart of the case for active multi-asset management.

Comparison of the manager's performance to peers is another type of benchmark in assessing the performance of individual investment managers. Almost every investment category has managers that can be grouped within it. Peer comparisons require recognition that two biases are present:

- Survivorship bias: Only the good managers remain in the peer group, while the poor performers have dropped out of the group.

- Backfill bias: Managers track hypothetical or seed account performance onto their live, client-based track record. Not surprisingly, only strategies with strong backfill performance see the light of day.

These biases are especially prevalent in less efficient asset classes like absolute return and private equity (Swensen 2009).

Volatility, Efficiency, and Rates of Return

Quantitative measures of volatility, efficiency, and rates of return also may be used to assess performance. Risk is generally measured in terms of standard deviation (also referred to as historical volatility), calculated as an investment's average deviation from its average price within a given time period. The problem with standard deviation, though, is that it doesn't tell us much about the fundamental risk in an investment strategy. It only tells us about the investment's fluctuation in value. What we really care about, however, is managing volatility because less volatility and better downside protection means compounding off higher lows.

A note on distinctions in discussing risk is helpful here. Volatility is described mathematically by the concept known as standard deviation. Standard deviation can describe the extent of fluctuation in the value of a security, an investment portfolio, or a capital market. Earlier in this book we focused on personalizing the definition of risk as the failure to achieve personal goals. Both are valid definitions of risk. They are linked by the investment policy statement. The investment policy statement transforms or converts the mathematical expression of risk into a description of the personal goals to be achieved.

Standard deviation is a statistical measurement that sheds light on historical volatility. For example, a volatile stock will have a high standard deviation whereas the deviation of a stable blue chip stock will be lower. A large dispersion tells us how much the return on the fund is deviating from the expected normal returns.

Investopedia 2014.

Sharpe ratio is another important quantitative tool that identifies the generation of excess return. It is calculated by determining the difference between a strategy's actual return and the risk-free rate (treasuries) and then dividing by the strategy's standard deviation. The Sharpe ratio measures return per unit of risk, meaning it measures the productivity and efficiency of an investment. Like standard deviation, the Sharpe ratio, while generally accepted and useful, is backward looking and does not identify fundamental risk factors (Swensen 2009).

> *Sharpe ratio tells us whether a portfolio's returns are due to smart investment decisions or a result of excess risk. Although one portfolio or fund can reap higher returns than its peers, it is only a good investment if those higher returns do not come with too much additional risk. The greater a portfolio's Sharpe ratio, the better its risk-adjusted performance has been. A negative Sharpe ratio indicates that a risk-less asset would perform better than the security being analyzed.*
>
> Investopedia 2014.

Internal rate of return (IRR) and time-weighted return are used to calculate rates of return. IRR (also referred to as dollar-weighted rates of return) take into consideration the timing of the payment and amount of dollars invested and the timing of the payment and receipt of dollars returned. IRR, as a measurement of return, is best used when the investment managers control the cash flow decisions. This is the case with illiquid strategies like private equity partnerships. When the investment manager does not control the cash flow decisions, then the timed-linked return calculation method should be used. Time-linked return calculation calculates a series of periodic returns without the consideration of a portfolio size at any point in time (Swensen 2009).

> *Internal rate of return (IRR) is the rate of growth a project is expected to generate. Although the actual rate of return that a given project ends up generating will often differ from its estimated IRR rate, a project with a substantially higher IRR value than other available options would still provide a much better chance of strong growth.*
>
> *IRRs can also be compared against prevailing rates of return in the securities market. If a firm can't find any projects with IRRs greater than the returns that can be generated in the financial markets, it may simply choose to invest its retained earnings into the market.*
>
> Investopedia 2014.

Caveats of Quantitative Measures

Despite the importance of quantitative performance assessment, it is important to remember that they are inherently backward looking and, as we know, past performance does not predict future results. Therefore, investments made solely on the basis of numbers are likely to disappoint. It is important to understand the fundamental forces that have driven valuations in the past and then consider the forces that are likely to drive future valuations. For this reason, Swensen (2009) urged, "Successful portfolio management combines art and science, requiring qualitative and quantitative assessment of investment strategies," and further argued that, "Successful relationship management demands placing soft factors in a place of primary importance. The numbers, while important, play a supporting role."

Moreover, performance needs to be viewed through the prism of time. Investments last for varying periods of time. Money market instruments mature in days and months. Private equity lasts as long as 10 years. All other asset classes fall in between.

Asset class performance, driven by market forces, also can alternate. One asset class can fare well while another simultaneously does not. Then market forces shift, and asset class performance can reverse. Experience with growth and value investment strategies illustrates this investment phenomenon. Given the need to view investment strategies through the prism of time, it is wise not to make quick decisions to terminate investment managers.

Often, what emerges from performance assessment is the decision to rebalance. At Brinker Capital, when we see performance lags and a reduction in account values but confirm that the case remains firm for a particular investment manager and strategy, we may rebalance and add more to the underperforming strategy. Conversely, if a strategy has had a significant outperformance driven by market forces, winners may be pared back with assets repositioned to underperformers. Although this (and the underlying philosophy of "buy low, sell high") sounds simple, shifting assets from your winners to your losers is often difficult in the moment. Doing the work upfront and having confidence in your lagging strategies is vital.

When to Terminate an Investment Manager

In some cases, after monitoring, assessing, and considering the reasons for lagging performance, the urge may arise to terminate an investment manager. This decision must be made objectively. In assessing performance, the termination decision should be approached as a hiring decision. If, based on qualitative and quantitative factors, Brinker Capital reaches the judgment, it wouldn't hire the manager at that point it time, it will terminate the manager. Typically, Brinker Capital will terminate a manager for one of the following reasons:

- Fundamental change in personnel, philosophy, or process that we believe will negatively impact future performance.

- Performance that does not meet our expectations, indicating the team is not executing as we would like.

- A significant change to the fund characteristics or structure (e.g., expense ratio increase, excessive AUM growth) that we judge will negatively impact future performance.

Importantly, when Brinker Capital makes a decision to terminate, it reviews the reasons it hired the investment manager. These reviews provide insights that are helpful in future hiring decisions (Swensen 2009).

A Look at Brinker Capital's Performance

Brinker Capital's investment value proposition is its actively managed multi-asset class investment philosophy, which we believe creates more purchasing power than commonly used index strategies and also delivers returns which are competitive with popular indices with lower overall risk, measured by standard deviation. The result is more purchasing power with less risk than can be achieved by investing through popular indices.

Figure 6.1 shows that for the 42-year period ending December 2013, a portfolio equally weighted to Brinker Capital's six asset

FIGURE 6.1

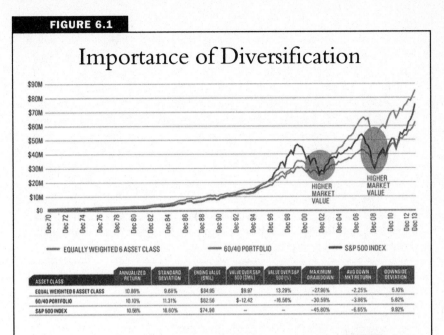

Importance of Diversification

...... EQUALLY WEIGHTED 6 ASSET CLASS   —— 60/40 PORTFOLIO   —— S&P 500 INDEX

ASSET CLASS	ANNUALIZED RETURN	STANDARD DEVIATION	ENDING VALUE ($MIL)	VALUE OVER S&P 500 ($MIL)	VALUE OVER S&P 500 (%)	MAXIMUM DRAWDOWN	AVG DOWN MKT RETURN	DOWNSIDE DEVIATION
EQUAL WEIGHTED 6 ASSET CLASS	10.86%	9.68%	$84.95	$9.97	13.29%	-27.96%	-2.25%	5.10%
60/40 PORTFOLIO	10.10%	11.31%	$62.56	$-12.42	-16.56%	-30.59%	-3.86%	5.82%
S&P 500 INDEX	10.56%	16.60%	$74.98	–	–	-45.80%	-6.65%	9.92%

ASSET CLASS	MARKET INDEX	START–END	EQUAL-WEIGHTED 6 ASSET CLASS	60/40 PORTFOLIO
U.S. EQUITY	DOW JONES TOTAL STOCK MARKET	JAN 71–DEC 13	16.67%	60.00%
INT'L EQUITY	BLEND	JAN 71–DEC 13	16.67%	0.00%
	MSCI EAFE (DEVELOPED)	JAN 71–DEC 87	16.67%	0.00%
	MSCI ACWI EX U.S. (DEVELOPED + EMERGING)	JAN 88–DEC 13	16.67%	0.00%
FIXED INCOME	BLEND	APR 73–DEC 13	16.67%	40.00%
	BARCLAYS TREASURY (TREASURY ONLY)	APR 73–DEC 75	16.67%	40.00%
	BARCLAYS AGGREGATE (BROAD TAXABLE FIXED INCOME)	JAN 76–MAR 97	16.67%	40.00%
	BARCLAYS AGGREGATE (BROAD TAXABLE FIXED INCOME)	APR 97–DEC 13	8.33%	40.00%
	BARCLAYS TIPS (TREASURY INFLATION PROTECTED SECURITIES)	APR 97–DEC 13	8.33%	0.00%
REAL ASSETS	BLEND	JAN 78–DEC 13	16.67%	0.00%
	NCREIF PROPERTY INDEX (REAL ESTATE)	JAN 78–DEC 13	16.67%	0.00%
	NCREIF PROPERTY INDEX (REAL ESTATE)	APR 91–DEC 13	8.33%	0.00%
	DOW JONES AIG COMMODITY (COMMODITIES)	APR 91–DEC 13	8.33%	0.00%
PRIVATE EQUITY	CAMBRIDGE U.S. PRIVATE EQUITY	APR 86–DEC 13	16.67%	0.00%
ABSOLUTE RETURN	CREDIT SUISSE/TREMONT HEDGE FUND	JAN 94–DEC 13	16.67%	0.00%
		TOTAL	100%	100%

Source: Brinker Capital, Inc., Fact Set, Cambridge Associates, NCREIF. This Growth of $1M chart is for illustration purposes only. No representation that the results represent performance of actual client accounts is intended. The chart is intended to demonstrate the impact on a traditional portfolio of diversification through the inclusion of additional asset classes over a long-term investment horizon. The table discloses the time periods during which each asset class, as represented by the market index listed, was included or removed from the chart as more representative market indexes became available, as well as the weighting of each asset class during the period. When index data for certain asset classes was not available, the other asset class weightings were

(*continued*)

(continued)

scaled upward. The information depicted in the charts above is derived from this table. For example, the equal weighted portfolio was 50% U.S. Equity and 50% International Equity from January 1971 through March 1973. In April 1973, the equal weighted portfolio was 33.33% U.S. Equity, 33.33% International Equity and 33.33% Fixed Income until January 1978, when the next asset class, Real Assets (real estate) was available, and so on. The S&P 500 Index is a market value weighted index with each stock's weight in the Index proportionate to its market value. The S&P Index is one of the most widely used benchmarks of U.S. equity performance. Each index is a broad market index representative of its respective asset class which is utilized by Brinker as a benchmark for measuring the performance of such asset class. Unmanaged indices are for illustrative purposes only. An investor cannot invest directly in an index. Index performance does not reflect the deduction of fees and changes and does not reflect the reinvestment of dividends. Past performance is no guarantee of future results. Data from January 1, 1971 through December 31, 2013.

classes (top line), S&P 500 Index (middle line), and 60/40 portfolio (bottom line).

The chart shows that the multi-asset class investment strategy compounds more wealth and purchasing power than any other depicted strategy. Two characteristics explain this result.

1. Lower risk. The risk, reflected by the standard deviation, is lowest for the equally weighted six asset class strategy. The table immediately below the chart shows that the portfolio equally weighted to Brinker Capital's six asset class strategy had a standard deviation of 9.68 percent, compared to 11.31 percent for the balanced strategy and 16.60 percent for the S&P 500 Index. This leads to the second distinguishing characteristic of our strategy.

2. Compounding off higher lows. Because the equal weighted strategy offers more downside protection, the six asset class strategy compounds off higher market values during market bottoms like December of 2002 and March of 2009 (see circles in the chart).

The equal weighted six asset class strategy, since inception in January 1971, would have created $9.97 million more in value than the S&P 500 Index through December 2013.

Summary

Investors with skill and resources should pursue active management. Absent skill and resources, investors should pursue more passive strategies. Equipped with both skill and resources, Brinker Capital is able to construct broadly diversified portfolios using traditional and non-traditional asset classes. Non-traditional asset classes—absolute return, real assets and "liquid private equity"—we believe offer significant opportunities to manage risk and enhance return.

Successful deployment of skill and resources in executing a multi-asset class strategy requires a disciplined framework. A disciplined framework consists of the following:

- An established investment committee that oversees the investment staff that originates, maintains and drives the investment process.
- A rigorous investment process based on analysis.
- Analysis guided by fundamental investment principles.
- An investment group with an independent thought process.
- Qualitative and quantitative assessment tools.
- Regular meetings with managers.
- Rebalancing which buys low and sells high.

Assuring that one has carefully selected an investment firm and an investment manager that follow a disciplined investment process makes it much more likely that desired outcomes, the investor's goals, will be achieved.

References

Buffett, Warren. "Buffet's Job Description: 'They May Be Hard to Identify,'" Wall Street Journal. (April 28, 2007). http://online.wsj.com/news/articles/SB117768120385484833.

Ellis, Charles. *Successful Investing: Winning the Loser's Game.* New York: McGraw-Hill Education, 2013.

Investopedia. "Internal Rate of Return (IRR)." (2014). www.investopedia.com/terms/i/irr.asp.

Investopedia. "Sharpe Ratio." (2014). www.investopedia.com/terms/s/sharpe ratio.asp.

Investopedia. "Standard Deviation." (2014). www.investopedia.com/terms/s/standarddeviation.asp.

Schein, Edgar H. *Organization Culture and Leadership*. San Francisco: Jossey Bass, 2010.

Swensen, David F. *Pioneering Portfolio Management: An Unconventional Approach to Institutional Investment*. New York: Free Press, 2009.

PART 3

How Can We Execute a Purpose-Driven Investment Strategy?

CHAPTER 7

Using a Goals-Based Approach

Dr. Daniel Crosby

Obstacles are those frightful things you see when you take your eyes off your goal.
                                                                        —Henry Ford

If you're like so many Americans, you probably make a list of your goals at the beginning of each year. Whatever form those resolutions take—whether the goals are physical, financial, or relational, they likely have two foundational elements: (a) they are specific to you, meaning they have personal value for you, and (b) they are aspirational, meaning they have an element of being emotional and inspirational.

For example, this year, I decided set the goal to lose 15 pounds so that I could have more energy to keep up with my 5-year-old. Personal value? Check. I am sick of hearing, *"Come onnn, Daddy!"* Aspirational? Absolutely—I want to finally win one of our backyard races.

Some time later in the year, you may or may not be on track to meet your resolutions. A recent hop on the scale tells me that I am not. But regardless of your current progress, your goals will stand as ever-present reminders of the person you could be, if you were willing to do the necessary work. As silly as it may sound, let's imagine goals that violate the two foundational elements we mentioned above: That is, let's assume you created an impersonal goal that lacked aspiration. For example, one year I set the goal of being able to play the longest running game of Monopoly in my group of friends. My friend, Bobby held the record—17 hours. In the end, I realized it was a case of keeping up with the Joneses, or the Bobby's, as it were. But hey, I was young, I got involved in the wrong crowd, and ultimately, it didn't stick. Have you ever set a goal that had nothing to do with your particular needs?

Although it defies logic, millions of us do so when it comes to planning our financial futures! How so? By comparing our investment performance against a broad market index like the S&P 500 Index. In doing so, we compare our performance against the performance of the market as a whole rather than something that is relative to our specific needs. The index, whether up or down, has become the de facto gold standard. It is an impersonal benchmark, as its performance in any given year may or may not even approximate our own performance needs.

Let's reapply this widely accepted logic of an impersonal benchmark to our other resolutions and see how it stands up. If you are like most people, you set some sort of weight loss or fitness goal at the beginning of the year. The CDC reports that the average man over 20 years of age is 5'9" and weighs 195 pounds. According to body/mass index (BMI) measures based on height and weight, he has a BMI of 28.8, meaning he is overweight and nearly obese! If we were to use this benchmark as a goal-setting index, the same way that we do financial benchmarks, the average American male would need to lose 27 pounds just to make it under the wire of normal. With a little digging, however, we find that the BMI can overestimate body fat in athletes and others who have a muscular build.

Now let's consider how the BMI benchmark might apply to other average 5'9" American males currently weighing 195. Some may feel optimally energetic and healthy at 178 (still solidly overweight by BMI standards). Others, such as a rather tall jockey (most are 4'10" to 5'6"), would consider anything above 125 a career-limiting move. Still others, such as bodybuilders or linebackers, may weigh well in excess of 200 pounds. For example, 5'9" Jay Cutler from Sterling, Massachusetts, is a four-time Mr. Olympia winner (2006, 2007, 2009, 2010) who weighed 274 pounds in contest condition. A profound fatty by BMI standards. If he set his weight goal based on the BMI, the only title he would be taking home is the latest blockbuster from the Redbox outside 7-Eleven. (Yes, that's right. His goal would be so mediocre that not only would he be a nondescript 168 pounds or so, it would also transport him to a time before video streaming.)

When applied to a highly personal goal such as bodyweight, we clearly see the illogic of following a "herd goal" linked to a benchmark. Why then do we struggle to see the illogic in such an arbitrary reference point when applied to our financial lives?

A second problem is that affixing your goals to a benchmark tends to lack inspiration. The goals we set should represent a tension between the people we are today and the people we hope to become. Remember my goal at the outset of this chapter? Who I am today: getting smoked, regularly, by a 5-year-old. Who I hope to become: a winner in our backyard sprint, at least once! This tension between the present and desired state is what propels us forward to make the sacrifices necessary to get from here to there. When we use an average like a market index for setting our financial goals, we lose sight (if we had any idea to begin with) of what we really want. We are settling in a very real sense.

No one sets out to live an average life. We don't dream of average happiness, average fulfillment or an average marriage, so why should we settle for an average portfolio? There is a sad irony in the fact that so many professionals, excellent in their other endeavors, spend so much time and energy worrying about how they stack up relative to such a mean hurdle.

The Allure of Determinism in Economics and Psychology

At this point, it is worth considering how we arrived at a place in the financial services industry where we have resisted our personal goals as a guide in favor of an arbitrary and impersonal measure like a market index. After all, I imagine you need little convincing that setting goals is a positive thing to do in most areas of your life. Setting and pursuing goals is very much a part of the way we govern our personal and professional lives. The reasons for the industry's impersonal approach have their roots in the philosophical underpinnings of efficient market theory, heretofore the ascendant paradigm from which advisors, analysts and gurus of all stripes have taken their marching orders. These roots, which we will discuss in some depth here, have privileged the past over the future and have favored the needs of economists over individual investors.

It may seem at first blush that an examination of the philosophical foundations of traditional conceptions of finance would hold little relevance and even less interest to the typical investor. However, it is from these often unexamined assumptions that theories are built and these theories, in turn, inform recommendations that directly impact the lives of those receiving said advice. As Slife and Williams (1995) say of such fundamental assumptions, "All theories have implied [hidden] understandings about the world that are crucial to their formulation and use." They go on to say that theories (e.g., EMH) must be examined thoroughly to assure that our adoption of them is not leading us down unintended paths.

The Basics

The idea of determinism, one of the most fundamental assumptions of traditional economic approaches, can be defined as the philosophical idea that every event or state of affairs, including every human decision and action, is the inevitable and necessary consequence of antecedent states of affairs. The two foundational ideas here, representative of determinism more broadly, are:

1. The observed reality is the only possible reality.
2. It was causally determined by a chain of past events.

To greater concretize this notion of determinism, let's look at a familiar example: human behavior. Deterministic notions of human behavior, much like deterministic ideas about market valuation, contend that the past determines the present and that whatever occurs is all that could have occurred. Take the case of someone who has committed a crime. A deterministic view of criminal activity says that criminals are formed by historical events, perhaps a life of want, abuse, and neglect.

If we look at criminal behavior through a deterministic lens, criminals didn't choose a life of crime per se; rather, they were led there inevitably by a previous chain of events. What they have become is all they could have ever become, given the undesirable circumstances under which they were raised.

The reason we are spending the time to examine assumptions like the above is that the assumptions we make about our behavior ought to have practical implications for decision-making. Consider the actions of society, especially the judicial system, if we espouse a deterministic worldview. Can we justly imprison someone who was only doing what their history programmed them to do? Can we vilify someone whose actions were causally determined? Surely not! An agentive, or free will, view of human nature says that criminals ought to be punished. After all, they made a poor choice among better possible alternatives. A deterministic view leads us to make other recommendations altogether, as the actions are not seen as chosen, and thus cannot meaningfully be vilified. To do otherwise is the rational equivalent of getting angry at your knee for extending when tapped by a doctor's mallet!

In this way, the philosophical foundation we choose to adopt informs the actions we take as a society, and so too it goes in the world of high finance. Efficient market theorists believe in the deterministic notion that the "price is always right" in equity markets. In a phrase, whatever the current price of an equity, that is all it could ever be in that moment, given the information available to market participants. Market participants, for their part, have very little control over their lives under this deterministic worldview and are simply maximizing utility without much say in the matter. They are subject to primitive impulses that lead them to act as they do in ways that keep markets at a near constant state of equilibrium. In keeping with the pillars of determinism, these security prices are determined by a causal chain of past events, all of which have culminated in the price you see before you on the computer. In a very real sense, the sum total of the past market fluctuations and the unfailingly predictable behavior of market participants has brought about an unchangeable present.

Just as the ideas we espouse about the drivers of human behavior inform the way we ought to prosecute crime, so ought our ideas of what drives stock prices influence our financial decision making. So, what is required of true believers in the deterministic undergirding of market efficiency?

First, the past ought to serve as a reliable roadmap for the future. Since the present unfolds as a direct consequence of the chain of events that make up the past, we could reliably look to the past to predict the future.

Second, it would make little sense to look for bargains or value in financial markets since "the price is always right."

Third, it would make very little sense to try and measure our performance relative to personal financial goals since a market index like the S&P 500 Index is the best to which we could reasonably aspire. Not to mention the fact that, as utility maximizing automatons ourselves, we can do very little to change our own behavior. Just as it is foolish for an avowed determinist to "blame" a criminal, it is foolish for an EMH advocate to talk of letting future dreams inform present realities, rooted as they are in the past.

The Upshot

So, what of the empirical results of these assumptions? It is not for nothing that every piece of financial literature you will ever read begins and ends with, "past results are not indicative of future performance." The fact is that the past is no predictor of the future, as much as we may mourn the supposed loss of prediction that comes with that realization. Wrong too is the notion that "the price is always right." After all, the price to equity ratios of some tech stocks soared into the thousands at the height of the NASDAQ bubble only to fall back into the single digits (if not to zero) just a few months later. It seems laughable to suggest that at all points along that journey, the price was an accurate reflection of value.

And what of market indices as our personal North Star in the investment process? The fact remains that most investors, including professional money managers, fail to beat the benchmark with any degree of regularity. EMH proponents point to this as proof of market efficiency.

However, benchmark adherence itself may be one of the very culprits of underperformance. As ubiquitous as it is, the performance of, say, the S&P 500 Index is available to investors at any hour of the day. Manager and investor performance is always being discussed relative to the benchmark, leading investors to make shortsighted, counter-productive moves in an effort to "keep up." The losses that may result spur further and excessive dabbling. Not only might investors lose money in absolute terms, they might also underperform the benchmark, causing them to veer from their plan in an effort to keep up with the market Joneses.

A truism in finance is that the more often investors check the markets, comparing their performance relative to the benchmark, the worse off their performance. Is beating the benchmark difficult? No doubt. Is using the benchmark as a gauge of personal performance a large contributor to this underperformance? Indubitably.

The Fine Print

If deterministic notions of financial markets that move us away from a more goal-based approach are so deeply flawed that they actually hurt individual investors, why do they persist? The truth is that they continue to exist for the benefit of economists and market prognosticators, albeit to the detriment of Joe Investor from Des Moines. The idea that the past begets a predictable future is what allowed economists and financiers to build beautiful models and take outsized bets . . . until the music stopped playing.

Two such deterministic models were authored by 1990 Nobel Prize Winners Harry Markowitz, who developed the theory of portfolio choice, and William Sharpe, who contributed to the theory of price formation for financial assets (CAPM). Their beautifully Platonic models were built on a Gaussian base and contributed to what is called Modern Portfolio Theory. Impressive, right?

Nassim Nicholas Taleb minced no words in his commentary: "if you remove their Gaussian assumptions and treat prices as scalable, you are left with hot air. . . . they work like quack remedies sold on the Internet." I guess I'll have to make room in the closet for these models beside my set of Shake Weights and Sauna Belt. And I guess even the Nobel Committee can sometimes get it wrong. Taleb further noted that The Nobel Committee could have discovered this bombast themselves, had they tested the Sharpe and Markowitz models, "but nobody in Stockholm seems to have thought about it."

Reluctant to surrender what seems less and less like a crystal ball and more like a Magic 8 Ball, determinists have chosen a philosophical framework that makes them look and feel omniscient, even if it hurts the little guy. After all, to make an omelet, you gotta crack some eggs.

Phillip Pilkington (2011), Dublin-based journalist who examines the intersection of finance, economics, politics, and power, speculates that the allure of deterministic models is the taste of control and power for their true believers, however illusory it is. He explains, "It provides a sort of imaginary [perch] in which the adherent can sit and watch humanity and ensure that they are acting in the appropriate manner. From such a position the neoclassical can then dictate to governments and populations what sorts of policies should be enacted to ensure that everyone acts as much in line with their fantasies as possible." Such a fantasy makes things deceptively simple, as "one only need to think about so-called 'market forces' to understand the big questions of why everything happens—and where everything should go."

Parallels in Psychology

Although psychology existed in some form or another as early as Wilhelm Wundt's lab in nineteenth-century Germany, it is hard to credit anyone other than Freud with being the grandfather of the discipline. Although he was Jewish by heritage, herr doktor was no fan of religion. Freud saw religion as a crutch for the weak-minded. Among his many diatribes against faith is perhaps his most famous from

Civilization and Its Discontents, "The whole thing is so patently infantile, so foreign to reality, that to anyone with a friendly attitude to humanity it is painful to think that the great majority of mortals will never be able to rise above this view of life. It is still more humiliating to discover how a large number of people living today, who cannot but see that this religion is not tenable, nevertheless try to defend it piece by piece in a series of pitiful rearguard actions."

Freud built a deterministic model of human behavior, partially as a consequence of his personal beliefs and also as a means of aligning himself with the more rigorous "hard sciences," in which linear, causal relationships are well known and predictions are possible.

Here's an experiment: If you combine two hydrogen molecules with one oxygen molecule, what do you get?

Water. Every. Single. Time.

Who can resist the simplicity and predictability of this applied to human behavior? Anyone with a toddler or a teenager certainly couldn't. (Freud, by the way, sired six children, which may further explain the appeal.)

Hence, Freud went to work mapping the human psyche in a way that was more reminiscent of physics or math than philosophy or religion. He wanted to combine two Hs and one O to make water. He sought to leave behind the superstitions of his forebears in favor of the predictive simplicity of determinism and his academic legacy bears that fingerprint.

Like a true determinist, Freud believed that the present was a causal representation of the past. This explains the Freudian school's emphasis on spending years exhuming a person's past in great detail. If present behavior is wholly explainable as the sum of past events, it makes sense to gain a deep understanding of what has gone before.

Psychological clinician Jacob A. Arlow (1991) explained that in psychoanalytic theory, "Thoughts, feelings, and impulses are events in a chain of causally related phenomena. They result from experiences in the life of the individual." See the parallel with making water? He continues, "Through appropriate methods of investigation, the connection between current mental experience and past events can be established."

Freud's deterministic leanings are no coincidence. His writings reveal the conscious decisions of a man trying to create a scalable and simple model of human behavior.

So it turns out that psychoanalysts and neoclassical economics alike have created deterministic systems they hoped would rival the forecasting power of their hard science counterparts. This is unceremoniously called "physics envy" in academic circles.

Such views posit that by examining the past, we can make predictions about an immutable future. This sort of linear predictability means that those who can "do the math" or "speak the language" are imbued with prophetic capabilities and are compensated and empowered accordingly. The seductions of such perks are too much to resist for the gurus and talking heads of these fields.

However, the home truth for determinists is that the messiness of lived experience calls such overly simplifying approaches into question. So what's the alternative?

The Economy of One

More recent developments in both psychology and economics point in a new direction, one in which the world is less predictable, peopled by individuals with diverse wants, needs, and even irrationalities. Because this new world is less predictable, it wrests the prophetic mantle from the gurus and returns it back to the individuals who populate it.

This behavioral awakening is both a blessing and a curse. The curse is that the world is not as sterile or "knowable" as we might have hoped or imagined. The blessing is that by reclaiming and personalizing the investment process, we can chart a course that works for us over the long term, even though this path may not have universal appeal. By benchmarking to the specifics of our lives, rather than vague generalities, we can become a new type of expert. An expert in the Economy of One, otherwise referred to as goal-based investing.

But understanding that a personalized, aspirational, and goals-based approach rather than a deterministic index-based approach to investing makes sense is only the first step. Separating from the herd of your own volition is difficult (usually, you need a dog, a horse, and a cowboy to do that) and there are bound to be obstacles.

You don't have to look too far to locate those obstacles. Benjamin Graham (2005), the father of value investing, once said, "The investor's chief problem—and even his worst enemy—is likely to be himself."

In my former professional life as a clinical psychologist, I often met with clients who were engaging in behavior that was maladaptive and led them away from living the life they wanted. Such behaviors ranged from the extreme (e.g., not being able to achieve sexual climax without holding a door knob) to the mundane (e.g., consistently procrastinating schoolwork). The commonality across all these was that the "misbehavior" made some sense when considered in appropriate context. Make no mistake, it was still a bad idea, but a deeper understanding led to an, "Oh, I get it" moment and the eventual fix.

For instance, in the "Doorknob Case" (since I know you're wondering), the patient had grown up in a conservative religious household where even kissing at a young age was considered taboo. Thus, his early romantic forays were always engaged surreptitiously, with a great fear of being caught. As a hedge against being discovered, he would tightly grip the door to his room while kissing his young love. Decades later, as a married man and otherwise well-adjusted professional, he would need to cling to a doorknob to achieve the appropriate level of relaxation while making love. While this behavior was odd and maladaptive, it at least made sense in terms of his historical experience, which allowed us to work toward freeing him of this odd addiction.

Similarly, our tendency to slavishly plan our financial lives around an impersonal index instead of our personal needs and wants can be explained on psychological grounds, even if it is not in our best interests. Thus, while the truth of Graham's words (we are our own problem) is undeniable, we believe the inverse is also true. Whereas the behavioral biases to which we all sometimes succumb can most certainly derail our financial lives, so too can our ability to focus on what matters most deeply to propel us toward a fulfilling and rewarding investing life.

The following pages will help you know your best friend and your worst enemy: yourself. Let's begin by examining some of the psychological reasons we are wed to the impersonal benchmark, en route to freeing ourselves from this self-defeating addiction.

Our Inner Demons: A Field Guide

If you're ever having trouble sleeping, spend some time researching financial goal setting online and you're sure to be snoozing in no time. It's not that the advice you'll find is bad per se, it's just that it is fundamentally disconnected from an understanding of how people behave. Most resources will give you some great meat and potatoes stuff about setting specific, attainable, and timely goals. You will nod your head, eventually doze off, forget all about it, and resume doing what you've always done before the next day.

But saying that talking about financial goals is a boring exercise in futility fails to account for some of the deeper reasons why we may be averse to personalizing the investment and financial planning process. There are at least three significant reasons we resist contemplating our personal financial goals: it can be stress-inducing, we dislike numbers, it is socially taboo, and we are slaves to "right now." Let's examine each of these in further detail.

Money Stresses Me Out

A recent survey conducted by the American Psychological Association (2004) says that 73 percent of Americans name money as the number one factor that affects their stress level. That's right, Number 1. *The New York Times* reports (Rampell 2009) that couples who reported disagreeing about finance once a week were over 30 percent more likely to get divorced than couples who reported disagreements a few times a month. So, in addition to being stress-inducing Public Enemy Number 1, money is also highly implicated in whether or not we stay married. No wonder we tread lightly!

There are a couple of ways in which we attempt to manage the anxiety brought about by financial concerns, neither of which ultimately helps our cause. First, we may ignore them entirely and fail to set any specific financial goals. After all, we erroneously suppose, "If I ignore it, it will go away." As anyone who has ever put off a project can attest, it never goes away and anxiety is only compounded as a deadline approaches. In college, this may have been as inconsequential as pulling an all-nighter and receiving a subpar grade. In our financial lives, ignoring appropriate planning and financial goal setting can have far more damning consequences.

The second ill-advised approach to reduce our stress is to outsource planning to the herd in the form of setting goals relative to market indices. As discussed previously, our goals may have nothing to do with the goals or performance of the greater investing public, but there is some psychological balm to be had from running with the pack. Sir Isaac Newton, brilliant as he was elsewhere, succumbed to such behavior when he lost a fortune (millions in today's dollars) by investing in what is now known as the "South Sea Bubble" (O'Farrell 2007). Newton, who originally resisted the mania, was eventually sucked in, complaining that it was hard to sit idly by and watch his friends get richer than he. He is quoted after the fact as saying, "I can calculate the movement of the stars, but not the madness of men."

Newton's inability to watch his friends' wealth increase relative to his is a symptom of our flawed humanity: We tend to frame wealth relative to our neighbors rather than in terms of our personal needs. Meir Statman (2010) found in conducting the research for his book, *What Investors Really Want*, that survey respondents would prefer to make $50,000 in a community where the average salary is $25,000 than make $100,000 in a community where the average salary is $250,000.

Our tendency to monitor benchmarks instead of attending to our own personal needs is symptomatic of this madness. We know that we will feel regret and anxiety about missing out or underperforming the herd, thus, we throw up our hands and settle for the status quo rather than striving for the returns we need to meet our personal dreams. In this respect, checking out entirely and outsourcing our goals to the masses are two sides of the anxiety management coin.

I Hate Numbers

Computer scientist Douglas Hofstadter first originated the term "innumeracy" which he defines as "a person's inability to make sense of the numbers that run their lives" (as cited in Paulos 2001). Notice that Mr. Hofstadter is not advocating that each of us understand math at his level or that each of us strive to be a mathematician. Rather, he suggests that there is a level of facility with math that is required to successfully navigate the tasks of daily living, including planning for a personal financial future. Just as one can benefit from literacy without aspiring to be Faulkner, one can benefit from numeracy without aspiring to be Einstein.

While illiteracy primarily impacts low socio-economic status individuals in the United States, innumeracy is far more widespread and impacts a greater percentage of middle class and even upper middle class people than presumed. Just look at our children: In the United States, the biggest economic engine in the world, they lag behind in math, as our 4th graders ranked 11th in the world and our 8th graders ranked 9th in the world based on the *Trends in International Mathematics and Science* 2011 Study (Mullis et al. 2011). Worse yet, only 7 percent of students in the United States reached the "advanced" level, compared to 48 percent in Singapore (Rich 2012).

Myriad studies have shown that the tendency toward socializing girls away from math and science is especially pronounced. Girls are, formally and informally, taught that science and math are the purview of boys and men. As a result, they show decreasing interest and scores beginning in early middle school.

Whatever the sociological or educational roots of our distaste for numbers, the impact of innumeracy on our ability to create meaningful financial goals cannot be overstated. We avoid what we don't understand. Instead, we fall back on what we are fed by the financial news outlets, which often care more about sensationalism than substance (If it bleeds, it leads!). The reason for this is that they are selling ad space, not giving you meaningful data from which to build a financial roadmap. Just think about it: Which are you more likely to watch and talk about the day after: David Attenborough's educational and beautifully shot series "Planet Earth" (2006) or the much-hyped action movie, "The Dark Knight" (2008)? For the same reasons that compel most people to "The Dark Knight" (hype, action, excitement) versus "Planet Earth," financial media outlets are not motivated to present the educational material you may need.

I Can't Talk About That!

One needn't look any further than the most recent U.S. Presidential election to witness the sloughing off of some historical conversational taboos. In the not-too-distant past, topics such as race, religion, and politics would have been considered impolite. In an era of increasing transparency and acceptance, however, old mores are being replaced by new standards. But despite our increased fluency in the language of what once was verboten, one topic remains touchy and awkward, especially within families. Indeed, in an era when sex is discussed freely on the nightly news, we still don't know how to talk to one another about money. If you demand further proof of the matter, remember that some organizations legally compel their employees to keep quiet about their salary at the risk of losing their jobs.

A recent study by the American Institute of CPAs (AICPA 2012) found that speaking to children about money was among parents' lowest priorities. In fact, money issues were trumped in terms of perceived importance by good manners, sound eating habits, the need for good grades, the dangers of drugs and the risks of smoking. Our reticence to talk about money is certainly not out of lack of need. An Accenture report (2012) states that Baby Boomers will leave $30 trillion to their children over the next 30 years. This doesn't even take into account the almost $12 trillion that MetLife predicts Boomers will receive from their parents. The fact is, money will be changing hands within families at an unprecedented rate in the years to come and we are ill equipped to make the exchange.

There are a number of reasons why talking about money may be so difficult. One is that there has been a vitriolic reaction against the wealthy in the wake of the Occupy movement and the global financial crisis. This sentiment was illustrated quite vividly in the September 24 *Fortune* magazine article, "Stop Beating Up the Rich" (Easton 2012). Another reason for this taboo may have a higher source.

By my count, the Bible, the best-selling book of all time and a foundational text for a majority of Americans, mentions money no less than 250 times. While not all Biblical references to money are negative, there are certainly enough references to "filthy lucre" to give pause. Not to mention verses such as Matthew 19:24 that says, "And again I say unto you, it is easier for a camel to go through the eye of a needle, than for a rich man to enter into the kingdom of God." To a nation founded on Protestant ideals about work and morality, the notion of wealth as potentially corrosive is one that is deeply embedded in the collective American consciousness. But social taboos around money are not strictly religious. Sigmund Freud, an avowed atheist, identified money with feces and connected it with an anal retentive personality, in plain terms, meaning someone who is obsessed with detail to a fault (Hall 1954).

Dr. Richard Trachtman, a psychotherapist and money counselor has some fascinating thoughts on his blog, www.moneyworkandlove.com, that center on wealth as it relates to another social taboo: sex. Trachtman (1999) observes that in some ways, money is very much a part of our social every day. We commiserate with our friends about not having enough money, we let out collective groans about the burdens of taxes and dream together about how to spend fictional lottery winnings. But in terms of the more common and serious matters that form the basis of our actual financial lives, we are conditioned toward silence. As Trachtman says of the sex vs. money taboo, "It is rare for a couple to marry without having had at least some sexual contact, but it is not rare at all for couples to marry without discussing financial matters."

John Levy, a counselor to people who have recently inherited money found the following reasons for the money taboo among his clientele (as cited in O'Neil 1993):

- Good taste—"It's just not done."
- Fear of manipulation—"It will give them power over me."
- Concern for spoiling children—"If they know how much we've got, they will never make anything of themselves."
- Embarrassment—"I don't deserve to be so much better off than others."
- Fear of being judged—"All they can see is my money."

Whatever the causes of our awkwardness around conversations about money, an increased dialogue around the subject is a necessity. Passing on wealth to subsequent generations will be beneficial only to the extent that are well educated financially. Without the proper financial grounding, they may be ill equipped to handle their newfound assets and may actually do themselves harm with what ought to have been a great gift.

Perhaps some of the reasons above are resonant with your personal situation and perhaps not, but it is to deny that the topic of money puts us all on eggshells. Consider a handful of your best friends. No doubt you could tell me much about their lives: the joys and struggles, the highs and lows. But I doubt if you could tell me their exact salary, savings, or other relevant financial indicators, because we simply don't talk about them. While this is fine in polite company, this tendency toward silence can extend beyond the cocktail party circuit. When we bring this same shame to our personal planning lives, we tend not to take a deep look at our own goals and motivations and instead tend to become enthralled in the larger financial conversation, which may have very little to do with our own circumstances at all.

I Want It NOW!

British economist Nassau Williams, Sr. knew of what he spoke when he famously said, "To abstain from enjoyment which is in our power, or to seek distant rather than immediate results, are among the most painful exertions of the human will." But not all great truths are taught by way of flowery quotations. Sometimes great life lessons can be taught by something wholly common—like a marshmallow. In 1972, Stanford psychologist Walter Mischel set out, marshmallows in hand, to test the resolve of a group of children. Each child was invited into the testing room and offered a marshmallow. They were informed that they could eat it immediately, but that, if they waited a bit, they could have *two* marshmallows! At that point, the tester left the room (usually for 15 minutes) and the battle of self-discipline began.

Of the 4-year-olds tested, 70 percent couldn't wait. Only 3 out of 10 showed enough self-restraint to earn the coveted second confection. Interestingly, the experiment has been replicated all over the world and consistently, two-thirds of those tested cannot wait and one-third can. More fascinating still is the far-reaching impact of the ability to consider future happiness. At a 15-year follow up, researchers found that those kids who waited are more successful in a number of domains, including academic and personal achievements. In an eerie real-life parallel to the marshmallow studies, the McKinsey Global Institute predicts that two out of three Baby Boomers will not be able to meet their retirement needs. In marshmallows as in life, good things come to those who are able to wait.

So it is that every day, beneath your awareness, a battle is raging. That is the battle between your present and future selves. Your present self wants the donut but your future self implores you to eat the celery. Your present self wants to date the "bad boy," but your future self begs you to seek out that studious guy in the front of the class. The "right now" you wants to blow your whole bonus check, while the rational future voice opines that you might want to put at least some of it away. It's a battle alright, but a lopsided one in which the future you is often left defenseless.

Consider the behavior of those joining a health club, when offered the choice of a monthly subscription rate and a pay-as-you-go option. In the moment, they feel resolved and as though they'll spend every waking moment in the gym. The reality is, it costs 70 percent more on average to choose the subscription model because attendance tends to dwindle over time. Similarly, you may fill your bookshelves with thick leather volumes of classic works, but find that when the time comes to read, you fall back on the latest Tom Clancy novel. Sure you mean well, but the chasm between your current and forecasted self remains gaping.

One of the reasons why the present self usually wins the day is that pain and pleasure are felt in the present. In order for financial goals to have any real resonance, they must have strong personal and emotional ties. This leads to the concept of "autonomy," a word derived from the Greek *autonomia*, the literal translation of which is "one who gives oneself their own law" (Harper 2001–2014). Identifying one's goals creates one's own law. Importantly, this does not necessitate going it alone. It is enough to understand at least some financial best practices so that you can select financial professionals whose goals and approaches mimic your own.

That's the ideal. But in reality, most of us operate absent a deep-seated, personally meaningful goal. Even the most numerate, stress-free investor with no real taboos around money is rudderless without the kind of goals just mentioned. Thus being without a North Star, we are left to be tossed to and fro by the daily buckings of the market bull (or bear). We tend to react as a group, in the moment, and are enabled to do so by the constant availability of an index. All we need to do is turn on Bloomberg News or navigate to cnnmoney.com to get our "gotta have it now" fix and we will know just how we are doing, relatively speaking. The result can be disastrous. Now, having revealed and debunked our inner demons let's take a look at the alternative so the exorcism may be complete.

Let Your "Why" Teach You "How"

Daniel Pink is a *New York Times* bestselling author whose books on sales, entrepreneurship and motivation have all been wildly popular. Perhaps

Pink's most read work is *Drive* (2011) which attempts to deconstruct human motivation, finally arriving at three pillars: mastery, autonomy and purpose. We'll leave mastery and autonomy, both fascinating topics in their own respect, for another day and focus our efforts instead on purpose. Pink defines purpose simply as, "the yearning to do what we do in the service of something larger than ourselves." Sure you say, that sounds great for a charity fundraiser, but what the hell does purpose have to do with the cost of tea in China (or my investment decisions)?

The fallacious notion that your personal goals have nothing to do with being a successful investor is a vestige of deterministic, EMH ways of thinking about performance. After all, if you're an efficiency-maximizing automaton who reacts with deft efficiency to arbitrage away momentary mispricings, who cares about what matters deeply to you, you're going to do what robots do. However, we know now that's not the case. In fact, the benefits to a goal-driven approach are myriad, with but a few discussed below.

Pop quiz: What is the best predictor of the size of a retirement nest egg? What's that you say, performance? Wrong! I'm sorry but the correct answer was "deferral rate," but thanks for playing. The way that goals-based investing increases deferral rates (and thus, wallet share) is by couching investments in terms of personal meaning.

Consider the lengths to which you would go to send your children to the college of their dreams. To retire with your spouse to an island in the Caribbean. To give philanthropically to a cause close to your heart.

Now consider the lengths to which you would go to beat the S&P 500 Index. Not quite the same is it?

The fact is, investors understand that money is only as good as the goals it helps you reach. Rather than speaking in sterile terms that rob wealth of its holistic meaning, use your goals as the benchmark and see how much easier saving becomes.

We have already touched on the extraordinarily myopic view most investors take, a tendency that is only furthered by the ubiquity of reports on how the market fared on any given day (or hour, or minute . . .). The fact is, most deeply meaningful goals exist a few years, if not a few decades down the road. If saving for your kid's college is the benchmark, what do you care if the S&P 500 Index is down 200 points today? That's not the game you're playing.

Perhaps the biggest benefit of all is the way in which a goals-driven approach provides shelter in the storm. Benchmark investors, anchored as they are to the index and the actions of others, tend to lose focus in market downturns which accounts for the "behavior gap trap" documented so well by Dalbar and others.

Purpose-driven investors, on the other hand, have a "why" that helps them deal with almost any "how." We've all had the experience of sacrificing our personal comfort to do something deeply meaningful, but it seems silly to suffer pointlessly. Thus, those with an important reason for staying invested, one that is bigger than the momentary discomfort of a paper loss, are more likely to do so, whereas those affixed to an arbitrary indicator have no real reason to stay the course.

Indeed, one of the biggest culprits in bad financial planning is disconnecting the process from the things that matter most to the person making the decisions. Coco Chanel said it best when she said, "The best things in life are free. The second best are very expensive." By connecting the best things in life (family, friends, education, philanthropy) to the next best things (the ones that actually cost money), the planning, investing and saving processes all become part of a seamless whole. Once dreams have been connected to financial realities, sensible behavior ceases to be a chore and begins to be a natural extension of a life well lived.

Summary

No one sets out to live an average life. Why should we settle for an average portfolio? Yet, that is often the outcome when we adopt deterministic models of investing and seek to beat the market according to some impersonal benchmark. The key to mastering our ability to defer gratification and formulate our financial goals based on what matters most to us, the ones making the decisions. When we do so, saving and achieving those goals will be far easier.

References

Accenture. "The 'Greater' Wealth Transfer: Capitalizing on the Inter-generational Shift in Wealth." Accenture. (June 2012). www.accenture .com/SiteCollectionDocuments/PDF/Accenture-CM-AWAMS-Wealth -Transfer-Final-June2012-Web-Version.pdf.

AICPA. "AICPA Survey: Money Among Lowest Priorities in Talks Between Parents, Kids." AICPA. (August 9, 2012). www.aicpa.org/press/ pressreleases/2012/pages/aicpa-survey-money-among-lowest-priorities-in -talks-between-parents-kids.aspx.

American Psychological Association. "Money Issues Leading Cause of Holiday Stress for Americans." American Psychological Association. (December 3, 2004). www.apa.org/news/press/releases/2004/12/holiday-stress.aspx.

Arlow, Jacob A. *Psychoanalysis: Clinical Theory and Practice*. Madison: International Universities Press, Inc., 1991.

Easton, Nina. "Stop beating up the rich." (September 6, 2012). Fortune, 166(5): 114. http://finance.fortune.cnn.com/2012/09/06/stop-bashing-rich/.

Freud, Sigmund. *Civilization and Its Discontents*. London: Imago, 1941.

Graham, Benjamin. *The Intelligent Investor: The Classic Text on Value Investing*. New York: HarperBusiness, 2005.

Hall, Calvin S. (1954). *A Primer of Freudian Psychology*. New York: New American Library.

Harper, Douglas. Autonomy. (2001–2014). Online Etymology Dictionary. www.etymonline.com/index.php?term=autonomy.

Mischel, Walter, Ebbe B. Ebbesen and Antonette Raskoff Zeiss. "Cognitive and attentional mechanisms in delay of gratification." (January 1972). Journal of Personality and Social Psychology, 21(2): 204–218. doi: 10.1037/h0032198.

Mullis, Ina V. S., Michael O. Martin, Pierre Foy and Alka Arora. TIMSS 2011 International Results in Mathematics. Chestnut Hill, MA: TIMSS & PIRLS International Study Center, Boston College, 2012. http://timssandpirls.bc .edu/timss2011/downloads/T11_IR_Mathematics_FullBook.pdf.

O'Neil, John. *The Paradox of Success*. New York: Putnam, 1993.

O'Farrell, John. *An Utterly Impartial History of Britain — Or 2000 Years of Upper Class Idiots In Charge*. New York: Doubleday, 2007.

Paulos, John Allen. *Innumeracy: Mathematical Illiteracy and Its Consequences*. New York: Hill and Wang, 2001.

Pilkington, Phillip. "Marginal Utility Theory as a Blueprint for Social Control." Naked Capitalism. (October 3, 2011). www.nakedcapitalism.com/2011/10/philip-pilkington-marginal-utility-theory-as-a-blueprint-for-social-control.html.

Pink, Daniel H. *Drive: The Surprising Truth About What Motivates Us*. New York: Riverhead Books, 2011.

Rampell, Catherine. "Money Fights Predict Divorce Rates." The New York Times. (December 7, 2009). http://economix.blogs.nytimes.com/2009/12/07/money-fights-predict-divorce-rates/?_php=true&_type=blogs&_r=0.

Rich, Motoko. U.S. Students Still Lag Globally in Math and Science, Tests Show. The New York Times. (December 11, 2012). www.nytimes.com/2012/12/11/education/us-students-still-lag-globally-in-math-and-science-tests-show.html.

Slife, Brent Donald, and Richard N. Williams. *What's Behind the Research?: Discovering Hidden Assumptions in the Behavioral Sciences*. Thousand Oaks: Sage, 1995.

Statman, Meir. *What Investors Really Want: Know What Drives Investor Behavior and Make Smarter Financial Decisions*. New York: McGraw-Hill, 2010.

Taleb, Nassim Nicholas. *The Black Swan: The Impact of the Highly Improbable*. New York, NY: Random House, 2007.

Trachtman, Richard. "Money, Work, and Love." Money, Work, and Love." (1999). www.moneyworkandlove.com.

CHAPTER 8

Pursuing Your Personal Benchmark

Dr. Daniel Crosby

To forget one's purpose is the commonest form of stupidity.

—Friedrich Nietzsche

I was recently asked to speak at a conference in Dublin, Ireland, a city I had never before visited. Although I was excited to visit a new country, in my uninformed imaginings, Dublin was little more than a mid-sized American city with better accents. I did very little research to prepare for my trip, a truth that is confirmed by the fact that I left my passport at home and failed to call my bank to ensure that my cards would not be frozen for "fraudulent activity" once abroad. Notwithstanding my absentmindedness, I arrived in Dublin safe and sound and, after over-coming my initial jet lag and the aforementioned banking mishap, ventured onto the cobblestone streets of the city to do a little exploring.

About a block from my hotel, I came across a fastidiously graffitied fence surrounding an aborted commercial real estate project. The graffiti read, "Back in the day you were born with original sin, now it's original debt. Every man, woman and child in this country is footing the bill for a load of empty buildings. Who listens to the little guy?" I was immediately struck by the message and the way it wove together Ireland's religious heritage seamlessly with their current economic hardships.

What I did not yet know was what the graffiti portended—the worst economic hardship I'd ever witnessed in a developed country. As I walked the streets of Dublin, I felt like an extra in an apocalyptic movie where some strange disease had stripped the world of its' inhabitants. I observed blocks full of opulent luxury condominiums boarded up and without a single tenant. I witnessed weathered signs promising the opportunity to "Live-Work-Play" in the city's "hottest new location" adorning half-started construction sites with heavy equipment rusting on site. I entered a spacious mall to purchase a present for my daughter (I promised her a leprechaun) only to find that 75 percent of the stores, including all of the retailers, had gone out of business. Everywhere I turned, I saw vestiges of the old abundance mentality that were all the more depressing, given the stark milieu in which I now found them. There had clearly been a time where the future looked bright, but that dreamed-of someday now seemed a long way off.

As I buttoned my coat against the cold Irish night and began the long walk back to my hotel, I was struck forcibly by a simple truth: "All of this hardship was borne from a frame of mind." The suffering I witnessed was very real and I, in no way, mean to make light of that. But the circumstances that caused the ephemeral rise and precipitous crash are very much rooted in psychology—namely, in a mindset that "what goes up may never come down." The thought that "this time is different." The belief that financial hardships happen to others, but never to us.

You see, in a very real sense, "the economy" and all its trappings are an entirely psychological construct. No one has ever unearthed a beautiful credit default swap or picked a perfectly ripe derivative. Financial systems are borne of humankind's genius and fail as a consequence of our fear, greed, and irrationality. Simply put, only we can dream them up and only we can screw them up. The "Celtic Tiger," the rapid growth of the Irish economy from 1995 to 2008, was a product, at least in part, of business-friendly taxation policies, a talented Anglophone workforce and the hard work of hundreds of thousands of Irish citizens. The subsequent precipitous crash, however, was a result of a belief that these things would always be enough to sustain the previous years' record economic growth numbers.

Bubbles like the one I witnessed in Ireland are formed on a foundation of half-truths. It is true that Ireland enjoyed legitimate success as a result of some actual competitive advantages. It is similarly true that the Internet has changed the way we live and do business. The fallacy behind both the Celtic Tiger and the NASDAQ bubble was the idea that this was a new era in which personal accountability, restraint, and economic fundamentals no longer matter.

This simple but powerful epiphany continues to affect how I go about all of my work, which primarily revolves around educating investors and designing investment products that minimize irrationality. I came to the realization that night that by changing our minds, we can truly change our reality in meaningful ways. If irrational exuberance can bring about financial calamity, then it stands to reason that rational adherence to a set of rules can save our financial lives. It's not a complex idea, but it's one that can have profound implications for the personal and financial wellbeing of our families and even our nations. And it all begins with a focus on—you guessed it—ourselves. As with all bubbles, the Irish crisis arose as emotion fueled connecting to personal needs as investors began trying to "get a piece of the action."

The Difference a Frame Makes

In Chapter 2, we previously touched on the human tendency to simplify, one of the Three S's of investor behavior. The need to simplify or use "heuristics," a psychobabble term for "rules of thumb," is obvious: There is simply too much information to consume in the always-connected era of the 24-hour financial news channel and smartphones. As Tversky and Kahneman (1974) suggest, we also use benchmarks, a form of heuristic, as an anchoring point for comparative use. After all, it makes sense that investors would want some grounding as well as a means of making investment decision-making more parsimonious.

As intuitive as this idea may seem to you, it has not always been the prevailing notion of how investors made decisions. Remember that hardcore EMH enthusiasts propose that investors are "informationally efficient," which is to say they incorporate all existing data into their financial decisions. Behavioral finance enthusiasts, for their part, responded with an onslaught of heuristic irrationalities aimed at blaspheming the gospel of informational efficiency.

To be honest, neither approach when taken to extreme is helpful to Suzie Q. Investor. EMH approaches paint Suzie as an automaton with lightning fast processing power and unlimited storage capacity for information. Older behavioral approaches emphasize the ways in which Suzie is fallible, but do little to assist her in the decision making process. As is so often the case, the truth lies somewhere in the middle: We are neither robotically systematic nor wholly idiotic when making investment decisions. To be sure, we do our best to remain objective and make good decisions, but we are strongly influenced by our cognitive limitations and the cloudy lens through which we all see the world. But behavioral approaches, which showcased the limitations of our mental computers, simultaneously gave us the notion that what we consumed mattered greatly. As the old programming maxim goes, "garbage in, garbage out."

Offering a more nuanced view, behavioral economics pioneers Tversky and Kahneman (1974) discovered that decisions are often made in relative terms, with a "frame" serving as a point of reference against which options can be weighed. An easy demonstration of the framing concept can be shown using something as benign as the sensation of temperature.

My wife and I are of differing opinions as to what constitutes "room temperature" (her ideal is in the high 70s, mine in the high 60s), but we have compromised by leaving our home thermostat at 73 degrees Farenheit. Thus, each morning I work in what seems like my fairly comfortable, if slightly stuffy, home office. Just before lunch, I go for a run in the Alabama heat and then return to my now frigid home office.

What happened? The temperature didn't change: It is still 73 degrees, just as it was 30 minutes earlier. The answer is, my frame changed and, with it, my experience.

Investors are much the same way: They do not experience the market or make financial decisions independent of their chosen frames.

As such, it behooves investors to thoughtfully choose a frame that maximizes rational behavior and leaves behind frames that encourage maladaptive performance, no matter how widely used they may be.

Limitations in Our Decision Making

Bounded rationality, first introduced by social scientist Herbert Simon in 1955, is one of the most widely accepted models of decision making known today. Bounded rationality simply means that the quality of a decision will be influenced by the information consumed, the cognitive limitations of the human mind and any time constraints that might exist (Gigerenzer and Selten 2002). Bounded rationality serves as the intellectual latticework for the behavioral notion that outputs are determined partially by the framing of inputs.

Simon says that rather than making optimal decisions all of the time, humans settle for "satisficing," or doing the best they can with the limitations at hand. To use a silly example, for you to accurately make the statement, "I don't like brussel sprouts," you would need to eat every brussel sprout in the world, which is difficult, at best. (But if you're keen on doing so, we suggest you try them roasted with kosher salt, freshly cracked black pepper, and a bit of bacon). Absent that, you satisfice by making the statement based on your experience of eating brussel sprouts to date. Similarly, Simon suggests that most people can only attend to 5 to 7 variables at once when making an important decision, far short of the 45,000 pieces of economic data available to consumers each month. Just as one needn't and couldn't eat every vegetable to make a well-informed decision about its taste, one cannot process every bit of financial trivia that accompanies a financial decision.

Lest you think we delight in shooting down old paradigms for its own sake, let's examine some of the practical fallout of moving from an efficient to bounded rationality framework as it concerns investing. To do so, we will dissect the original definition of bounded rationality in terms of its three constituent parts: timing, cognitive limitations, and information consumed.

Regarding timing, we previously mentioned that the time horizon against which most investors evaluate their decisions has shrunken drastically in the last few decades. These horizons only continue to shrink as technology advances. So what is the impact of this ever-nearing horizon in terms of bounded rationality? Simon suggests that rationality becomes increasingly "bound" or encumbered as the urgency of a decision increases. Simply put, the more pressing a decision is perceived to be, the less rational the decision. There can be little doubt that benchmarking to the moment rather than long-term personal goals has a net negative impact with respect to maintaining an optimal time frame.

The reality of our cognitive limitations should be no surprise to anyone over the age of 30, as brain capacity begins to diminish (and forgetfulness increases) from a relatively early age. Our limitations are evidenced in everything from our phone numbers to our childhood mnemonics. Phone numbers are presented in "chunks" of 3 and 4 numbers rather than as 10 independent digits because we are typically only able to hold 7 or so such chunks at any given time. For fun, try giving your number as 10 equally spaced digits the next time some knuckle dragging cretin hits on you at the bar and see if he (or she) is able to keep up! Similarly, we learn mnemonics such as "My Very Educated Mother Just Served Us Nachos" in an effort to remember the eight planets in our solar system (RIP Pluto).

Thus brings us to the third constraint: information consumption. Because we are unable to hold and process all relevant data, we must choose the subset most germane to our specific needs. Although the variables most important to you are best left to a discussion between you and your advisor, I can say with some confidence that the economic forecast for the nation of Cyprus does not qualify. Very often, a slow news day in the markets will prompt talking heads to reach for stories so far removed from the personal needs of the average investor as to be laughable. However, this sort of alarmist reporting can loom large in the minds of investors doing their best to stay informed and consider all angles en route to protecting the capital for which they have worked so hard. It is a shame and a hindrance to waste our limited cognitive real estate on things of so little importance to our personal financial purpose.

All is not lost, however. Given an appropriate timeline and a small number of relevant variables, investors ought to be able to make decisions that approach rationality. Conversely, if investors stay squarely within the aim of the firehose of financial news and allow their emotions to rise and fall with the benchmark, they are likely to make hasty decisions that have little to do with their long-term financial wellbeing. The keystone determinant of financial rationality then, is not *if* investors simplify their decisions, but *how* they simplify them. We can be owned by our benchmarks or own them—the decision is up to us.

The Joneses, Jealousy, and Missteps

I once sat down next to a woman on a plane and, upon hearing that I was a psychologist, she opened up to me about a history of childhood abuse and neglect. Although I treated her story with the appropriate circumspection and respect, it was nonetheless jarring to experience that degree of vulnerability without the appropriate relational foundation. Most of us do not share intimate details with the public, so what does get shared can look a little bit like a highlight reel of our lives rather than a play-by-play. The other person, whomever that may be, then becomes our external benchmark. Being exposed to the best of what is going on with others and juxtaposing that with our intimate familiarity with every disappointing detail in our own lives is a recipe for feeling like a failure. A recent study showed that people who spent a great deal of time on Facebook were more depressed than their peers who did not (Konnikova 2013). The reason is that Facebook is little but a brag sheet where people boast about the good things happening in their lives, often omitting the sad or boring parts that happen every day.

You Win, I Lose

Inter-individual comparison is a deck that is stacked against us: We know all of our own highs and lows, but tend to see only (or mostly) the highs of those to whom we compare ourselves. This being so, it makes sense that the most realistic barometer of our personal wellbeing lies in comparing the person we are today with the person we were yesterday rather than to our neighbor.

The same goes for investing. Take a moment and recount how many times a friend or acquaintance (the external benchmark, in this case) has trumpeted his or her successful stock picking acumen after a recent success. Now recall how often someone at a barbecue has related with sadness a story of having unsuccessfully navigated the vagaries of the financial markets. One needn't be an expert in human behavior to guess that the first number is larger than the second. We are simply socialized that "if we don't have something nice to say, we should say nothing at all," a logic that leads us to broadcast gains and bury losses.

Perhaps we already have a sense that benchmarking to our drinking buddies is a bad idea; but what of the ubiquitous and seemingly respectable market index as a comparative benchmark? It turns out that comparing to an index can lead to an unsatisfying experience in much the same way that Facebook can. Just as Facebook pictures show perfectly coifed children (omitting the hour-long, tearful hair combing battle it took to get there), market indices report returns without any of the attendant heartache. Index returns cannot meaningfully be separated from the risk borne to achieve them, but the oversimplified approach of benchmarking to an index leads us to pine for the returns while ignoring our ability to bear the necessary risk over a period of time.

I Win, I'm at Par

Equally problematic is that index benchmarking, externally focused as it is, activates our tendency to want to keep up with the Joneses. If we underperform the benchmark, we feel as though we are being lapped by our fellow investor in the wealth accumulation game. But, if we receive benchmark returns, we receive no great joy since we are only seen as treading water or at "par." External comparisons are inherently unsatisfying, in life as in investing. Worse still, they lead us to act irrationally.

We're all familiar with the phrase "keeping up with the Joneses," but we might not understand just how deeply it is ingrained in our concept of wealth and success. Each year, a Gallup poll asks Americans to determine "What is the smallest amount of money a family of four needs to get along in this community?" Gallup finds that the answers to this question move up in line with average incomes of the respondents. In a developed country like ours, the notions of "relative wealth" and "relative poverty" are very much at play.

No doubt there is true hunger, poverty, and want in our country, and I don't want to minimize that. But among the middle and upper socio-economic classes, people tend to look to others to determine whether or not they are successful, rather than point to some static measure of wealth. Studies show that the most noticeable way in which money affects happiness is negative! We see that the very rich enjoy a slight bump in happiness given their comparative superiority, but the "have nots" are made absolutely miserable as they look up at their better resourced counterparts. Given that the increase in happiness is slight and that the rich make up a small fraction of the total population, in general, the tendency to view money in comparative terms is the source of a great deal of woe.

Given our tendency to compare our own incomes with what others have, we only feel better off if we move up relative to those with whom we compare ourselves. Thought of in this comparative light, wealth creation becomes a contest where "your gains" are tantamount to "my losses" and vice versa. In this paradigm, my striving for a greater income and working longer hours has decreased your happiness in aggregate.

In a very real sense, we attempt to climb to the top of the corporate ladder on the backs of those with whom we interact and, in so doing, we are sacrificing a great deal of what would really make us happy along the way. Given this human tendency to compare and construe wealth in relative terms, it's easy to see how the work/life balance we are constantly striving to achieve continues to shift increasingly toward work. After all, if we take a break, the people with whom we are comparing ourselves will be that much further ahead in the race upon our return. As long as work remains a "you win, I lose" scenario, our relationship with others will be strained, at best, as we continue to push each other in the direction of greater and greater imbalance.

The American tendency toward outward displays of wealth and comparative measurement is not endemic to all developed countries. Switzerland is just one example of a very wealthy country with a philosophy diametrically opposed view to showy wealth. As opposed to the American mantra of, "If you've got it, flaunt it," the Swiss take an "If you've got it, hide it" approach so as not to provoke envy in others. The Swiss approach demonstrates that our views are an outcropping of a specific way of viewing wealth rather than something fundamental about human nature. It is up to us to determine to support each other on the way to balance and true happiness rather than prodding each other toward jealousy and excess.

Keeping Up to Fall Behind

To concretely examine the negative power of external benchmarks, let's take a look at an imaginary investor named Katrina who represents a far from imaginary sequence that plays out daily. Katrina is a naturally conservative person in most aspects of her life, and her investments are no exception. She is working closely with an advisor who has devised a portfolio with returns that are keeping up with her modest goals. While out to dinner with friends, Katrina becomes aware that some of her friends are enjoying superior returns by investing in high-yield foreign bonds. Their rewards are doubly great since they have chosen not to diversify but go "all in" on what they think is an exciting opportunity.

Our placid heroine is not initially swayed, but her confidence in her plan has been eroded slightly, and she begins to dig into the financial news a bit to see what she has been missing. She reads a slew of articles with names like, "Secrets of the Three Best Hedge Fund Managers Alive" and "You'd Be a Millionaire Today If You'd Bought This Stock." She begins to ruminate on "what might have been" and becomes increasingly dissatisfied with her own modest life and the shortcomings she perceives in her less-than-omniscient advisor. This, combined with her friends' continued trumpeting of their own investment successes, takes Katrina's "eye off of the ball" and leads her to follow her friends into riskier financial waters. The bonds are now near their peak, but Katrina has no way of knowing that and sees the inflated price as a symbol of strength and reassurance that she's just following other savvy investors.

Soon, a coup occurs that destabilizes the region and shakes the confidence of Katrina, her friends and investors like them all over the world. Once again, influenced by the herd logic she has grown to rely on, Katrina sells at a 50 percent haircut and retreats to cash to lick her wounds. Thoroughly unsettled, yet oblivious to the herd logic that brought and continues to keep her down, she remains un-invested throughout the downturn, missing valuable opportunities to buy low.

Let's examine the irrationality of Katrina's decision in light of Simon's bounded rationality model:

1. Time: By taking her eye off her long-term investment goals and artificially truncating her timeline, Katrina felt a sense of "missing out" that was catalyzed by her use of a poor benchmark (in this case, her friends).

2. Cognitive limitations: Katrina must make decisions on a few pieces of data, the quality of which will shape the rationality of her decision.

3. Information: In the past, Katrina relied on data vetted by her advisor that corresponded nicely to her generally low appetite for risk. After reframing her benchmark from "taking care of myself" to "keeping up with others," she now was at sea, tossed about on the rogue waves of the financial media.

In short, whereas she used to enjoy peace of mind and returns that met her personal goals, now her portfolio greatly suffered and the quality of her decisions rapidly diminished.

We could dissect Katrina's decision from any number of angles: She suffered from unnecessarily bound rationality, fell prey to emotional contagion, succumbed to the availability heuristic and any number of other fancy sounding academic terms.

But the root of Katrina's problem and the wellspring of all of her irrationality was choosing to use an external rather than personal benchmark. The decisions she made were a direct result of the yardstick used to measure success. Use an arbitrary yardstick and you'll get arbitrary results. Medvec, Madey and Gilovich discovered something fascinating in their 1995 study of Olympic medalists that speaks forcefully to the power of benchmarks. Their study revealed that bronze medalists were happier than silver medalists. Sounds irrational, right? The reason is the chosen benchmark. Whereas silver medalists benchmark to just having missed the gold, bronze medalists benchmark to just having missed not placing at all. In much the same way, the benchmark you choose has profound implications, not only for the way you make decisions, but the pleasure you will experience along the way.

The Anatomy of Better Decisions

Drawing and expounding upon the idea of bounded rationality, Keith Redhead (2009), a principal lecturer in finance at Coventry University in the UK, set forth a behavioral view of how people make financial decisions in his paper of the same name (see Figure 8.1).

The first step in Redhead's (2009) model is what he calls "objective information," which is data in raw form, before it has been interpreted or manipulated by humans (as it must eventually be).

> It is worth a small digression here to remind the reader that raw data is essentially useless until it has been through a sensory filter. A raw data answer to the question, "How long until we get there?" might be "7," which could be 7 miles, 7 minutes, 7 meters or 7 hours. It is further worth noting that all of the systems by which we codify data are man-made: It is nowhere written in stone tablets by the hand of God that an hour is 60 minutes or that a mile is 5,280 feet. Data will always be limited by the transformations we make to classify it and the subjective lens through which we attempt to grasp it. If any investment professional attempts to sell you on a "wholly objective" platform, you ought to run far away, but not before insulting the intelligence of the same.

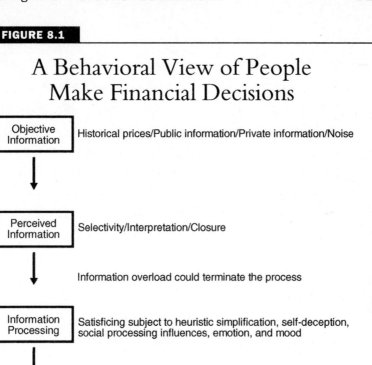

FIGURE 8.1

A Behavioral View of People Make Financial Decisions

Objective Information — Historical prices/Public information/Private information/Noise

Perceived Information — Selectivity/Interpretation/Closure

Information overload could terminate the process

Information Processing — Satisficing subject to heuristic simplification, self-deception, social processing influences, emotion, and mood

Decisions — Buy/Sell/Hold

Activation — Procrastination/Inhibition

Action — Decision implemented

Source: Redhead, Keith J. (2009) "A Behavioral View of How People Make Financial Decisions." *Journal of Financial Planning.*

The second step in Redhead's process is the transformation of the "objective information" into a more usable form through the process of perception. This produces what Redhead calls "perceived information." It is at this point that the author cautions that "information overload could terminate the process," meaning that the sheer volume of data could prove overwhelming and confusing for a great many investors. Here is where purpose-driven investing serves to simplify the process. For example, Suzie Q. Investor, who has identified an appropriate rate of return, time horizon, risk tolerance and the like, will realize that a great deal of the noise that dots the investment landscape is not for her. Thus, the process of perceiving is streamlined and loses its daunting quality.

The third step is "information processing" which is where the satisficing, or making "good enough" decisions takes place. It is in this third step that referential heuristics (rules of thumb), including emotions ("affect heuristic" for us nerds) becomes a critical part of the decision-making process. We have shown above that the question of heuristics is less one of "if" and more one of "how" or "which." Those not relying on a well-defined, goal-based heuristic are likely to rely upon the most salient heuristic at any given moment, and salience is largely determined by emotions like fear and greed. In a bull market, high levels of performance are likely to serve as the benchmark while bear markets will lead to a more defensive mentality. The danger of processing information using moving targets like these is obvious to anyone in the business of financial advice giving: The client will live in a state of perpetual dissatisfaction and miss the opportunities available in both good times and bad.

The fourth step, not covered in great detail here is "decisions" which is simply the resolution to buy, sell, or hold. The fifth step is activation, which refers to a stage of procrastination and inhibition, even after a decision is made. It is only until the sixth step that we reach action and implementation of the decision.

This model is helpful and illuminating in depicting how people make financial decisions. In particular, Redhead emphasizes that financial decision making is not simply a matter of perceiving, deciding, and action. Instead, many pitfalls are waiting for us along the way.

Avoiding Financial Inhibition and Overconfidence

As anyone who has ever set a goal and failed to reach it can attest, making up your mind to do something is not enough. And unless we have sufficient motivation to carry out our best laid plans, we will fall prey to what psychologists call the "status quo bias" or tendency to do as we've always done. Redhead describes three psychological dynamics of financial inhibition that make it difficult for us to embark on a new goal:

- Status quo bias, meaning our tendency to keep an existing investment rather than switch to a new one. Investments we have tend to seem more valuable than investments we don't, thus the saying "A bird in the hand is worth two in the bush."

- Conservatism, meaning our reluctance to change due to our fear of change or the process of change. For example, whether or not we fear weighing less (whatever that means), we might fear the emotional pain we will endure in saying no to dessert. Conservatism is particularly alluring when one is uncertain about the costs and benefits of a decision.

- Confirmation bias, which involves looking for information that reinforces the goals or investments we already have and can over emphasize the case against change.

This triad of status quo bias, conservatism, and confirmation bias can fail the best of our goals and our most iron-clad resolutions, resulting in paralyzing financial inhibition that discourages saving. In Neukam and Hershey's (2003) study, those who saved most for retirement were those with the strongest financial goals and the lowest level of fear. In short, they had the least financial inhibition. Defining the purpose for our investments help us ward off these three horsemen of our own financial apocalypse along with the consequent financial inhibition.

We are not out of the woods yet, however. We also must be wary of greed, which catalyzes the sort of overtrading and overconfidence that is at least equally damaging as financial inhibition. Thus, reaching the final step of action requires taking particular actions that help us stay true to the purpose and goals for our investing as well as maintain a future orientation and appropriate horizon.

The degree to which we successfully reach Redhead's sixth step of action will have everything to do with the heuristics we have chosen, the way in which we have processed information relative to these rules of thumb and the degree to which we are emboldened to act on our good ideas. In all of these things, purpose is our North Star and a lack thereof leaves us rudderless in a stormy sea.

Avoiding Advisors Who Revere the Market Benchmark

To this point, we have only talked about the dangers of benchmarking for individuals, but it is also worth examining the ways in which our slavish obedience to benchmarks distorts the performance of even professional money managers. It does so in at least two ways: by homogenizing returns and by distorting the true meaning of safety and risk during extreme market conditions.

"No one ever got fired for hiring IBM." If you've spent any time in the business world at all, you're likely familiar with this saying, which represents the idea that individual performers are safe when going with a known quantity. In much the same way that many a middle manager has played it safe by working with IBM, many professional money managers are loathe to deviate from the benchmark. This reluctance is not because they have their clients' best interests at heart, but because they are worried about their own professional success.

Christopher H. Browne put it extremely well in his address to Columbia Business School,

> *Investment performance is generally measured against a benchmark, and claims to being long-term investors aside, the typical institutional client tracks performance*

on a monthly or quarterly basis versus the benchmark. Performance that deviates from the benchmark becomes suspect and can lead to termination of the money manager. Consistency of returns relative to the benchmark are more important than absolute performance especially in a world dominated by the hypothesis that asset allocation is more important than stock selection. Once the advisor figures out how he or she is being measured, they realize that tailoring the portfolio to the benchmark reduces the risk of relative underperformance and loss of the account. Unfortunately, the chances of significantly outperforming the benchmark are equally diminished.

—Browne 2000

Authors Lakonishak, Schliefer and Vishny share a similar sentiment in their book, *What Do Money Managers Do?* (1997), stating, "The process of selection and evaluation of money managers may actually distort their investment strategies" by referring to the system of judging money managers relative to market indices, which forces them to bunch their stock picks near the middle of the benchmark to avoid tracking error. Similarly, they tend to pick popular stocks and avoid extremes of valuation, all of which combines to make exceptional absolute returns difficult. As Robert Kirby of Capital Guardian once said, "If you are going to look like the benchmark, you can't beat the benchmark" (cited by Browne 2000). Thus, investors are left with the worst of both worlds—high fees and no real active management!

A second danger of benchmark adherence comes in times of market extremes (which seem to be happening with greater frequency). During extreme market highs and lows, utilization of the benchmark as the gold standard may skew what are some fundamental principals when viewed along a longer time horizon. Once again, Christopher H. Browne is on point in saying,

Adhering to value investment principles in periods such as 1998, 1999, and the first quarter of 2000 required a tremendous amount of conviction. You are derided for not adapting to a changing world, for failing to understand "new paradigms." How many times did we hear that the old methods of valuation were not relevant to the "new economy?" We were told that "hits," not profits, were what was important in valuing Internet companies. However, a business strategy *that cannot ultimately produce a profit means the business is ultimately worth zero. For example, Priceline.com traded as high as $138 per share on May 7, 1999 for a market capitalization in excess of $22 billion. On November 14, 2000 it closed at $2.78 for an eye-popping drop of 98 percent. We asked ourselves, do we really want to fly from New York to Miami via maybe Minneapolis and Charlotte and risk getting in at midnight, or do we want a bit more specificity in our travel plans? However, we were told we were out of touch.*

Today, Internet companies are going bankrupt as fast as they went public just 12 short months ago. If nothing else, the speed with which the world changes is certainly accelerating. Money managers are not stupid. They realize that sticking one's neck out and producing short-term under performance that differs from an index that is used as the benchmark is risky.

—Browne 2000

In these two respects, reverence for the benchmark becomes a "limit to arbitrage" or a restriction placed on funds that would normally be arbitraged away by rational traders. As long as the benchmark remains the gold standard, savvy money managers will be reticent to take non-normative bets and go against the grain, no matter how big an opportunity they may sense. After all, to do so would risk tracking error (e.g., deviation from the benchmark) that might cost them their livelihood. Upton Sinclair's (1934) words ring truer than ever, "It is difficult to get a man to understand something, when his salary depends on his not understanding it." It may be for different reasons, but the use of market indices as the standard of measurement increases irrationality and dopey behavior in both the retail and institutional money management space.

Going Your Own Way

Imagine that you are out for a night on the town with your significant other and, in an attempt to show yourself to be a person of sophistication, you have taken them to your favorite Puccini opera (incidentally, La Boheme will be your favorite if you are truly a person of taste). You are moved throughout the show, and at the end of the performance, you quickly rise to your feet and begin to applaud wildly. After a ponderous 15 seconds you notice that your date and fellow opera goers still remain seated, they having not been moved as deeply. What do you do? How difficult would it be to remain standing?

Now take the opposite approach. Suppose you were offended by the poor costuming and the inauthentic accents of the performers and did not see fit to give a standing ovation, although the rubes around you feel differently. How hard would it be to remain seated in a sea of hundreds of others standing?

In both cases, I think you will agree that going against the crowd is most difficult indeed, no matter how deeply convicted you may feel. The same is true of financial markets, where not only your convictions but also your cash is on the line.

Solomon Asch (1951) of Swarthmore College convincingly illustrated our need to conform in what are now known as the "Asch Conformity Experiments." Asch began by enlisting the help of seven "confederates," a fancy word for people who are in on the joke. Confederates were told that they would be shown lines like the ones pictured in Figure 8.2 and that they would be asked to select the

FIGURE 8.2

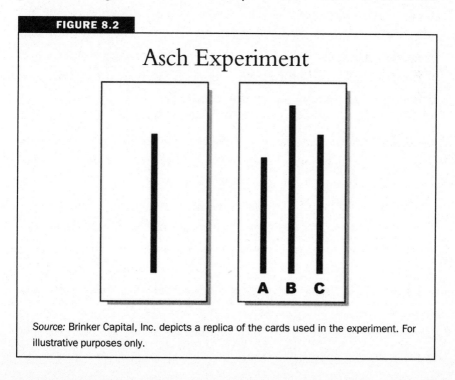

Asch Experiment

A B C

Source: Brinker Capital, Inc. depicts a replica of the cards used in the experiment. For illustrative purposes only.

line on the right that corresponded most closely with the one on the left.

So what was the catch? The seven confederates were told to "throw the contest" by giving an incorrect answer but doing so authoritatively. The one person not in on the joke went last, so that by this time, he had seen seven people respond conclusively in a manner inconsistent with what was right before his eyes. Much as in our opera example, personal convictions were placed in direct competition with the power of the crowd. In the Asch experiments, 75 percent of respondents succumbed to the herd on at least one occasion, showing how difficult it can be to stand alone, even when what is being asked is extremely simple. If it is difficult to swim upstream on such a simple task, how much more difficult is it to persevere in financial markets when so little seems certain?

Remaining a purpose-driven contrarian is not easy, but it is most certainly worth it. Not only does it have the immediate benefits thoroughly vetted in this chapter but it may also fundamentally change the way you think and lead to a virtuous cycle of "self-herding."

The neo-classical economic view is that economic decisions are reflective of hedonic utility, meaning you choose what you think will make you feel best (Ariely and Norton 2007). More recent research shows that both one's anticipated outcomes as well as past outcomes of related decisions inform our choices today.

This becomes more complicated when you consider that our memories, rather than being stored perfectly in mental folders, are constantly evolving and being shaped and reshaped by the stories we tell ourselves about the things we've experienced.

We like to think of ourselves as rational, competent human beings. This is partly why, as we look at our past actions, we infer some kind of utility from the decisions we've made. Also, if we've done something consistently, there was probably a very good reason for it! In light of this, every current decision becomes a combination of a forecasted future utility as well as blasting back into the past, to see if "I am the kind of person who does xyz behavior." Whether we are or are not that kind of person will subsequently inform all of our future decisions.

Thus, in a very real way, all of our present decisions are the sum total of a perceptual past and an imagined future. In this respect, our actions not only reveal our preferences, they go a long way toward creating them! Every current decision you make with respect to everything from who you love to how you invest, will increase or decrease the likelihood that you'll act similarly at some future date.

Simply put, your decision combines what you think will make you happiest in the future with an examination of what you have done in the past.

Summary

It is a difficult thing to avoid the herd and make personal financial decisions that may be uncomfortably non-conformist in the moment. However, once you have trained yourself to do so, you set in motion a virtuous cycle of "self-herding" wherein your past good behaviors serve as justification for more of the same down the road. Before long, it will become routine for you to pass on the immediate gratification of knowing what the market is doing moment to moment as you become increasingly aware of how such self-restraint can make your day . . . and your tomorrow.

References

Ariely, Dan and Michael I. Norton. "How Actions Create—Not Just Reveal— Preferences. (December 2007). *Neuroeconomics*, 12(1): 13–16. http://people .duke.edu/~dandan/Papers/Other/actionsCreate.pdf.

Asch, Solomon E. "Effects of group pressure on the modification and distortion of judgments." In *Groups, Leadership and Men*, ed. by Harold Guetzkow, 177–190. Pittsburgh: Carnegie Press, 1951.

Browne, Christopher H. "Value Investing and Behavioral Finance." Presentation to Columbia Business School, November 15, 2000. www.tweedy.com/ resources/library_docs/papers/ChrisBrowneColumbiaSpeech2000.pdf.

Gigerenzer, Gerd, and Reinhard Selten. *Bounded Rationality: The Adaptive Toolbox*. Cambridge: MIT Press, 2002.

Kahneman, Daniel, and Amos Tversky. "Prospect Theory: An Analysis of Decision under Risk." (March 1979). *Econometrica*, 47(2): 263–291. doi: 10.2307/1914185. JSTOR 1914185. www.princeton.edu/~kahneman/docs/Publications/prospect_theory.pdf.

Konnikova, M. "How Facebook Makes Us Unhappy." The New Yorker. (September 10, 2013). www.newyorker.com/online/blogs/elements/2013/09/the-real-reason-facebook-makes-us-unhappy.html.

Lakonishok, Josef, Andrei Shleifer, and Robert Vishny. 1997. "What Do Money Managers Do?" (Working paper). Boston: Harvard University.

Medvec, Victoria Husted, Scott F. Madey, and Thomas Gilovich. "When Less Is More: Counterfactual Thinking and Satisfaction Among Olympic Medalists." (1995). *Journal of Personality and Social Psychology*, 69(4): 603–610. http://psych.cornell.edu/sites/default/files/Medvec.Madey_.Gilo_.pdf.

Neukam, Kirstan A., and Douglas A. Hershey. "Financial Inhibition, Financial Activation, and Saving for Retirement." (January 2003). *Financial Services Review*, 12(1): 19–37. http://psychology.okstate.edu/images/files/hershey/9.pdf.

Redhead, Keith J. "A Behavioural View of How People Make Financial Decisions." (2009). Coventry University. www.coventry.ac.uk/Global/06%20Life%20on%20Campus%20section%20assets/Faculty%20of%20Business%20Environment%20and%20Society/Departments/SAM/Research%20Papers/Research%20Paper%202009%206.pdf.

Simon, Herbert. "A Behavioral Model of Rational Choice." (February 1955). *Quarterly Journal of Economics*, 69(1): 99–188. doi: 10.2307/1884852. http://ptfs.library.cmu.edu/awweb/main.jsp?flag=browse&smd=1&awdid=1.

Sinclair, Upton. I. *Candidate for Governor: And How I Got Licked*. Berkeley and Los Angeles: University of California Press, 1934.

Tversky, Amos, and Daniel Kahneman. "Judgment under Uncertainty: Heuristics and Biases." (September 27, 1974). *Science*, 185(4157): 1124–1131.

CHAPTER 9

Providing an Easy-to-Understand Explanation

Chuck Widger

Lucy, you got some 'splaining to do!

—Dezi Arnez to his wife Lucy Arnez

By using the bucket framework I am using a type of mental accounting which makes it easy to communicate important behavioral finance concepts, and consequently, I easily connected with two important new clients I had been unable to connect with for years.

—Michelle Curry, Financial Advisor

U p to this point in the book, we have outlined the theory underlying our Personal Benchmark solution, from the reasons we need to look at investing differently (Part 1), to the components of the Personal Benchmark approach (Part 2), and, in Part 3, how we use a goals-based approach and find our personal benchmark.

The remaining two chapters offer advisors practical tools to use with clients. Here, in Chapter 9, we provide an easy-to-understand explanation of Personal Benchmark that advisors and clients may find useful.

Explaining and applying complex investment and behavioral finance concepts or principles is not always easy. Frequently, the art of communicating advice is best done through pictures, graphs and charts, or mathematical proofs. With that in mind, this chapter provides ample charts, graphs, pictures, and descriptions you can use daily. This chapter's content was developed by Brinker Capital's consultants and staff of professionals who help advisors understand and communicate Brinker Capital's investment offerings every day. Let's begin.

Your Best Investment

What is your best investment? Stocks? Bonds? Precious metals? Art or jewelry? A family business or maybe education? Or is it some combination of these? (See Figure 9.1.)

Most people say it's their house.

The problem with this is depicted in Figure 9.2. Over the 40-year period from 1973 to 2013, average home prices rose from $29,900 in 1973 to $152,000 in 2013. While this represents an impressive increase in nominal value (a whopping 508 percent!), adjusting the initial $29,900 for inflation based on CPI means that the house value needs to be $158,000 just to have preserved the same purchasing power (see Figure 9.2). In short, not only did we fail to reap any sort of return *over 40 years* in our great housing investment, we actually lost 3.08 percent of our original principal.

Let's compare this disappointing result to what would have happened had we placed the $29,900 in 1973 in a stock portfolio. It would have grown to $880,000 (see Figure 9.3)!

FIGURE 9.1

What Is Your Best Investment?

| Stocks | Bonds | Art/Jewelry |
| Family Business | Education | Gold |

Source: Brinker Capital, Inc. For illustrative purposes only.

FIGURE 9.2

1973 Home Value Adjusted for Today's Inflation

1973 average home price	$ 29,900
2013 average home price	$152,000
Inflation-CPI	$158,000

Source: Average home price represented by U.S. Census Bureau "Median and Average Sales Price of Homes" report, 2013. Inflation-CPI obtained from the Bureau of Labor Statistics in the Department of Labor.

FIGURE 9.3

1973 Investment Adjusted for Today's Inflation

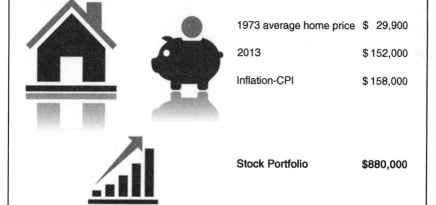

1973 average home price	$ 29,900
2013	$ 152,000
Inflation-CPI	$ 158,000
Stock Portfolio	**$880,000**

Source: Average home price represented by U.S. Census Bureau "Median and Average Sales Price of Homes" report, 2013. Inflation-CPI obtained from the Bureau of Labor Statistics in the Department of Labor. Stock portfolio results obtained from calculator. net and assumes a $29,900 initial investment in 1973 and 7.906% annual rate of return over 40 years.

FIGURE 9.4

The Problem, Opportunity and Solution in Investing

The Problem: Clients are Still Investing with Emotions

The Opportunity: It's time to Change the Conversation

The Solution: Brinker Capital My Personal Benchmark

Source: Brinker Capital, Inc. For illustrative purposes only.

In short, your house is not the best investment. An example of a better investment is an operating business, which compounds cash flow over time by reinvesting earnings into products and services in strong growing markets.

The choice seems to be clear: equities or equity-like investments are the right choice for growing purchasing power. So, why do investors still struggle with investment decisions? And why does the average investor underperform?

Because investment decisions often are made with our emotions steering the ship. As advisors, this presents an opportunity to change the conversation. The framework for doing so is Brinker Capital's Personal Benchmark (see Figure 9.4). Let's examine each of these in turn.

Once More, with Feeling

Time and again, investment after investment, emotions tend to drive investor behavior. Why? Daniel Kahneman, Nobel Prize winning expert on behavioral finance, puts it this way: "We are not usually rational or driven by logic. We humans are guided by the immediate and emotional impact of gains and loss, not the long term prospects of wealth." We learned in Chapter 2 that emotional decisions tend to be shortsighted, reactive, and associative. All of this means that we are more likely to eat the marshmallow we can get today, so to speak, rather than defer our gratification to get two tomorrow (see the discussion of Walter Mischel's 1972 marshmallow experiment in Chapter 7).

We're Not Dealing with Marshmallows Anymore

In Walter Mischel's 1972 work, the loss subjects incurred by making the emotional "now" decision was one marshmallow. In real life, the costs are usually far greater. A simple story demonstrates what our rather knee-jerk emotional investment decisions can lead to if we fail to think them through.

Before the days of modern plumbing, getting clean drinking water was no easy feat. And although the earliest evidence of plumbing was found in Mesopotamia dating back to around 3000 B.C.E., plumbing all but ceased during the Dark Ages following the fall of the Roman Empire in 476 C.E.

Thus, water developed a mystical status, due to its scarcity and people's vital need for it. Wells became a popular place for socializing and collecting water for drinking and bathing. According to European folklore, a wishing well was a sacred place where any spoken wish would be granted for a price (usually a penny). People still make wishes and drop coins today in fountains from New York's Bryant Park to Rome's Quirinale district, which houses the Trevi Fountain.

One day, two coworkers, Sam and Bob, approached the Bryant Park fountain, each with a penny in hand. It was a momentous time: in 30 days, they were both turning 65, mandatory retirement age at their organization and they would have to leave their jobs. It should have been a happy time, but each one held a secret: due to a series of poor decisions as well as unexpected economic downturns, neither of them were financially ready for this life change.

Sam stepped up to the fountain and whispered, "I want $1 million dollars" and dropped his coin in the fountain.

Nothing happened for a few seconds, but then suddenly, his pockets bulged and then they broke. Hundred dollar bills spilled down his pants legs. He was showered with money. He could not believe his eyes. His wish was instantly and completely granted!

Bob then stepped up to the fountain. He spoke, "I want just 1 penny. But I want the amount to double every day, for the next 30 days." With that, Bob threw in a penny, the only money he had, into the fountain.

Again, nothing happened for a few moments. The men looked at each other. Sam again was incredulous, this time because Bob would make such a foolish wish. Bob reached into his left pocket. Nothing. He reached into his right pocket. And he found . . . a single penny.

At that, Sam could no longer contain himself. He burst into uncontrollable laughter, equal parts relief, shock, and glee, tears streaming from his eyes. Dumbstruck at his own phenomenal success and his friend's sheer madness.

Eventually, Sam and Bob left the fountain, returning to their own homes. Each one safely put away his windfall: Sam, his $1 million and Bob, his one penny.

It must be said that the wishing well did work for Bob. The next day, he indeed did have two pennies where the previous day, he had one. And the day after that, he had four pennies where the previous day, he had two. This was nothing compared to Sam's amount, of course. He still had his $1 million dollars.

And so it went, day after day, with their fateful retirement day looming ever closer. Each day, Sam would ask, both teasing and jeering, "Hey, Bob, how's that wish coming?! What are you up to now?"

None of this bothered Bob, even though his responses of "16 cents" or even "$10.24" would send Sam into fits of laughter, every time.

But a funny thing happened as the days wore on. On Day 18, Bob's nest egg reached four figures: $1,310.72. And only 3 days later, it reached *five* figures: $10,485.76. Sam had to admit he was starting to get uneasy, seeing how fast Bob's single penny was growing. But he rapidly quashed any uneasy feelings with taking a peek at his own $1 million, still safe and sound.

But even this wouldn't calm Sam's anxieties with only 3 days to go till retirement. Bob arrived at work on time, sunny and whistling. *Whistling!* Sam felt sick to his stomach, his face ashen. "H–hey, Bob. H–how's your wish turning out?" he asked reluctantly, weakly.

"$1,342,177.28."

The windfall from Bob's penny, with the amount doubled daily, had exceeded Sam's $1 million just 28 days later by 34 percent!

After that, Sam stopped asking. And by Day 30, Bob's penny had matured into $5,368,709.12.

So demonstrates the illusory seduction of emotional thinking when investing. After all, on Day 1, who would choose to go home with one penny when they could go home with a fistful of dollars in the amount of $1 million? And up to Day 27, the emotionally driven investment would appear to be right. But that wasn't the end of the story. By Day 30, that penny, with the total amount doubled daily, exceeded the $1 million by 537 percent.

Thus is the power of compounding. Although we may not have a magic wishing well, we do have the capital markets. Investing in them does create astonishingly more over time than we may have ever asked for or imagined when we made our first investment, however meager.

The unfortunate truth, though, is that too many investors are Sam's, who focus on getting and simply saving a windfall, while too few are Bob's, who invest and capture the full benefits of the compounding of wealth and purchasing power by capital markets. Figure 9.5 shows how Sam and Bob's wealth grew day by day.

Figure 9.6 demonstrates the actual shortfall investors experienced in capital markets for the 30-year period ending December 31, 2013. The average fixed income fund investor yielded a mere 0.7 percent annualized return, in comparison to Barclays Capital Aggregate Bond Index (7.67 percent) and the S&P 500 Index (11.11 percent). Average individual investors have dramatically underperformed the market.

FIGURE 9.5

Sam's and Bob's Wealth Over 30 Days

Day	Sam	Bob
1	$1,000,000	$0.01
3	$1,000,000	$0.04
6	$1,000,000	$0.32
9	$1,000,000	$2.56
12	$1,000,000	$20.48
15	$1,000,000	$163.84
18	$1,000,000	$1,310.72
21	$1,000,000	$10,485.76
24	$1,000,000	$83,886.08
27	$1,000,000	$671,088.64
30	**$1,000,000**	**$5,368,709.12**

Source: Brinker Capital, Inc. For illustrative purposes only.

FIGURE 9.6

Performance of the Markets versus an Average Mutual Fund Investor

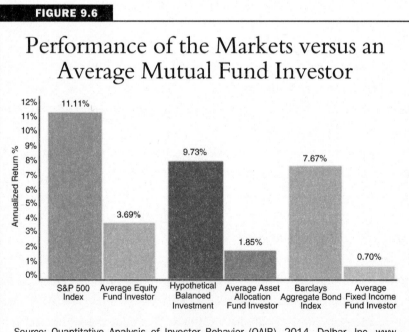

Source: Quantitative Analysis of Investor Behavior (QAIB), 2014, Dalbar, Inc. www
.dalbarinc.com. Data from January 1, 1984 to December 31, 2013. Average equity fund

(continued)

(continued)

investor and average bond fund investor performance results are based on the DALBAR 2014 QAIB study. DALBAR is an independent, Boston-based financial research firm. Using monthly fund data supplied by the Investment Company Institute, QAIB calculates investor returns as the change in assets after excluding sales, redemptions and exchanges. This method of calculation captures realized and unrealized capital gains, dividends, interest, trading costs, sales charges, fees, expenses and any other costs. After calculating investor returns in dollar terms, two percentages are calculated for the period examined: Total investor return rate and annualized investor return rate. Total return rate is determined by calculating the investor return dollars as a percentage of the net of the sales, redemptions, and exchanges for the period. Hypothetical Balanced Investment based on the performance of an investment weighted 50% to the S&P 500 index and 50% to the Barclays Aggregate Bond Index and rebalanced monthly. Equity benchmark performance is represented by the Standard & Poor's 500 Composite Index, an unmanaged index of 500 common stocks generally considered representative of the U.S. stock market. Fixed income benchmark performance is represented by the Barclays Aggregate Bond Index, an unmanaged index of bonds generally considered representative of the bond market. Indexes do not take into account the fees and expenses associated with investing, and individuals cannot invest directly in any index. Performance of an index is not illustrative of any particular investment. Past performance is no guarantee of future results.

We Haven't Got Time for the Pain

Whether it's investing in equities, forms of balanced investment funds or bond funds, the average investor simply underperforms. What explains this dubious track record? According to Shefrin and Statman's (2000) Behavioral Portfolio Theory, the pain of losses are more intolerable and acute than the pleasure of gains are gratifying. People feel awful when their investment account values fall −10 percent to −20 percent and just have to unload the failing investment to end the torture. Figure 9.7 makes the point that Brinker Capital's purpose is to help advisors narrow the investor "behavior gap trap."

Understanding that investors make emotional decisions is only a first step. You likely have seen this behavior in your own clients many times. So where do we go from here? We need to change the conversation.

FIGURE 9.7

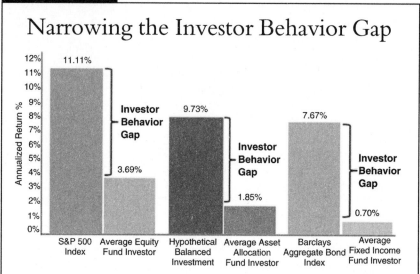

Narrowing the Investor Behavior Gap

Source: Quantitative Analysis of Investor Behavior (QAIB), 2014, Dalbar, Inc. www .dalbarinc.com. Data from January 1, 1984 to December 31, 2013. Average equity fund investor and average bond fund investor performance results are based on the DALBAR 2014 QAIB study. DALBAR is an independent, Boston-based financial research firm. Using monthly fund data supplied by the Investment Company Institute, QAIB calculates investor returns as the change in assets after excluding sales, redemptions and exchanges. This method of calculation captures realized and unrealized capital gains, dividends, interest, trading costs, sales charges, fees, expenses and any other costs. After calculating investor returns in dollar terms, two percentages are calculated for the period examined: Total investor return rate and annualized investor return rate. Total return rate is determined by calculating the investor return dollars as a percentage of the net of the sales, redemptions, and exchanges for the period. Hypothetical Balanced Investment based on the performance of an investment weighted 50% to the S&P 500 index and 50% to the Barclays Aggregate Bond Index and rebalanced monthly. Equity benchmark performance is represented by the Standard & Poor's 500 Composite Index, an unmanaged index of 500 common stocks generally considered representative of the U.S. stock market. Fixed income benchmark performance is represented by the Barclays Aggregate Bond Index, an unmanaged index of bonds generally considered representative of the bond market. Indexes do not take into account the fees and expenses associated with investing, and individuals cannot invest directly in any index. Performance of an index is not illustrative of any particular investment. Past performance is no guarantee of future results.

Changing the Conversation

Helping investors shift how they make investment decisions requires shifting how we talk to them about these decisions. This goes for new and existing clients. One place to start is exposing three common investing pitfalls, as identified by the co-author Dr. Daniel Crosby.

Staying Power

Proponents of efficient market theory would have us believe that financial asset prices are set by rational investors who process all current information available on an investment opportunity in the capital markets. This is a nice idea; however, investors simply do not weigh information objectively. Instead, decisions run amok based on recently processed and emotionally charged data.

Our saving grace is defined personal goals. Data shows that for purposeful investment solutions, like 529 plans and retirement plans, investors tend to ride their investments through various market conditions and resist the seduction of the information that would so easily lead them astray. Those investors who do have the wherewithal to do so often are handsomely rewarded. Figure 9.8 shows the steady growth of assets in retirement plans and 529 plans over a 13-year period.

What if we created purposeful goals for the investor's entire portfolio? Our experience shows that under such conditions, investors are more likely to put recent data in perspective and set aside emotionally charged data in favor of the purpose and logic of their stated portfolio investment strategy. They develop staying power.

A Different Kind of Bucket List

In Chapter 2, we first learned about mental accounting, which means that investors make decisions based on the label or purpose they put on a set of funds. For example, people spend "bonuses," but save "reimbursements" and "rebates." Chapter 5 elaborated on this idea in some detail.

The bottom line, when we want to shift the conversation with investors, we need to stop thinking about Our Investment (a singular

FIGURE 9.8

Growth of Assets in Retirement Plans and 529 Plans Over a 13-Year Period

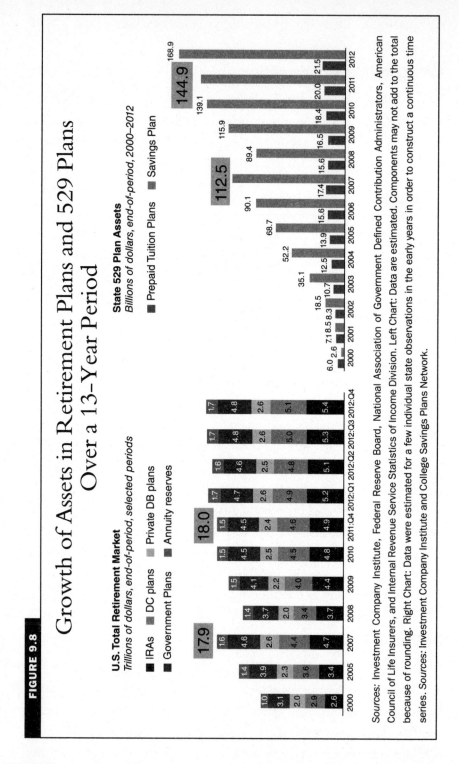

U.S. Total Retirement Market
Trillions of dollars, end-of-period, selected periods

■ IRAs ■ DC plans ■ Private DB plans
■ Government Plans ■ Annuity reserves

State 529 Plan Assets
Billions of dollars, end-of-period, 2000–2012

■ Prepaid Tuition Plans ■ Savings Plan

Sources: Investment Company Institute, Federal Reserve Board, National Association of Government Defined Contribution Administrators, American Council of Life Insurers, and Internal Revenue Service Statistics of Income Division. Left Chart: Data are estimated. Components may not add to the total because of rounding. Right Chart: Data were estimated for a few individual state observations in the early years in order to construct a continuous time series. *Sources:* Investment Company Institute and College Savings Plans Network.

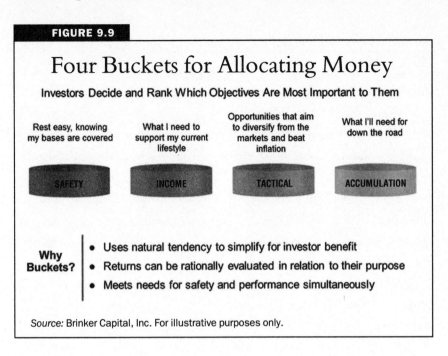

FIGURE 9.9

Four Buckets for Allocating Money

Investors Decide and Rank Which Objectives Are Most Important to Them

Rest easy, knowing my bases are covered	What I need to support my current lifestyle	Opportunities that aim to diversify from the markets and beat inflation	What I'll need for down the road
SAFETY	INCOME	TACTICAL	ACCUMULATION

Why Buckets?
- Uses natural tendency to simplify for investor benefit
- Returns can be rationally evaluated in relation to their purpose
- Meets needs for safety and performance simultaneously

Source: Brinker Capital, Inc. For illustrative purposes only.

amount of invested capital) and start thinking about the different uses, purposes, and consequent strategies for a diversified portfolio of investments. We suggest four mental buckets (see Figure 9.9):

1. Safety, which preserves principal and reduces overall portfolio volatility.

2. Income, which generates cash flow while limiting volatility.

3. Tactical, which manages volatility and focuses on opportunity for appreciation.

4. Accumulation, which involves appreciation and acceptance of greater volatility for the purpose of future purchasing power.

Deliberately creating these buckets then gives us a new way to think about, talk about, develop and report on an investor's portfolio strategy. More importantly, our experience shows that these buckets help investors resist emotional and investment volatility by properly framing their investment choices.

An Offer They Cannot Refuse

In addition to creating buckets, the principles of mental accounting remind us of the power of words.

Studies show time and again that we are duped pretty much every time when presented with two equal alternatives that are worded differently. Consider the following example from classic behavioral finance.

Psychology professor Thomas Gilovich surveyed people to find out how many agreed they could save 20 percent of their income and how many agreed they could live on 80 percent of their income. You'd expect the same results for both questions, right? Wrong. In fact, the results were downright astonishing (see Figure 9.10).

Out of every 10 people asked, only 5 agreed they could save 20 percent of their income. However, when the question was flipped and they were asked if they could live on 80 percent of their income, 3 people changed their answer: a full 80 percent agreed they could! This represents a 60 percent increase in a positive response.

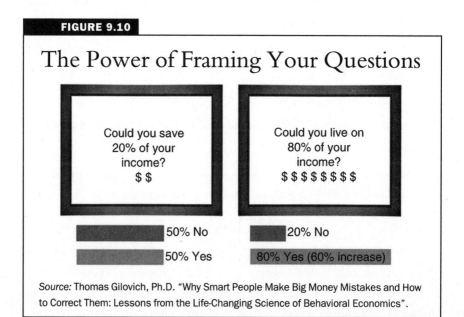

FIGURE 9.10

The Power of Framing Your Questions

Could you save
20% of your
income?
$ $

Could you live on
80% of your
income?
$ $ $ $ $ $ $ $

50% No

50% Yes

20% No

80% Yes (60% increase)

Source: Thomas Gilovich, Ph.D. "Why Smart People Make Big Money Mistakes and How to Correct Them: Lessons from the Life-Changing Science of Behavioral Economics".

The implication is clear: we, as advisors, must choose our words carefully, phrasing investors' best options and choices in ways they cannot refuse.

The Brinker Capital Personal Benchmark Solution

Warren Buffett is noted for saying, "There are two rules for making money." Rule #1 is "don't lose money." Rule #2 is "go back to rule number one." Brinker Capital has created a seamless investment offering called Personal Benchmark that offers support for front-end sales, portfolio construction, and back-end reporting (see Figure 9.11).

Personal Benchmark combines the power of Brinker Capital's time-tested multi-asset class investment philosophy with insights from behavioral finance theories—an innovative investment offering in the industry.

Personal Benchmark gives advisors a tool for changing the conversation with investors so that they avoid the emotional decision making that has undermined so many. The rest of this chapter reviews some of

FIGURE 9.11

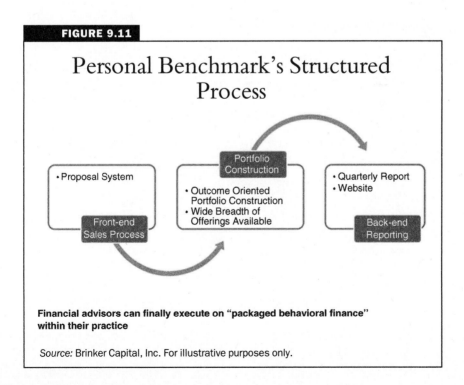

Personal Benchmark's Structured Process

- Proposal System

Front-end Sales Process

Portfolio Construction

- Outcome Oriented Portfolio Construction
- Wide Breadth of Offerings Available

- Quarterly Report
- Website

Back-end Reporting

Financial advisors can finally execute on "packaged behavioral finance" within their practice

Source: Brinker Capital, Inc. For illustrative purposes only.

the key ways Personal Benchmark helps investors manage volatility and capital losses en route to achieving attractive risk-adjusted returns.

Six Asset Classes

Brinker Capital's several investment offerings all practice its multi-asset class investment philosophy (see Figure 9.12), and each has actual track records of producing attractive risk-adjusted returns (see Chapter 4 for a full discussion). Several of Brinker Capital's investment offerings are used to implement Personal Benchmark.

This multi-asset class investment philosophy enables the investor to manage the volatility of the investment portfolio, which is key to creating purchasing power. When volatility is not managed, return is drained from the portfolio as investors cannot stick with their investment strategy and make decisions based on behavioral factors that jeopardize their ability to meet their long-term goals. As shown in Figure 9.13, although both Scenario A and B yield an average annual return of 0 percent, the

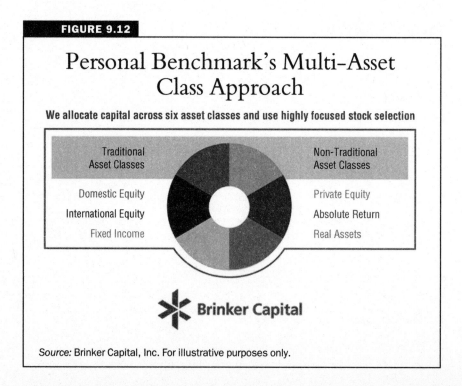

FIGURE 9.12

Personal Benchmark's Multi-Asset Class Approach

We allocate capital across six asset classes and use highly focused stock selection

Traditional Asset Classes	Non-Traditional Asset Classes
Domestic Equity	Private Equity
International Equity	Absolute Return
Fixed Income	Real Assets

Brinker Capital

Source: Brinker Capital, Inc. For illustrative purposes only.

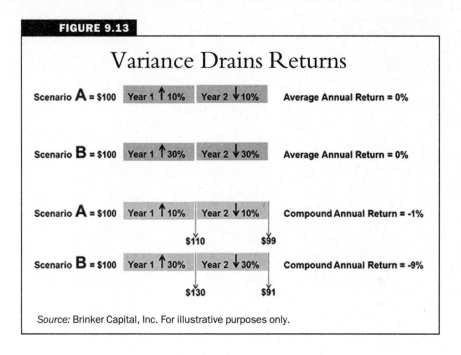

FIGURE 9.13

Variance Drains Returns

Scenario **A** = $100 | Year 1 ↑ 10% | Year 2 ↓ 10% | Average Annual Return = 0%

Scenario **B** = $100 | Year 1 ↑ 30% | Year 2 ↓ 30% | Average Annual Return = 0%

Scenario **A** = $100 | Year 1 ↑ 10% | Year 2 ↓ 10% | Compound Annual Return = -1%
$110 $99

Scenario **B** = $100 | Year 1 ↑ 30% | Year 2 ↓ 30% | Compound Annual Return = -9%
$130 $91

Source: Brinker Capital, Inc. For illustrative purposes only.

compound annual return for Scenario A (after a return of 10 percent in Year 1 and −10 percent in Year 2) is −1 percent, whereas compound annual return for Scenario B (after a return of 30 percent in Year 1 and −30 percent in Year 2) is −9 percent. The point to remember here is that wider swings produce a lower compounded annual return. Variance drains return and reduces ending portfolio values.

Mental Accounting and Buckets

Personal Benchmark utilizes the concept of mental accounting to help investors constrain irrational thought and emotional interference. The process begins by identifying their objectives (or several conflicting purposes) and determining the relative importance of each.

Mental accounting is enacted in Personal Benchmark when advisors work with investors to create an investment strategy based on the four buckets. This changes the conversation by allocating investor investment dollars based on the way investors actually think. Figure 9.14 illustrates the unique visual tool advisors use to help the investor initially identify an

FIGURE 9.14

Visually Intuitive Allocation Tool: Buckets Help Simplify the Process for Investors

Source: Brinker Capital, Inc. For illustrative purposes only.

asset allocation which suits the investor's risk tolerance and return objectives.

What's special about this tool is that the advisor can easily adjust the nature of the portfolio from more aggressive to more conservative using the digit on the risk–return continuum slide. Consider it the investor's own "sleep" number. They're not just for mattresses anymore! As the portfolio's composition shifts, the amount of assets allocated to each bucket adjusts and the cylinder diagram also adjusts accordingly.

What's more, by using this simple and intuitive tool, the traditional questions from the investment questionnaire are answered. Once the investor agrees to the visually depicted composition, the advisor confirms the answers to the questionnaire.

This unique application was made possible by the imagination of Andrew Rosenberger, a talented Brinker Capital portfolio manager, and the programming prowess of Brinker Capital's Web team.

FIGURE 9.15

Brinker Capital Investment Strategy Matrix

	Safety	Income	Tactical	Accumulation	Mix
Preservation and Income	35% Destinations Defensive	40% Crystal Diversified Income	25% Crystal Strategy I		20/80
Conservative	45% Destinations Defensive		25% Crystal Strategy I	30% Destinations Moderate	30/70
Conservative Income	25% Defensive	30% Crystal Diversified Income	20% Crystal Strategy I	25% Destinations Moderate	30/70
Stable Growth	25% Destinations Defensive		20% Crystal Strategy I	55% Destinations Moderate	40/60
Stable Growth and Income	10% Defensive	30% Crystal Diversified	10% Crystal Strategy I	50% Destinations Moderate	40/60
Balanced Growth	30% Destinations Defensive		20% Crystal Strategy I	50% Destinations Aggressive	50/50
Balanced Growth and Income	20% Defensive	30% Destinations Balanced Income	15% Crystal Strategy I	35% Destinations Aggressive	50/50
Growth	15% Destinations Defensive		20% Crystal Strategy I	65% Destinations Aggressive	60/40
Growth and Income	10% Defensive	20% Destinations Balanced Income	15% Crystal Strategy I	55% Destinations Aggressive	60/40
Accumulation	10% Destinations Defensive		10% Crystal Strategy I	80% Destinations Aggressive	70/30

Source: Brinker Capital, Inc. For illustrative purposes only. Holdings subject to change.

Embedded in the logic of the Personal Benchmark system are 10 possible investment strategies. Each strategy has a long-established track record, which makes it possible to reasonably determine the risk and return characteristics of the investor's portfolio strategy. Thus, each strategy can be carefully matched to the investors' profile of questionnaire answers and stated risk and return preferences.

Thus, once the nature of the portfolio is confirmed using the buckets, complete with risk and return objectives, the Personal Benchmark system pulls in the appropriate mix of Brinker Capital investment strategies from the Brinker Capital Investment Strategy matrix. This mix constitutes the investor's portfolio strategy (see Figure 9.15).

Now Sit Back, Relax, and Enjoy the Ride

With the mental accounting reconciled and the strategies chosen, it is time for the investor to sit back and enjoy the ride. Personal Benchmark reports provide intuitive illustrations of the performance of the different

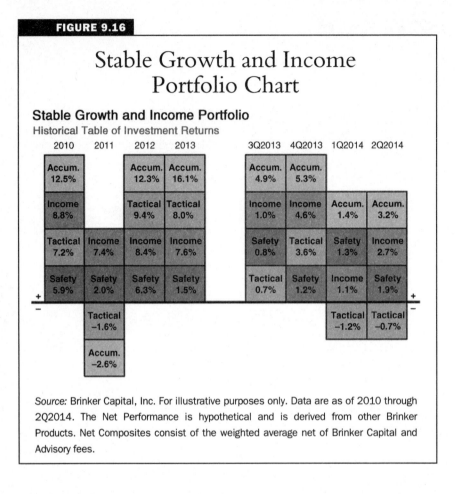

FIGURE 9.16

Stable Growth and Income Portfolio Chart

Stable Growth and Income Portfolio
Historical Table of Investment Returns

2010	2011	2012	2013		3Q2013	4Q2013	1Q2014	2Q2014
Accum. 12.5%		Accum. 12.3%	Accum. 16.1%		Accum. 4.9%	Accum. 5.3%		
Income 8.8%		Tactical 9.4%	Tactical 8.0%		Income 1.0%	Income 4.6%	Accum. 1.4%	Accum. 3.2%
Tactical 7.2%	Income 7.4%	Income 8.4%	Income 7.6%		Safety 0.8%	Tactical 3.6%	Safety 1.3%	Income 2.7%
Safety 5.9%	Safety 2.0%	Safety 6.3%	Safety 1.5%		Tactical 0.7%	Safety 1.2%	Income 1.1%	Safety 1.9%
		Tactical −1.6%					Tactical −1.2%	Tactical −0.7%
		Accum. −2.6%						

Source: Brinker Capital, Inc. For illustrative purposes only. Data are as of 2010 through 2Q2014. The Net Performance is hypothetical and is derived from other Brinker Products. Net Composites consist of the weighted average net of Brinker Capital and Advisory fees.

buckets for the time period requested by the advisor. The resulting easy-to-use charts help advisors explain the relative performance of the buckets to investors.

For example, Figure 9.16 displays the Stable Growth and Income Portfolio for calendar years 2010, 2011, 2012, and 2013. Quarterly performance is also displayed for the most recent four quarters (in this case, the third quarter of 2013 through the second quarter of 2014).

Examining the figure, we find that all the buckets did well in 2013's third and fourth quarters. Looking back further, we see that 2011 was a challenging year for risky assets. However, the negative year for risky assets was nicely offset by the Income and Safety buckets, thereby preserving capital and reducing volatility.

Did you notice anything missing throughout this discussion? There was no mention of alpha, Beta, Sharpe ratio or beating indices. Rather, at Brinker Capital, we emphasize that the advisor–investor conversation and the entire investment experience begins and ends with the investor's personal goals. Our philosophies, tools, and advisory approaches provide a consistent message that when it comes to capital markets, it is all about the individual investor, not the herd.

Persuasive Phrases

Bob Fillmore, a very sophisticated and seasoned advisor with offices in Denver and Las Vegas, reviewed this chapter as part of the development process of the book. He offered some great suggestions on persuasive phrases advisors can use in communicating the Personal Benchmark concepts. Bob called them "power phrases."

Bob's great suggestions on how to change the investment advisory conversation are as follows:

- Acknowledge that emotions drive investor behavior.

- Leverage Daniel Kahneman's quote: "We are not usually rational or driven by logic. We humans are guided by the immediate and emotional impact of gains and loss, not the long term prospects of wealth."

- Compounding creates more and investing in capital markets in fact does create more.

- All too frequently, investors sell low and buy high. Why? Because decisions get made on the basis of emotion rather than logic.

- Personal Benchmark is packaged behavioral finance.

- The key to achieving attractive returns is to manage risk, both volatility and the more fundamental risk of losing money.

- Managing volatility is the key to creating purchasing power. It's not about eye-catching returns.

Summary

At Brinker Capital, we understand that, as humans, we are prone to multiple emotional stumbling blocks that ultimately undermine our investment performance. Thus, we recognize the need to change the conversation. It begins by defining the investor's personal goals and then framing investments in ways that match how investors think and help them develop the inner fortitude to weather the inevitable storms of the capital markets.

Brinker Capital's Personal Benchmark solution gives advisors an intuitive set of tools to guide them through the process of defining the investor's preferred risk–return profile and selecting an appropriate strategy that is time-tested to deliver the desired investment experience. The next chapter examines this solution in greater detail.

References

Dalbar, Inc. *Quantitative Analysis of Investor Behavior*. Boston: Dalbar, 2014.

Mischel, Walter, Ebbe B. Ebbesen and Antonette Raskoff Zeiss. "Cognitive and attentional mechanisms in delay of gratification." (January 1972). Journal of Personality and Social Psychology, 21(2): 204–218. doi: 10.1037/h0032198.

Shefrin, Hersh, and Meir Statman. (2000). "Behavior Portfolio Theory." Journal of Financial and Quantitative Analysis, 35(2): 127–151. doi: 10.2307/2676187 www.scu.edu/business/finance/research/upload/bpt.pdf.

CHAPTER 10

Leveraging a Scalable Offering for Investors and Advisors

Chuck Widger

I have been using different investment strategies to achieve the different purposes established in the financial plans I do for clients. Brinker Capital's Personal Benchmark formalizes the multiple strategy investment advisory process and provides consolidated reporting, thereby enhancing the entire investment advisory process.

—David Poole, Financial Advisor

In the preceding chapters, we provided an overview of the Personal Benchmark solution and a detailed discussion of Brinker Capital's investment philosophy. We also offered advisors an easy-to-understand and easy-to-use explanation of Personal Benchmark.

In this chapter, advisors are provided with a practical illustration of the scalable system through which an advisor implements Personal Benchmark. Lastly, the benefits of this system to an advisor's practice are discussed.

Using Personal Benchmark

The Personal Benchmark solution is illustrated next through a case study. Chapter 1 introduced you to Jim Dodd, a hypothetical client. In this chapter, we discuss Jim in two scenarios:

- Scenario 1: Jim has $800,000 in assets in a single registration. His goals are to have current income and growth to create future purchasing power. Jim can accept some volatility or fluctuation in investment values.

- Scenario 2: Jim's wife Jane is introduced. In this scenario, Jim has $300,000 individually and $100,000 in an IRA. His wife Jane has $500,000 in her own name and $100,000. Family assets total $1,000,000.

Beginning the Process

An advisor begins the process by signing onto Brinker Capital's proposal generation system, ProGen, via the Brinker Capital website (see Figure 10.1). Upon signing in, you will see the opening screen, which presents a list of your completed proposals and proposals in progress (see Figure 10.2). At this point, you could select one of these proposals, create a new proposal, or complete the Brinker Capital questionnaire for a single or multiple registration.

Accessing the Investor's Portfolio

Alternately, to rapidly access Personal Benchmark, you may click the "Quick Track" button (see Figure 10.3). This action will produce a

FIGURE 10.1

Personal Benchmark Sign-In Page

Proposals

Welcome to ProGen Systems, Your Enhanced Proposal Generation System

Source: Brinker Capital, Inc. Hypothetical example for illustrative purposes only.

FIGURE 10.2

List of Completed Proposals and Proposals in Progress

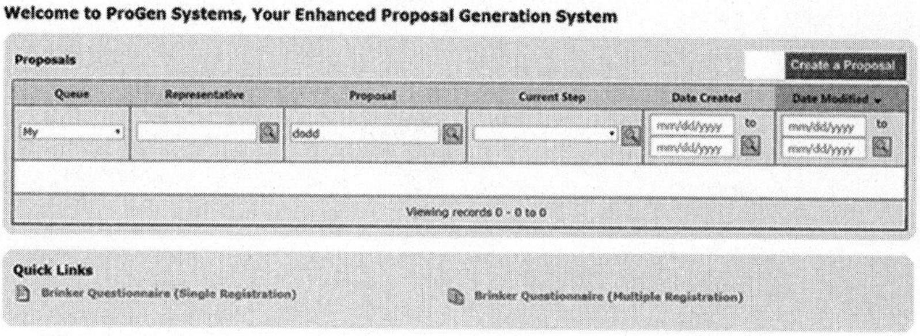

Welcome to ProGen Systems, Your Enhanced Proposal Generation System

Proposals						Create a Proposal
Queue	Representative	Proposal	Current Step	Date Created	Date Modified ▾	
My ▾	🔍	dodd 🔍	▾ 🔍	mm/dd/yyyy to mm/dd/yyyy 🔍	mm/dd/yyyy to mm/dd/yyyy 🔍	

Viewing records 0 - 0 to 0

Quick Links

📄 Brinker Questionnaire (Single Registration)   📄 Brinker Questionnaire (Multiple Registration)

Source: Brinker Capital, Inc. Hypothetical example for illustrative purposes only.

FIGURE 10.3

Rapid Access to Personal Benchmark

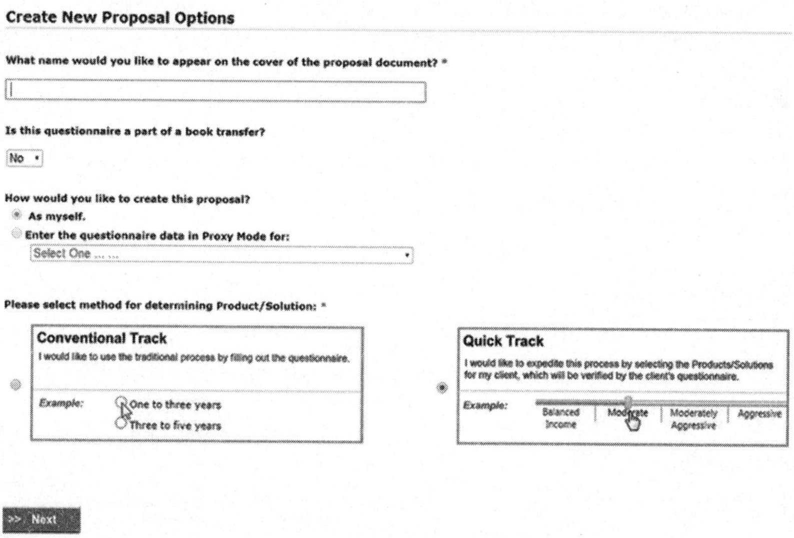

Create New Proposal Options

What name would you like to appear on the cover of the proposal document? *

[ ]

Is this questionnaire a part of a book transfer?

[No ▾]

How would you like to create this proposal?
- ● As myself.
- ○ Enter the questionnaire data in Proxy Mode for:
  [Select One ... ... ▾]

Please select method for determining Product/Solution: *

Conventional Track
I would like to use the traditional process by filling out the questionnaire.

Example: ● One to three years
○ Three to five years

Quick Track
I would like to expedite this process by selecting the Products/Solutions for my client, which will be verified by the client's questionnaire.

Example:
| Balanced Income | Moderate | Moderately Aggressive | Aggressive |

>> Next

Source: Brinker Capital, Inc. Hypothetical example for illustrative purposes only.

FIGURE 10.4

Brinker Capital's Products and Solutions

Source: Brinker Capital, Inc. Hypothetical example for illustrative purposes only.

display of the portfolio of Brinker Capital Products and Solutions, one of which is Personal Benchmark (see Figure 10.4).

In our case, we are interested in viewing Jim Dodd's registrations. Therefore, on the opening screen, we clicked on Jim Dodd's entry. We are then presented with the complete information we have on file for this client. The data is organized in 12 tabs, starting with Proposal Options and ending with the list of Documents. Here, we will walk you through some of the key tabs.

Clicking on the "Product" tab, we see that the Dodds have four registrations: an individual and an IRA registration each for Jim and Jane (see Figure 10.5).

FIGURE 10.5

The Dodds' Registrations

Proposal Options	Rep Info	Registration	Product	Objective	Client	Addl Info	Distribution Info	Summary	Asset Allocation	Fees	Documents

Registration Name	Registration Type	Proposal Amount	Product	
Jim Dodd	Individual	$300,000.00	Personal Benchmark - Household (Product Min. $1M, Registration Min. $100K)	▼
Jane Dodd	Individual	$500,000.00	Personal Benchmark - Household (Product Min. $1M, Registration Min. $100K)	▼
Jim Dodd IRA	IRA	$100,000.00	Personal Benchmark - Household (Product Min. $1M, Registration Min. $100K)	▼
Jane Dodd IRA	IRA	$100,000.00	Personal Benchmark - Household (Product Min. $1M, Registration Min. $100K)	▼

Source: Brinker Capital, Inc. Hypothetical example for illustrative purposes only.

Viewing and Creating the Investor's Personal Benchmark

Clicking on the "Objective" tab presents Personal Benchmark for the Dodd account in total (see Figure 10.6). Please note that this screen allows you to adjust the risk–return continuum for each registration.

It is important to note that people always have a mix of short- and long-term risk preferences and that the time horizon for each goal determines the level of risk. For example, funding a college education over the next few years requires an allocation to safety and perhaps income. Investment for retirement in 15–20 years requires allocations to accumulation and perhaps tactical.

To adjust the profile, you would move the indicator right or left until the right risk–return balance for the client is achieved. The percentage allocated to each of the buckets in the pictured cylinder changes as the profile shifts. A description of the portfolio (in the Dodds' case, "Stable Growth and Income") also is presented.

Also on this tab is the traditional investment questionnaire (see Figure 10.7). Note that the questionnaire has been pre-populated based on the risk–reward balance selected on the previous screen. After you confirm the questionnaire answers with the investor, you must click the box indicating, "I confirm that the answers to these questions reflect my

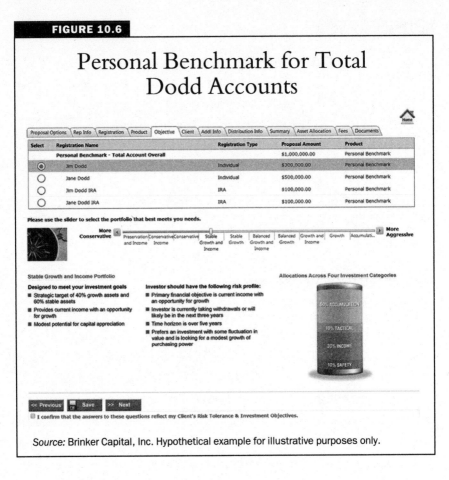

FIGURE 10.6

Personal Benchmark for Total Dodd Accounts

Source: Brinker Capital, Inc. Hypothetical example for illustrative purposes only.

Client's Risk Tolerance & Investment Objectives" and then click "Next" to proceed to the selected Portfolio Investment Strategy Summary.

Reviewing the Investor's Portfolio Investment Strategy

You may view a summary of the Investment Strategy by clicking the "Asset Allocation" tab (Figure 10.8). Here the registrations for Jim and

FIGURE 10.7

Traditional Investment Questionnaire

Please complete the following questions as they apply specifically to the assets under consideration for this investment strategy proposal. **Brinker Capital will identify your overall investment objective based on your responses to the following questions.** Please consider your response to each question carefully to avoid responses that conflict with one another. **Fields marked with * are required.**

1. Financial Objective (choose one)*
- ○ Income
- ◉ Income and capital appreciation
- ○ Capital appreciation and income
- ○ Capital appreciation
- ○ Substantial capital appreciation

2. What is your investment time horizon for these assets? *
- ○ One to three years
- ○ Three to five years
- ◉ Five to ten years
- ○ Ten years or more

3. Please rank your top two items of relative importance to you from the following choices: Rank as #1 your most important item and #2 as your second most important item. *

1.	Liquidity (ability to convert assets to cash within a short time frame)
2.	Inflation protection (rate of return required to offset inflation over time)
3.	Current income
4.	Income and capital appreciation
5.	Capital appreciation and income
6.	Substantial capital appreciation

Rank #1 ○1 ○2 ◉3 ○4 ○5 ○6

Rank #2 ○1 ○2 ○3 ◉4 ○5 ○6

4. For this portfolio, you would like to invest in assets that offer: (choose one) *
- ◉ Current income with modest fluctuation in value
- ○ Competitive total return (appreciation and some income) with moderate fluctuation of principal
- ○ The potential for high capital appreciation with possibility of substantial fluctuation in principal

5. Which of the following hypothetical investment scenarios most appeals to you (choose A, B or C)? *

	Annualized Return Goal	Return During a Positive Year	Return in a Negative Year	Chance of Losing Money in a year
A	10%	40%	-20%	1 in 4
B	8%	26%	-10%	1 in 5
C	6%	18%	-6%	1 in 6

Source: Brinker Capital, Inc. Hypothetical example for illustrative purposes only.

Jane are reviewed and the allocation for all four registrations are depicted. The Portfolio Investment Strategy listed in the table at the top is characterized as Stable Growth and Income. The cylinder reveals that this strategy allocates 10 percent to Safety, 30 percent to Income, 10 percent to Tactical, and 50 percent to Accumulation. The particular investment strategy per bucket also is displayed (e.g., the Accumulation bucket is using Brinker Capital's Destinations Moderate-Taxable strategy). If you are satisfied with the summary, you may click the "Next" button to proceed to the document selection screen.

FIGURE 10.8

Summary of the Dodds' Investment Strategy

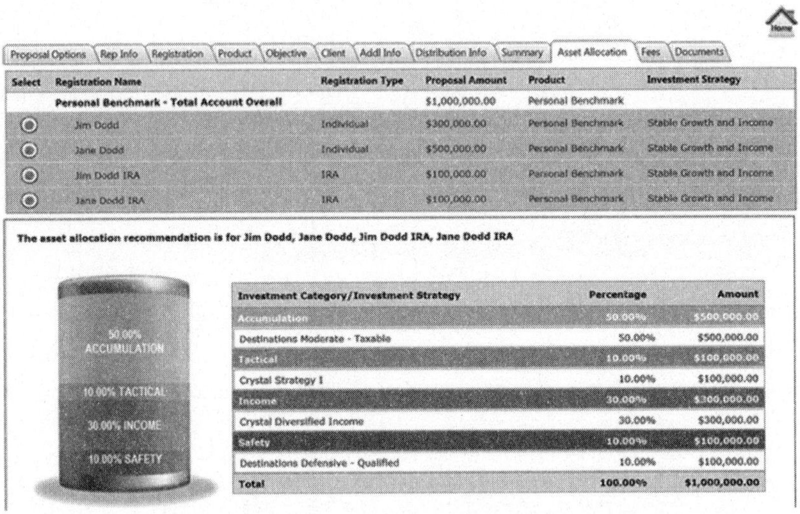

| Proposal Options | Rep Info | Registration | Product | Objective | Client | Add'l Info | Distribution Info | Summary | Asset Allocation | Fees | Documents |

Select	Registration Name	Registration Type	Proposal Amount	Product	Investment Strategy
	Personal Benchmark - Total Account Overall		$1,000,000.00	Personal Benchmark	
◉	Jim Dodd	Individual	$300,000.00	Personal Benchmark	Stable Growth and Income
◉	Jane Dodd	Individual	$500,000.00	Personal Benchmark	Stable Growth and Income
◉	Jim Dodd IRA	IRA	$100,000.00	Personal Benchmark	Stable Growth and Income
◉	Jane Dodd IRA	IRA	$100,000.00	Personal Benchmark	Stable Growth and Income

The asset allocation recommendation is for Jim Dodd, Jane Dodd, Jim Dodd IRA, Jane Dodd IRA

Investment Category/Investment Strategy	Percentage	Amount
Accumulation	50.00%	$500,000.00
Destinations Moderate - Taxable	50.00%	$500,000.00
Tactical	10.00%	$100,000.00
Crystal Strategy I	10.00%	$100,000.00
Income	30.00%	$300,000.00
Crystal Diversified Income	30.00%	$300,000.00
Safety	10.00%	$100,000.00
Destinations Defensive - Qualified	10.00%	$100,000.00
Total	100.00%	$1,000,000.00

(Pie chart: 50.00% ACCUMULATION, 10.00% TACTICAL, 30.00% INCOME, 10.00% SAFETY)

Source: Brinker Capital, Inc. Hypothetical example for illustrative purposes only.

Reviewing the Investor's Documents and Proposal

The "Documents" tab lists the various paperwork available for our selected client (see Figure 10.9). In our case, we simply want a proposal at this point in the investment advisory process. Under the "Proposals" tab, we see the entry for Jim Dodd and click "View/Print" so we may have a printed proposal to present to the investor.

The proposal, called the *Investment Strategy Recommendation*, is roughly 20 pages in length. The first part of the proposal includes standard educational pieces that all investors receive, including:

- The advisor's role and the roles Brinker Capital and the investment managers play.

FIGURE 10.9

Documents Available for the Dodds' Account

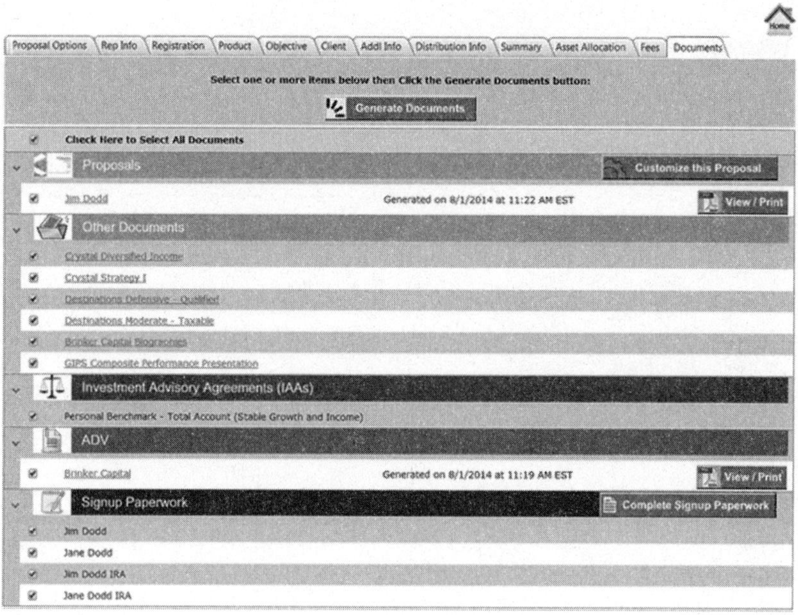

Source: Brinker Capital, Inc. Hypothetical example for illustrative purposes only.

- The investment advisory process and principles that guide Brinker Capital's portfolio construction process.
- Brinker Capital's multi-asset class investment philosophy in a clear and succinct fashion, along with calendar annual performance of Brinker Capital's six asset classes.
- Empirical proof statement for multi-asset class investing (see Chapter 6 for a discussion of the empirical support for multi-asset class investing).
- Brinker Capital's current key investment themes.
- The broad array of communication tools Brinker Capital makes available to advisors and investors.

FIGURE 10.10

Dodds' Combined Recommended Strategy

Detailed Investment Strategies

Account Registration	Brinker Program	Assets
Jim Dodd	Personal Benchmark - Crystal Diversified Income	$300,000
Jane Dodd	Personal Benchmark - Destinations Moderate - Taxable	$500,000
Jim Dodd IRA	Personal Benchmark - Crystal Strategy I	$100,000
Jane Dodd IRA	Personal Benchmark - Destinations Defensive - Qualified	$100,000
Total		$1,000,000

Overall Diversification

- Domestic Equity 26.59%
- International Equity 11.94%
- Fixed Income 42.35%
- Absolute Return 8.35%
- Real Assets 7.65%
- Private Equity 3.12%

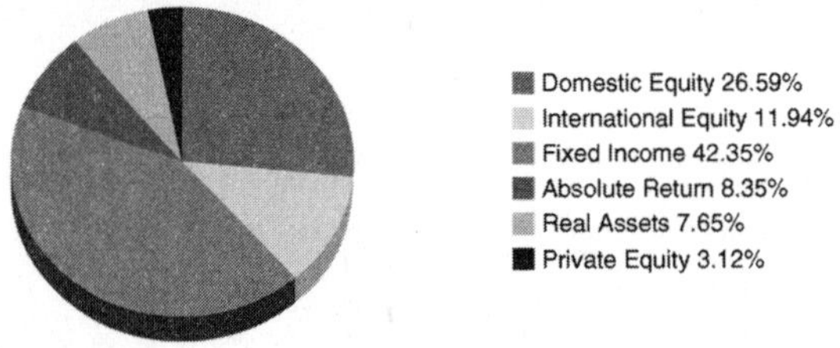

Source: Brinker Capital, Inc. Hypothetical example for illustrative purposes only.

The second half of the proposal includes information for the specific investor, customized based on the selected profile and investment strategy. This section includes:

- A summary of the registrations, the Brinker Capital program selected for each, and a visual display of the overall diversification approach (see Figure 10.10).

- Report of the overall investment objective, framed in terms of the four buckets, along with a description of this investment objective (see Figure 10.11).

- Year-to-date, 1-year, 3-year annualized and since inception performance of the chosen investment strategy (see Figure 10.12).

- Illustrated growth of a $100,000 investment of the previous 5 years (see Figure 10.13).

- Full disclosure of program fees (see Figure 10.14).

FIGURE 10.11

Dodds' Recommended Investment Strategy: Personal Benchmark

Portfolio Holdings

Investment Category/Strategy	Registration Name	Target Allocation	Target Allocation
Accumulation		$500,000	50.00%
Destinations Moderate - Taxable	Jane Dodd	$500,000	50.00%
Tactical		$100,000	10.00%
Crystal Strategy I	Jim Dodd IRA	$100,000	10.00%
Income		$300,000	30.00%
Crystal Diversified Income	Jim Dodd	$300,000	30.00%
Safety		$100,000	10.00%
Destinations Defensive - Qualified	Jane Dodd IRA	$100,000	10.00%
TOTAL		$1,000,000	100.00%

Overall Investment Objective: Stable Growth and Income

Designed to meet the following investment goals:
- Strategic target of 40% growth assets and 60% stable assets
- Provides current income with an opportunity for growth
- Modest potential for capital appreciation

Investor should have the following risk profile:
- Primary financial objective is current income with an opportunity for growth
- Investor is currently taking withdrawals or will likely be in the next three years
- Time horizon is over five years
- Prefers an investment with some fluctuation in value and is looking for a modest growth of purchasing power

Source: Brinker Capital, Inc. For illustrative purposes only. The categorizations are based upon data provided by Morningstar, Inc. as interpreted by Brinker Capital. The investment style categorization is based upon the primary asset class/style represented by a fund or manager, even though it may not be the exclusive asset class/style represented by the fund or manager.

The content and format of the *Investment Strategy Recommendation* is clear and crisp, having been tested and refined for over 27 years of practice in support of various Brinker Capital investment products, through numerous Personal Benchmark focus groups, and now in the ongoing successful offering of Personal Benchmark in the marketplace.

FIGURE 10.12

Dodds' Recommended Investment Strategy Historical Performance

Performance Through 06/30/2014

Annualized	QTD	YTD	1 Year	3 Year	Since Inc. (1/1/2009)
Recommended Investment Strategy	2.59%	3.77%	11.62%	7.40%	9.93%
CPI	0.87%	1.32%	2.08%	1.85%	2.15%
Calendar Year	2013	2012	2011	2010	2009
Recommended Investment Strategy	11.06%	9.92%	1.49%	9.43%	19.66%
CPI	1.51%	1.76%	3.02%	1.42%	2.81%

Historical Table of Investment Returns

2010	2011	2012	2013		3Q2013	4Q2013	1Q2014	2Q2014
Accum 10.96%		Accum 11.69%	Accum 15.67%		Accum 4.83%	Accum 5.28%		
Income 8.80%		Tactical 9.38%	Tactical 7.95%		Income 1.04%	Income 4.62%	Accum 1.62%	Accum 3.31%
Tactical 7.18%	Income 7.43%	Income 8.37%	Income 7.59%		Safety 0.77%	Tactical 3.60%	Safety 1.31%	Income 2.66%
Safety 5.95%	Safety 2.04%	Safety 6.29%	Safety 1.53%		Tactical 0.68%	Safety 1.15%	Income 1.11%	Safety 1.91%
	Accum -1.57%						Tactical -1.23%	Tactical -0.68%
	Tactical -1.61%							

Source: Brinker Capital, Inc. For illustrative purposes only. The performance information for the Personal Benchmark strategies presents back-tested performance of a hypothetical account invested with the specific investment strategies (or a proxy thereof) included in the Recommended Investment Strategy and not the historical performance of actual accounts invested in the Recommended Investment Strategy. Calculations assume annual rebalancing of the account to the target allocations in the Recommended Investment Strategy. No representation that any actual account has achieved such performance is intended. The performance information does not reflect the deduction of advisory fees payable to Brinker Capital or other expenses for services not covered by the advisory fee. These fees and expenses will reduce an investor's return.

FIGURE 10.13

Historical Performance Of Dodds' Recommended Investment Strategy: Personal Benchmark

Jim Dodd, Jane Dodd, Jim Dodd IRA, Jane Dodd IRA

Growth of $100,000

January 2009 - June 2014

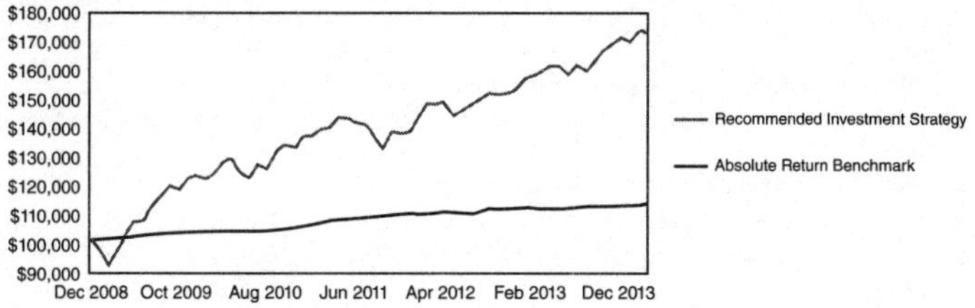

Calendar Year Gross Performance

	YTD	2013	2012	2011	2010	2009
Recommended Investment Strategy	3.77%	11.06%	9.92%	1.49%	9.43%	19.66%
Absolute Return Benchmark	1.32%	1.51%	1.76%	3.02%	1.42%	2.81%

Gross Annualized Return though Jun 2014

	YTD	1 Year	3 Year	5 Year	Std.Dev.
Recommended Investment Strategy	3.77%	11.62%	7.40%	9.70%	7.00%
Absolute Return Benchmark	1.32%	2.08%	1.85%	2.05%	0.67%

Source: Brinker Capital, Inc. Hypothetical example for illustrative purposes only. The performance information for the Personal Benchmark strategies presents back-tested performance of a hypothetical account invested with the specific investment strategies (or a proxy thereof) included in the Recommended Investment Strategy and not the historical performance of actual accounts invested in the Recommended Investment Strategy. Calculations assume annual rebalancing of the account to the target allocations in the Recommended Investment Strategy. No representation that any actual account has achieved such performance is intended. The performance information does not reflect the deduction of advisory fees payable to Brinker Capital or other expenses for services not covered by the advisory fee. These fees and expenses will reduce an investor's return. The standard deviation shown is for the length of time displayed on the Growth of $100,000 Chart.

FIGURE 10.14

Disclosure of Program Fees

Your Program Fees

Based upon this proposal of $1,000,000.00, the blended fee payable to Brinker Capital for all assets in your Personal Benchmark accounts is 0.55% annualized. This blended fee will vary based upon the investment strategy selected and total account value (resulting from appreciation, depreciation, liquidations, or additional contributions) in accordance with Brinker Capital's fee schedule for the Personal Benchmark program. Brinker Capital may change the fee schedule for the Personal Benchmark program on 30 days advance written notice to you.

Your fee covers the following costs associated with your investments:

- Compensation to Brinker Capital and Avery Cook for assisting in the development and ongoing monitoring of your investment strategy
- Your investment strategy recommendations
- Compensation to the coordinating sub-adviser for portfolio implementation and coordination services
- Fees paid to your investment managers for asset management services
- Transaction costs generated in the purchase and sale of equity securities in your portfolio
- Customized quarterly reporting, monthly statements and trade confirmations
- Access to Brinker Capital Online Services
- All ongoing asset manager and mutual fund due diligence provided by Brinker Capital
- Custody of the assets in your portfolio

Account Registration	Investment Strategy	Assets	Fee
Jim Dodd	Personal Benchmark	$300,000.00	0.55%
Jane Dodd	Personal Benchmark	$500,000.00	0.55%
Jim Dodd IRA	Personal Benchmark	$100,000.00	0.55%
Jane Dodd IRA	Personal Benchmark	$100,000.00	0.55%

The total annual fee is exclusive of mutual fund expense ratios and ETFs, which are set forth in the prospectus for each fund. A fund expense ratio represents the percentage of the fund's assets that go toward the expense of running the fund. A fund expense ratio reflects the fund's investment advisory fee, administrative costs, distribution fees and other operating expenses, which are paid by the fund and reduce the fund's net asset value. A higher percentage of smaller Personal Benchmark accounts will be invested in funds rather than allocated to separate account managers in order to obtain greater diversification among asset classes and investment styles.

Brinker Capital will debit your account at the beginning of each quarter based on the previous quarter's ending balance. Your initial quarterly fee will be pro-rated based upon the beginning value of your account and Brinker Capital will debit your account the month following your initial investment.

Asset allocations will be reviewed annually on the approximate anniversary of the opening of the Personal Benchmark account, and following an addition or withdrawal to the Personal Benchmark account which would result in an adjustment to Brinker Capital's fee.

Source: Brinker Capital, Inc. Hypothetical example for illustrative purposes only.

Implementing the Strategy and Monitoring Investor Performance

Once the Investment Advisory Agreement between the investor, advisor and Brinker Capital is signed and the investor's assets are transferred to the investor's account at the custodian bank, Brinker Capital directs the investment of the investors' transferred amounts into the securities, as dictated by the selected Brinker Capital investment strategy.

Thereafter, when the investment process is completed, advisors and investors can access relevant account information 24/7 via Brinker

FIGURE 10.15

Dodds' Account Snapshot

<< Back to last search result
Account Snapshot for Dodd Total Account

Account Name	Account Number	% Allocation	Market Value
Dodd Total Account		100.00%	$1,508,790.00
Jim Dodd IRA	Show Less ▲		

Account Name	Account Number	% Allocation	Market Value
Crystal Strategy I	DODPBM02	8.8%	$133,054.00
Jim Dodd	Show Less ▲		

Account Name	Account Number	% Allocation	Market Value
Crystal Diversified Income	DODPBM03	27.5%	$415,106.00
Jane Dodd	Show Less ▲		

Account Name	Account Number	% Allocation	Market Value
Destinations Moderate - Taxable	DODPBM01	56.2%	$847,461.00
Jane Dodd IRA	Show Less ▲		

Account Name	Account Number	% Allocation	Market Value
Destinations Defensive - Qualified	DODPBM04	7.5%	$113,169.00

⦿ Personal Benchmark View ○ Six Asset Class View

56.2% ACCUMULATION
27.5% INCOME
8.8% TACTICAL
7.5% SAFETY

Investment Category/Strategy	% Allocation	Market Value
Accumulation		
Destinations Moderate - Taxable	56.2%	$847,461.00
Income		
Crystal Diversified Income	27.5%	$415,106.00
Tactical		
Crystal Strategy I	8.8%	$133,054.00
Safety		
Destinations Defensive - Qualified	7.5%	$113,169.00

Performance Summary	MTD	QTD	YTD	Since Inception**	Inception Date
Total Portfolio		2.7%	3.9%	10.1%	12/31/08
Accumulation					
(DODPBM01) Destinations Moderate - Taxable		3.3%	5.0%	12.3%	12/31/08
Income					
(DODPBM03) Crystal Diversified Income		2.7%	3.8%	8.5%	12/31/08
Safety					
(DODPBM04) Destinations Defensive - Qualified		1.9%	3.2%	4.7%	12/31/08
Tactical					
(DODPBM02) Crystal Strategy I		-0.7%	-1.9%	7.6%	12/31/08

** Annualized for accounts invested over one year.
*Market values for equities, corporate, government and agency bonds are typically updated by 9AM Tuesday-Saturday. Prices for securities listed on non-U.S. based exchanges may be additionally delayed due to time zone differences. Municipal bond values are updated monthly.

Source: Brinker Capital, Inc. Hypothetical example for illustrative purposes only.

Capital's website. Among the most utilized pieces of information is the account snapshot (see Figure 10.15).

Beginning the first full quarter after the account is established, the investor and the advisor receive a Personal Benchmark Performance Report. Brinker Capital conducted numerous focus groups to assure that the report includes the right mix of information and is presented in an intuitive, easy-to-deliver, and clear format.

The Account Summary page of the performance report presents three types of data pertinent to investment performance (see Figure 10.16). The

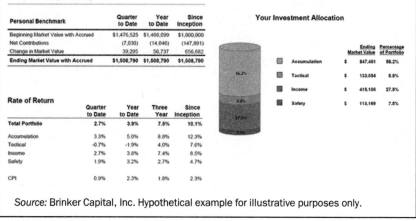

FIGURE 10.16

Dodds' Account Summary

Account Activity Summary

Personal Benchmark	Quarter to Date	Year to Date	Since Inception
Beginning Market Value with Accrued	$1,476,525	$1,466,099	$1,000,000
Net Contributions	(7,030)	(14,046)	(147,891)
Change in Market Value	39,295	56,737	656,682
Ending Market Value with Accrued	$1,508,790	$1,508,790	$1,508,790

Rate of Return

	Quarter to Date	Year to Date	Three Year	Since Inception
Total Portfolio	2.7%	3.9%	7.6%	10.1%
Accumulation	3.3%	5.0%	8.6%	12.3%
Tactical	-0.7%	-1.9%	4.0%	7.6%
Income	2.7%	3.8%	7.4%	8.5%
Safety	1.9%	3.2%	2.7%	4.7%
CPI	0.9%	2.3%	1.8%	2.3%

Your Investment Allocation

		Ending Market Value	Percentage of Portfolio
Accumulation	$	847,461	56.2%
Tactical	$	133,054	8.8%
Income	$	415,106	27.5%
Safety	$	113,169	7.5%

Source: Brinker Capital, Inc. Hypothetical example for illustrative purposes only.

first section investors and advisors generally consult is the Account Activity Summary. It answers their number one question: "What did I make in absolute or dollar terms?" In this case, Jane and Jim are up $508,790 quarter to date.

The second section, Rate of Return, presents the return information for the total portfolio and for each of the buckets. In this case, the total portfolio is up 2.7 percent for the quarter and 10.1 percent since inception. Importantly, this section also reports the CPI, the benchmark for the portfolio investment strategy. It is the central thesis of Personal Benchmark that an investors' key goal is—to increase their purchasing power, which is to compound above the rate of inflation. Given that the CPI is 0.9 percent for the quarter and 2.3 percent since inception (compared to the Dodds' portfolio performance of 2.7 percent and 10.1 percent, respectively, the Dodds' portfolio investment strategy is creating purchasing power).

The third section, Investment Allocation, reiterates the percentage allocated to each bucket and reports the ending market value of each bucket.

The performance report also includes a Risk Return Plot (see Figure 10.17), which graphically indicates the annualized return for the total portfolio as well as the four buckets. This is included in the report only when the account has been established for more than a year. In the Dodds

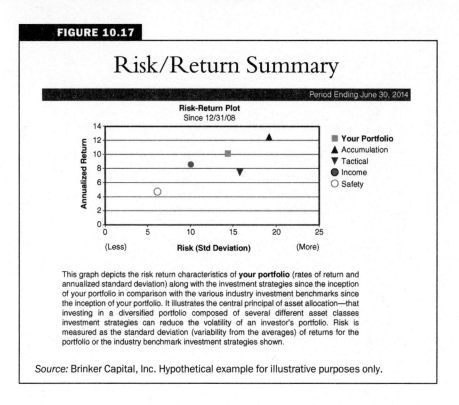

FIGURE 10.17

Risk/Return Summary

Period Ending June 30, 2014

Risk-Return Plot
Since 12/31/08

■ Your Portfolio
▲ Accumulation
▼ Tactical
● Income
○ Safety

Annualized Return

Risk (Std Deviation)
(Less)   (More)

This graph depicts the risk return characteristics of **your portfolio** (rates of return and annualized standard deviation) along with the investment strategies since the inception of your portfolio in comparison with the various industry investment benchmarks since the inception of your portfolio. It illustrates the central principal of asset allocation—that investing in a diversified portfolio composed of several different asset classes investment strategies can reduce the volatility of an investor's portfolio. Risk is measured as the standard deviation (variability from the averages) of returns for the portfolio or the industry benchmark investment strategies shown.

Source: Brinker Capital, Inc. Hypothetical example for illustrative purposes only.

case, the Plot shows that the annualized return for Accumulation is greater than the other buckets. The lower returns for the other three buckets pulled down the returns for the total portfolio.

The performance report presents the investor's progress in increasing purchasing power for each bucket and context (see Figure 10.18).

The left side of the page displays a summary of the investor's performance versus plan both in two formats. First, a written summary reiterates the goal for each bucket and summarizes the performance to date. Second, a table presents each bucket's performance year-to-date and since inception.

In this case, all four buckets are exceeding the purchasing power goal of meeting or exceeding the CPI. For example, the goal for the Accumulation bucket was CPI +4 percent over a 10-year period. The summary indicates "YTD Return in the Accumulation pool exceeds the stated goal" and "Since Inception Return in the Accumulation pool exceeds the stated goal" and the table shows the supporting figures that

FIGURE 10.18

Personal Benchmark Evaluation

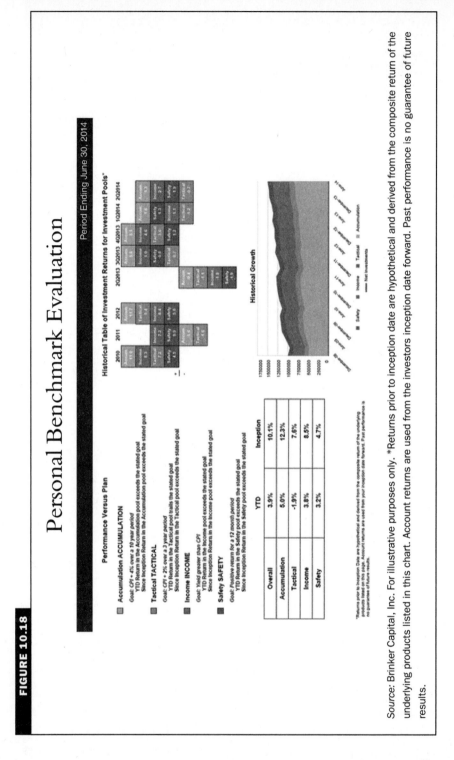

Source: Brinker Capital, Inc. For illustrative purposes only. *Returns prior to inception date are hypothetical and derived from the composite return of the underlying products listed in this chart. Account returns are used from the investors inception date forward. Past performance is no guarantee of future results.

Accumulation is compounding at 5 percent year-to-date and 12.3 percent since inception.

The upper right, or northeast quadrant depicts the performance for each bucket for the three preceding calendar years. Quarterly performance for the previous five quarters also is presented. Buckets are presented in descending order based on return.

This quilt chart communicates context by illustrating that the relative performance of each bucket can vary quarter-to-quarter and year-to-year. For example, in 2011 the accumulation bucket was down 1.6 percent and down 0.4 percent in 2Q2013. However, it was the top-performing bucket for all other periods. It also reports the strongest since-inception performance (12.3 percent) than any other bucket. Thus, although each bucket's performance will vary over time, ultimately, Brinker Capital's time-tested investment strategies should generate returns that exceed the rate of inflation, as measured by the Consumer Price Index (CPI).

The graph in the lower right or southeast quadrant presents a picture of how each bucket contributes to the growth of the portfolio's assets.

Importantly, the Personal Benchmark Performance Report does not include as performance benchmarks for any capital market indices. This is deliberate, as Brinker Capital's philosophy is that index-guided investment strategies mislead investors. When investors focus on, "How did I do in comparison to the S&P 500 Index?" they select investment strategies that will achieve that outcome. This means investors tend to assume greater levels of risk than they actually understand and can accept when the "risk hits the fan." For example, virtually no investor considered the more than 50 percent drop in equity market prices during 2008–2009 acceptable.

Therefore, the Personal Benchmark Performance Report directs the investor's focus toward the true desired outcome: the creation of purchasing power to fund investor's lifestyle.

To help you guide investors through this goals-based performance report, Brinker Capital provides a guide with each performance report (see Figure 10.19). Among other things, the guide explains that framing

FIGURE 10.19

Guide to the Performance Report

Brinker Capital

Personal Benchmark

Guide to
Goals–Based
Performance
Reporting

2Q2014

Brinker Capital designed Personal Benchmark to be an investment strategy that helps create purchasing power and manage the behavioral conflicts which surface while advising investors.

This guide will help you better understand the enhancements to the Performance Report and can be used as a tool to deepen the relationship with your client.

Frame the discussion: It's a joint commitment

Historically, investment performance rather than good investor behavior has thought to be the primary determinant of investment success. However, we now know that investor behavior accounts for at least half of performance success, meaning that both the financial advisor and the client have an important role in ensuring that goals are met.

Take this opportunity to make a joint commitment with your client. Reinforce the value you bring to the relationship is to help them make sound investment decisions, provide encouragement and education as well as serve as a resource and sounding board for all financial decisions. Reinforce that your client's commitment should be to maintain a long–term focus, adhere to personal (rather than market) benchmarks, make ongoing contributions as necessary and avoid emotion–laden irrational behavior. Framing the conversation this way is not only more accurate, it also empowers the investor, who may not have realized the positive power he or she can exert over the process.

By framing long-term goals into smaller buckets, the advisor provides more opportunities for success, which is likely to encourage further rational investment behavior.

Be sure to congratulate your client as they achieve small milestones in each of their buckets and provide them with a sense of how far they have come and how far they have yet to go.

– Daniel Crosby, Ph.D.

Use mental accounting to help investors understand the investment strategy: Make it personal

Investors tend to mentally account for money relative to the goals they have assigned to a certain bucket of money. Money that is lumped into one large account, as is typically done at investment houses, has no particular power to motivate. However, money that has been segmented into buckets that have deep personal meaning can serve to "bake in" good behavior. There are three primary reasons why this is the case – personal goals are likely to be long or medium term, they have the salience to increase saving and they provide more chances for measurable, incremental progress. Take the time each quarter to reinforce the investor's purpose for each investment category – or "bucket" – and how it performed.

Investment Allocations	Purpose	Quarterly Commentary (As of 6/30/14)
SAFETY	The safety bucket focuses on protecting purchasing power	The safety bucket generated a modest return for the second quarter, helped by strong performance of equity strategies, closed–end funds and yield advantaged fixed income. The safety bucket is designed to provide stability in times of market stress, and will typically provide a modest return when market returns are strong.
INCOME	The income bucket focuses on providing current income	The income bucket posted solid gains as interest rates have settled into a range and investors have again embraced yield producing assets, including REITs, MLPs and dividend paying stocks. Overall, income generated by income strategies has been lower than the historic average, investors have to be careful not to over–extend risk to make up for lower yields in this environment.
TACTICAL	The tactical bucket focuses on responding to the markets	The tactical bucket was slightly negative as the addition of equity hedges in the portfolio detracted from performance in a rising market. Moving into the third quarter, the strategy remains conservatively positioned with a focus on adding value through country and security selection rather than adding outright equity exposure.
ACCUMULATION	The accumulation bucket focuses on growing purchasing power over time	Global equity markets continued to climb higher in the second quarter, a positive for accumulation assets. While we continue to be positive on risk assets going forward, investors should remember that building wealth is not a linear process and to expect bumps in the road in the future.

Source: Brinker Capital. Holdings subject to change.

Brinker Capital, Inc., a Registered Investment Advisor.   800.333.4573   1055 Westlakes Drive / Suite 250 / Berwyn, PA 19312

For one–on–one use with financial advisors.   PB_GUIDE_QRTLY

Source: Brinker Capital, Inc. For illustrative purposes only.

FIGURE 10.19

Continued

Personal Benchmark

Guide to Goals-Based Performance Reporting

Focus on what matters most: Resolve simultaneous risk preferences

Rather than having a single risk preference, which can be mapped along an efficient frontier, a client's willingness to take risk is impacted by the way in which they have framed their goal. The more important a goal is and the nearer the timeline, the less risk they ought to take, and vice versa. Traditional portfolios have lumped all accounts into a single performance measure, typically compared to a benchmark to gauge performance. The problem with this practice is that clients tend to want risk in bull markets and safety in bear markets, regardless of what they said in early conversations around risk.

A bucketed approach allows advisors to continuously measure and adjust the balance of a portfolio specifically to meet the goals of the client and provides them with opportunities for safety and risk in all markets. Whereas traditional portfolios lead to almost constant dissatisfaction because they are "never quite right". A Personal Benchmark portfolio accounts for investors' simultaneous preferences and provides the advisor with safety and risk talking points in all markets. Instead of using a market index as a benchmark, be sure to compare the results of the bucket to the specific goal it is supposed to be meeting and make adjustments accordingly.

Portfolio Management Team

Jeff Raupp, CFA
Sr. Investment Manager
MBA, Villanova Univ.
B.S., Univ. of Delaware

Amy Magnotta, CFA
Sr. Investment Manager
B.S., Lehigh University

Andy Rosenberger, CFA
Sr. Investment Manager
B.S., The Pennsylvania State University

Firm Overview

Brinker Capital is an investment management firm and one of the nation's leading independent providers of managed account and mutual fund investment services. Through our innovative investment products, we seek to provide real purchasing power for investors and sustainable purchasing power for future generations. Brinker Capital was founded in 1987 by Charles Widger and is located in suburban Philadelphia.

Historical Table of Investment Returns

Source: Brinker Capital.
Performance shown is for the BalancedGrowth & Income Qualified Strategy.

As you begin the discussion to review the quarterly report with your client, remember to reinforce this is part of a joint commitment, personalize the purpose for each "bucket" and frame the discussion to compare results to the specific goal it is supposed to be meeting.

For More Information

Contact a member of your Brinker Capital Client Service Team at 800-333-4573

Advisory fees are described in Brinker Capital's Form ADV, Part 2A. Returns for periods exceeding one year are annualized. Past performance is no guarantee of future results. Brinker Capital does not have composite historical performance information for the Personal Benchmark Program. The performance results contained herein do not represent the actual trading or investment performance of actual accounts invested in accordance with the Recommended Investment Strategy but were produced through the retroactive application of the Recommended Investment Strategy using the target allocations to the specific investment strategies included in the Recommended Investment Strategy as currently configured, which was developed with the benefit of hindsight. No representation that any actual account has achieved such performance is intended. All calculations are based on monthly data and assume annual rebalancing of the account to the target allocations in the Recommended Investment Strategy. The calculations do not reflect the rebalancing methodology that Brinker Capital intends to utilize in connection with the management of accounts invested in its Personal Benchmark Program, which methodology allows for some "drift" from the targeted allocations of an Investment Strategy and, therefore, may permit greater variation from the target allocations than are reflected in the back-tested performance results included herein. However, Brinker Capital believes that annual rebalancing of the hypothetical account for purposes of back-testing performance of the recommended Investment Strategy will provide the closest approximation of the performance of an account invested in the recommended Investment Strategy.

Returns are calculated gross (before the deduction) of advisory fees payable to Brinker Capital and any other expenses for services not covered by the advisory fee including administrative costs, which would reduce your return. The net effect of the deduction of Brinker Capital's fees on annualized performance, including the compounded effect over time, is determined by the relative size of the fee and the account's investment performance. The chart below depicts the effect of a 1% management fee on the growth of one dollar over a ten year period at 10% (9% after fees), 5% (4% after fees) and 3% (2% after fees) assumed rates of return.

Year	1	2	3	4	5	6	7	8	9	10
10%	1.10	1.21	1.33	1.46	1.61	1.77	1.95	2.14	2.36	2.59
9%	1.09	1.19	1.30	1.41	1.54	1.68	1.83	1.99	2.17	2.37
5%	1.05	1.10	1.16	1.22	1.28	1.34	1.41	1.48	1.55	1.63
4%	1.04	1.08	1.12	1.17	1.22	1.27	1.32	1.37	1.42	1.48
3%	1.03	1.06	1.09	1.13	1.16	1.19	1.23	1.27	1.30	1.34
2%	1.02	1.04	1.06	1.08	1.10	1.13	1.15	1.17	1.20	1.22

 Brinker Capital   brinkercapital.com   800 333 4573   1055 Westlakes Drive / Suite 250 / Berwyn, PA 19312

For one-on-one use with financial advisors.

the portfolio investment strategy through mental accounting helps advisors and investors reconcile differing simultaneous risk preferences.

Reaping Benefits for Advisors

Personal Benchmark holds the promise of many benefits for advisors. Below, we have listed just 10 of the benefits advisors may anticipate by using the solution.

1. Different way to frame, structure, and monitor investments: In Personal Benchmark, the advisory experience begins by framing investments in light of investors' goals, yielding a highly personalized approach. The investors' goals are then reflected in allocations to four buckets, each of which has a specific purpose. Investors then are able to monitor their progress against their stated goals rather than against capital market indices. This is a dramatic and beneficial departure from how traditional investing portfolios are planned, executed, and monitored.

2. Manage behavioral biases: The advisory process embedded into Personal Benchmark helps advisors and investors discuss, recognize, and manage behavioral biases. As a result, investors may avoid the typical pitfalls of wanting risk in bull markets, safety in bear markets, and overall failing to achieve expected returns because they do not properly manage risk.

3. Develop staying power: Over time, as investors readily see they have preserved principal through the allocation to the safety and income buckets, they are more likely to remain invested in the more volatile accumulation bucket that provides greater returns and, therefore, more purchasing power over time.

4. Simplified strategy selection and investment rebalancing: Brinker Capital assumes discretion for allocation and manager selection. This means that advisors can avoid both the time consuming effort of initially making these critical decisions and the ongoing rebalancing effort to assure that the portfolio's asset allocation stays on

track with the desired level of risk exposure. Rebalancing can quickly turn into what is called the "rebalancing nightmare" because getting rebalancing calls right requires time, expertise, and discipline, and errors are common. Rebalancing involves not only making the right calls on when to reposition assets in a portfolio; it also requires being right on which asset class or sub-asset class to reduce and to which asset class or sub-asset class to add. In cases where an account has periodic distributions, Brinker Capital manages the timely distribution of the desired amount and manages the reallocation to the safety bucket, which is the source of the withdrawal.

5. Ease of use and fewer entry barriers for smaller accounts: Many of the advisors we work with find that Personal Benchmark is extremely useful with smaller accounts. Its scalability and personalization simply makes it easier to properly manage these important relationships efficiently.

6. Personal Benchmark allows smaller accounts to be established in certain Brinker Capital products that typically have higher minimums: For example, Personal Benchmark's minimum is $250,000. If the selected portfolio investment strategy directs a 10 percent allocation to the tactical bucket, which is implemented by Brinker Capital's Crystal Strategy I Absolute Return portfolio, the investor has gained access to this strategy with only $25,000, even though this strategy normally has a $100,000 minimum.

7. Simplified account consolidation: For some advisors, consolidating investor accounts held at different custodians can produce troubles with efficiently and correctly aggregating total values and returns. With Personal Benchmark, portfolio totals and returns are efficiently accounted for and calculated through Brinker Capital systems.

8. Continuous access: Through the Brinker Capital website, advisors and their investors may gain 24/7 access to proposals, investment advisory agreements, account data, and performance reports.

9. Clear, thorough reporting: The inclusion of the risk-adjusted return chart after the first year provides the advisor with a valuable tool for initiating objective discussions with investors about risk and return. Annualized returns are clearly depicted as a graph. A picture is worth a thousand words.

10. Service differentiation: Through the various benefits advisors reap using Personal Benchmark, a primary one is using the solution—this will distinguish advisors in the marketplace. Personal Benchmark can help advisors achieve considerable efficiency and scales of economy in their advisory practice while maintaining high quality and providing personalized services. We know of no other offering that so effectively embeds behavioral finance in a managed solution executed through proven multi-asset class investing. Personal Benchmark does the right thing for investors and advisors. It seeks to help establish advisors as thought leaders in their marketplace.

Summary

This chapter emphasizes that Personal Benchmark can help advisors achieve considerable efficiency and scale in their advisory practice, all the while delivering highly personalized advice.

Through the Brinker Capital website, advisors and their investors may gain 24/7 access to proposals, investment advisory agreements, account data, and quarterly reports.

The process begins by framing investments in light of investors' goals. These goals are then translated into allocations to four buckets, each of which has a specific purpose. This approach enables investors to monitor their progress against their goals rather than against capital market indices. This is a dramatic and beneficial departure from how traditional investing portfolios are planned, executed, and monitored. Brinker Capital's approach helps investors avoid the typical pitfalls of wanting risk in bull markets, safety in bear markets and, overall, failing to achieve expected returns because they do not properly manage risk.

Conclusion

Wealth is the ability to fully experience life.

—Henry David Thoreau

By integrating behavioral finance and investment management, Personal Benchmark enables advisors to create for investors the purchasing power that finances the life styles or experiences investors aspire to create for themselves. Framing investment strategies through the prism of your personal goals, or purpose, manages the frequently counterproductive behavioral biases that throw investors off course. Utilizing a personal benchmark does everything from helping you manage behavioral irrationalities to protecting you against some of the return-damning flows of efficient market theory.

By combining proven behavioral management tools with Brinker Capital's tested multi-asset class investment strategies (many with 19-year track records), Brinker Capital is offering a simple abstract paradigm that connects finance with the way people actually live their lives. We believe this enhancement is an advance in investment theory because it increases the explanatory and predictive power of investment theory by including plausible psychological premises.

We are highly confident that Personal Benchmark's enhancements to investment theory will improve the investment results for many, many investors. But, to emphasize only the financial advantages of a goals-based approach is to overlook its greatest richness of all, one more consistent with the epigraph above.

Simply put, personal benchmarking is about so much more than merely being a rational investor; instead, it is about redefining what it means to be wealthy. Real wealth is about more than dollars and cents, it is about using those means in the service of something bigger than oneself and using that burning desire as a centerpiece for all decision making, financial and otherwise. To employ a great quote from the Good Book, "For what shall it profit a man, if he shall gain the whole world, and lose his own soul?" (Mark 8:36, King James Version). Purpose-driven investing speaks to both the mind and soul of investing and suggests that the two can be seamlessly interwoven for synergistic benefit.

Earlier in this work, you were introduced to the concept of "operationalization," where one concrete variable serves as proxy for a fuzzier, harder-to-measure construct. It is no secret that for many, the amount of wealth they have amassed serves as shorthand for happiness, but such is hardly the case. Although wealth is positively correlated with wellbeing to a point, disconnecting money from purpose is a formula for emotional bankruptcy.

One such self-delusional variant of chasing money for happiness is the "I'll stop ignoring my happiness when I reach xyz number." Your magic number may be a salary or it may be a wished-for dollar amount to have in the bank. Whatever it is, I can promise you that when you get there, it won't seem like enough. You see, we are not conditioned to think of money in terms of "enough."

The scientific name for this phenomenon is the "hedonic treadmill" or "hedonic adaptation," referring to the fact that we must make more and more money to keep our level of happiness in the same place. What tends to happen is that our expectations rise and fall with our earnings (as well as other circumstances in our life), keeping our happiness at a relatively stable place. To demonstrate this effect, I'd like for you to consider two groups that seemingly have little in common—paraplegics and lottery winners.

Suppose I asked you, "Which would make you happier, winning the lottery or being in a crippling accident?" Not too tough, right? So, we would hypothesize that one year after the life-changing event, lottery winners would be much happier and paraplegics would be much sadder. But this is simply not the case. One year after their respective events, it makes little difference whether you are riding in a Bentley or a wheel-chair—happiness levels remain relatively static.

Why? We tend to over predict the impact of external events on our happiness. One year later, paraplegics have found out their accidents were not as catastrophic as they may have feared and have coped accordingly. Similarly, lottery winners have found out that having money brings with it a variety of complications. No amount of spending can take away some of the tough things life throws at each and every one of us. As the saying goes, "Wherever you go, there you are."

In much the same way, we tend to project forward to a hypothesized happier time, when we have more money in the bank or are making a bigger salary. The fact of the matter is, when that day arrives, we are unlikely to recognize it and will simply project forward once again, hoping in vain that something outside of ourselves will come and make it all better.

A recent Princeton study set out to answer the age-old question, "Can money buy happiness?" Their answer: sort of. Researchers found that making little money did not cause sadness in and of itself, but it did tend to heighten and exacerbate existing worries. For instance, among people who were divorced, 51 percent of those who made less than $1,000 a month reported having felt sad or stressed the previous day, whereas that number fell to 24 percent among those earning more than $3,000 a month. Having more money seems to provide those undergoing adversity with greater security and resources for dealing with their troubles. However, the researchers found that this effect (mitigating the impact of difficulty) disappears altogether at $75,000 dollars per year.

At this salary range, individual differences have much more to do with happiness than does money. Although the study makes no specific inferences as to why $75,000 dollars is the magic number, I'd like to take a stab at it. Most families making $75,000 a year have enough to live in a safe home, attend quality schools, and have appropriate leisure time. Once these basic needs are met, quality of life has less to do with buying happiness and more to do with individual attitudes. After all, someone who makes $75,000 can buy a faster car than someone who makes less, but his or her ability to get from point A to point B is not substantially improved. Once we have our basic financial needs met, the rest is up to us. Hard work provides the means, but we must find our meaning.

So, if happiness does not come from hitting the lottery and sadness is not borne of personal tragedy, what does make us happy? Well, fortunately (or unfortunately, depending on how well-adjusted your parents are), a great deal of happiness comes from our "hedonic set point," which is genetically determined. A 10-year, longitudinal study of 1,093 identical twins found that between 44 percent and 52 percent of subjective wellbeing is accounted for by genetic factors. This means that roughly half of what makes you happy is out of your control, I'm sorry to say.

Of the remaining 50 percent, roughly 10 percent is due to external circumstances and a whopping 40 percent is due to intentional activities, meaning the choices we make and the purpose we create. We previously discussed how we tend to overrate the importance of the things that happen to us and, sure enough, only 10 percent of what makes us happy is accounted for by lucky and unlucky breaks. A full 80 percent of the non-genetic components of happiness can be controlled by our attitude and by making choices that are consistent with finding true joy. The first step in this pursuit is ensuring that the goals we are setting for ourselves are consistent with finding true happiness.

If 80 percent of the happiness that is in our control comes from setting and working toward positive goals, what sort of goals should we be setting? Headey et al. (2008) found that goals focused on enriching relationships and social resources are likely to increase wellbeing. That makes sense—we connect with a number of close friends and find joy within those relationships. In friendship, we "consume" limited, but satisfying quantities. Having a core group of close friends satiates us: It is sufficient to meet our social needs and typically, we do not pine for ever-greater numbers of friends.

However, goals based around monetary achievement is another matter entirely. Headey et al. (2008) found these types of goals have a negative effect on overall wellbeing. This is because financial goals inherently seem unattainable: Just as we reach our former goal, the hedonic treadmill kicks in and our excitement over having "arrived" is gone in an instant. The goal moves, whether that move is barely noticeable or whether it takes the form of a mad sprint down the field.

Dr. Daniel Gilbert, a happiness expert at Harvard, says that pursuing wealth at the expense of more satisfying goals has a high opportunity cost. "When people spend their effort pursuing material goods in the belief that they will bring happiness, they're ignoring other, more effective routes to happiness." The simple fact is this: chasing money and material goods is an itch that our flawed psychology will never let us scratch, unless we can define our financial goals in terms of the personal ends they will meet.

In a money-obsessed world that has socialized us to chase the almighty dollar, it can be weirdly unsettling to learn that money isn't everything. As much as we whine about money, having something that is the physical embodiment of happiness is, well, nice. We can hold it, save it, get more of it, all while mistakenly thinking that getting paid is how we "arrive." Realizing that money does not directly equate to meaning can leave us with a sense of groundlessness. But once we've stripped away that faulty foundation, we are able to replace it with things that lead to less evanescent feelings of happiness. Breaking your overreliance on money as a substitute for real joy is a great first step, a second step is learning to spend your wealth in ways that matter.

Lest we swing from the extreme of "money is the only good" to the opposite extreme of "money is no good," it is worth noting that there are ways in which money can be spent to improve happiness. A lot of our troubles with money stem from the way we spend it, thinking that buying "things" will make us happy. We engage in retail therapy, which is quickly followed by feelings of regret at being overextended. Before we know it, we're surrounded by the relics of our discontent; the things we bought to be happy become constant reminders that we're not.

Instead of amassing a museum of junk, spend your money on things of real value. Spend a little more on quality, healthy food and take the time to savor your new purchases. Use your money to invest in a dream—pay yourself to take a little time off and write that novel about which you've always dreamt. Give charitably and experience the joy of watching those less fortunate benefit from your wealth. A growing body of research suggests that the most important way in which money makes us happy is when we give it away. Finally, spend money on having special experiences with your loved ones. It's true that money doesn't directly buy happiness, but it can do a great deal to facilitate it if you approach it correctly.

The Centrality of Purpose

While we hope you are now convinced of the importance of defining your goals as an aid to your financial decision making, it is also worth considering the centrality of purpose in creating a life that is rich in the most meaningful sense of that word. In almost every endeavor, successful people answer "Why?" and let that define their "How?" and "What?" In his simple but profound TEDx talk, Simon Sinek lays out a model for purpose-driven action that he calls the Golden Circle, pictured in Figure C.1.

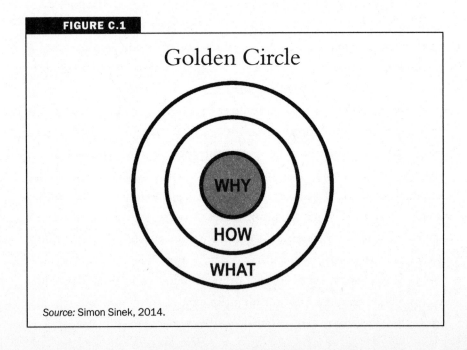

FIGURE C.1

Golden Circle

WHY

HOW

WHAT

Source: Simon Sinek, 2014.

Sinek suggests that uninspired behavior, whether corporate or personal, begins with "What?" instead of "Why?" He suggests that most communication begins with an explanation of what someone is involved in, touches briefly on how it is accomplished, but seldom addresses why it is done. This milquetoast approach is uninspiring and seldom leads to the kind of influence that meaningfully moves the needle. Inspired leaders and exceptional organizations on the other hand, start with their purpose and let that answer the other questions. Sinek uses the example of Apple circa 2009 and says they answer the three questions as such:

Why?—"Everything we do, we believe in challenging the status quo."

How?—"By making our products beautifully designed and user friendly."

What?—"We just happen to make great computers."

Sinek convincingly suggests that we are less persuaded by what is being sold than the reasons underlying it. In his words, "People don't buy *what* you do, they buy *why* you do it."

But we as individual investors aren't trying to be influential, are we? The *Merriam-Webster* (2014) definition of *influence* is, "the act or power of producing an effect without apparent exertion of force or direct exercise of command." Influence underlies so much of the important work we do in our businesses. What is leadership, but persuading a group of people to work in service of a common goal? What is change management, but influencing people to do things differently than they have done in the past? But we needn't suppose that influence always be externally facing. Sometimes the person we most need to influence is ourselves.

If our investment process is not firmly rooted in a meaningful "Why?" it will be as uninspired and unpersuasive as a bad sales pitch. Reexamine the definition of influence briefly, focusing on ". . . without apparent exertion of force . . ." Ensuring that our own decisions are consistent with our long-term best interests can be extremely difficult and we have all had the experience of trying to force ourselves to make good decisions at a time of fear. But when our financial lives are anchored in something that matters to us personally—our very own "Why?"—it becomes almost effortless to do what is right. We would never sacrifice something so important for some short-term comfort. Just as Sinek says, once we have discovered our financial meaning, our "What" and "How" won't be far behind.

But Sinek is hardly alone in putting forth the centrality of purpose in living a meaningful and productive life. Stephen Covey, the author of *The 7 Habits of Highly Effective People: Powerful Lessons in Personal Change,* suggested, "You have to decide what your highest priorities are and have the courage—pleasantly, smilingly, nonapologetically—to say 'no' to other things. And the way you do that is by having a bigger 'yes' burning inside. How different our lives are when we really know what is deeply important to us, and, keeping that picture in mind, we manage ourselves each day to be and do what really matters most."

The path to your financial dreams is beset on all sides with temptations. At times, these temptations will take the form of consumption— spending for today's pleasure and forgetting about the Future You. At other times, it will require that you silence the panicked voice inside your head that tells you to run at exactly the inopportune moment. In all events, having that bigger "yes" burning inside of you is what will positively influence your ability to endure.

Malcolm Gladwell, author of *Outliers: The Story of Success* (2011), an examination of exceptional achievers in all walks of life, found that "meaningful work" was one of the key differentiators between those who excelled and those who did not. Imbuing your investing life with meaning may not make you Warren Buffett, but it is predictive of both enjoyment and success in many walks of life. Organizational development guru Patrick Lencioni advocates in *Silos, Politics and Turf Wars: A Leadership Fable About Destroying the Barriers That Turn Colleagues Into Competitors* (2006) the creation of thematic goals, which he calls a "rallying cry," in addition to the more traditional numerical benchmarks. As he says, "The thematic goal is not a number, and it is not even specifically measurable. It is a general statement of a desired accomplishment. It requires a verb, because it rallies people to do something.

Improve, increase, reduce, grow, change, establish, eliminate or acceler-
ate." Imagine two different rallying cries, the first, "Keep up with the
benchmark!" and the second, "Improve Charlotte's life by sending her to
college!" Which flag would you follow into battle?

Finally, there is the awesomely named Mihaly Csikszentmihalyi
(pronounced "Chick-sent-me-high"), who studies what he calls
"flow," often referred to colloquially as "being in the zone." Flow is
achieved when an athlete can't miss or when you look up at work and the
day is already over, time having flown by (yeah, I know, it's never
happened to me either). Dr. Csikszentmihalyi has consistently found that
"making meaning" is one of the components necessary to achieve the
psychology of optimal experience. As he states on page 217 of his seminal
work, *Flow: The Psychology of Optimal Experience* (2008), "Creating
meaning involves bringing order to the contents of the mind by
integrating one's actions into a unified flow experience . . . people
who find their lives meaningful usually have a goal that is challenging
enough to take up all of their energies, a goal that can give significance to
their lives . . . Purpose, resolution and harmony unify life and give it
meaning by transforming it into a seamless flow experience . . . Every
living moment will make sense and most of it will be enjoyable."

If "purposeful," "resolute" and "harmonious" are not three adjec-
tives you would use to describe your participation in capital markets, not
having taken a purpose-driven approach may be partly to blame.

Viktor Frankl, with whom you are now becoming very familiar,
famously said, "Ultimately, man should not ask what the meaning of life
is, but rather he must recognize it is he who is asked." As George Bernard
Shaw said in a similar vein, "Life is not about finding yourself. Life is
about creating yourself."

For quite some time now, the prevailing doctrine of capital markets
has been of a decidedly "find yourself" model. They believed that there
was an efficient allocation of resources that could be plotted along a curve
that would best serve your needs, we simply needed to find it.

But it is time we took back the process from the economists and
talking heads and reestablished our centrality in making our financial lives

work (or not). In this new model, risk is simply the likelihood that we will underperform our dreams. Irrationality is acting in ways that thwart our ability to reach those dreams. And the optimal portfolio is not the one that generates the highest return in abstraction, it is the one that helps us meet our goals without killing our nerves before we get there.

Finding Meaning in the Mundane

Dr. Alex Pattakos, in his excellent book, *Prisoners of Our Thoughts: Viktor Frankl's Principles for Discovering Meaning in Life and Work* (2010), tells the story of a woman who benefitted greatly from making meaning central in her own life. The woman in the story was a mail carrier, hardly a job most of us aspire to. If you doubt my assertion, I'd remind that we have a euphemism for maddeningly tedious work that drives one insane— "going postal."

When asked how she kept her spirits up despite nipping dogs, bad weather and what would seem to many of us a boring routine, she replied, "I don't just deliver mail. I see myself helping to connect people to other people. I help build the community. Besides, people depend on me and I don't want to let them down." She then went on to draw on the proud history of her profession, quoting first century Greek historian Herodotus, who said of letter carriers, "Neither snow nor rain nor gloom of night stays these couriers from the swift completion of their appointed rounds." By couching her efforts in terms of the immense good they did in the community, our heroine was able to find meaning in the mundane, and her outlook was impacted accordingly.

All too often, we find ourselves in the process of "de-meaningful-izing" our endeavors by viewing them microscopically, fragmented from the actual good they do. A therapist may sullenly go about doing her paper-work, failing to realize it is the vehicle by which she heals a community. A parent may begrudgingly make dinner for his family, not realizing that it is small moments like these that will matter most over a lifetime.

So, too, does the investment process become arduous when it becomes decoupled from the larger purpose it serves. Even seemingly small investment decisions will take on a dynamism and life of their own when viewed through the appropriate lens. Perhaps making investment decisions will never be the reason you get out of bed in the morning, but whatever does get you out of bed can certainly be at the forefront of how you make decisions!

Doing what we know to be in our long-term best interest can be hard, especially when others are screaming that the sky is falling, but it becomes less difficult when it's attached to something meaningful. As Frankl says, ". . . suffering ceases to be suffering at the moment it finds a meaning . . ."

We at Brinker Capital are confident that a purpose-driven approach to investing can provide you shelter in tough times and energize positive behavior, making a sometimes boring process more meaningful, and all the while making the whole experience more enjoyable. We've got you covered on the "How?". Now, go find your "Why?", and never let it go.

References

Covey, Stephen R. *The 7 Habits of Highly Effective People: Powerful Lessons in Personal Change.* Simon & Schuster, 2013.

Csikszentmihalyi, Mihaly. *Flow: The Psychology of Optimal Experience.* Harper Perennial Modern Classics; 1st edition, 2008.

Gladwell, Malcolm. *Outliers: The Story of Success.* Back Bay Books, 2011.

Headey, Bruce, Juergen Schupp, Ingrid Tucci, and Gert G. Wagner. (2008). "Authentic Happiness Theory Supported by Impact of Religion on Life Satisfaction: A Longitudinal Analysis with Data for Germany." *IZA Discussion Papers*, no. 3915. Retrieved from: http://nbn-resolving.de/urn:nbn: de:101:1-20090119113.

Influence. In *Merriam-Webster Dictionary.* Retrieved from www.merriam-webster .com/dictionary/influence.

Lencioni, Patrick. *Silos, Politics and Turf Wars: A Leadership Fable About Destroying the Barriers That Turn Colleagues Into Competitors.* First edition. Jossey-Bass; 2006.

Pattakos, Alex. *Prisoners of Our Thoughts: Viktor Frankl's Principles for Discovering Meaning in Life and Work.* Second edition. Berrett-Koehler Publishers, 2010.

About the Authors

Chuck Widger, Executive Chairman, Brinker Capital

Chuck Widger is the founder and executive chairman of Brinker Capital, an investment management firm with $17 billion in assets under management (as of June 30, 2014). Chuck is currently chair of the Villanova University School of Law Board of Consultors. Mr. Widger is a past chair of the Gettysburg College Board of Trustees and is chair-emeritus of the Money Management Institute's Board of Governors. The Money Management Institute is the industry association for the $3.5 trillion managed solutions industry. Chuck holds a B.A. from Gettysburg College, a J.D. from Villanova University School of Law, and an L.L.M. (Taxation) from Boston University's School of Law. He served as a Lieutenant in the U.S. Navy.

Dr. Daniel Crosby, President, IncBlot Consulting

Educated at Brigham Young and Emory Universities, Dr. Daniel Crosby is a psychologist and behavioral finance expert who helps organizations understand the intersection of mind and markets. Dr. Crosby constructed the "Irrationality Index," a sentiment measure that gauges greed and fear in the marketplace from month to month. His ideas have appeared in the *Huffington Post* and *Risk Management Magazine*, as well as his monthly columns for WealthManagement.com and Investment News. Daniel was named one of the "12 Thinkers to Watch" by Monster.com and a "Financial Blogger You Should Be Reading" by AARP.

Dr. Crosby's well-reviewed first book, *You're Not That Great* (2012) applies elements of behavioral finance such as loss aversion and the availability heuristic to the pursuit of a meaningful life.

When he is not consulting around market psychology, Daniel enjoys independent films, fanatically following St. Louis Cardinals baseball, and spending time with his wife and two children.

About the Companion Website

This book has a companion website, which can be found at www .wiley.com/go/benchmark. Enter the password: widger123.

The companion website provides resources available for this book that can be accessed directly from the URLs provided. The site contains sample reports, white papers, overviews, and links to articles and websites. Please continue to visit this site for additional resources.

Index